# THE ARTS OF MINISTRY

# THE ARTS

# OF MINISTRY

*Feminist-Womanist Approaches*

## Christie Cozad Neuger

*editor*

Westminster John Knox Press
Louisville, Kentucky

Scripture quotations from the New Revised Standard Version of the Bible are copyright © 1989 by the Division of Christian Education of the National Council of the Churches of Christ in the U.S.A. and are used by permission.

Grateful acknowledgment is made to Alfred A. Knopf, Inc. for permission to reprint an excerpt from "For Strong Women," in *The Moon Is Always Female* by Marge Piercy, copyright © 1980 by Marge Piercy.

*Book design by Jennifer K. Cox*
*Cover design by Fearless Designs*
*Cover photography by Charles Krebs, courtesy of the The Stock Market®.*

*First edition*

Published by Westminster John Knox Press
Louisville, Kentucky

This book is printed on acid-free paper that meets the American National Standards Institute Z39.48 standard. ∞

PRINTED IN THE UNITED STATES OF AMERICA

00 01 02 03 04 05 — 10 9 8 7 6 5 4 3 2

**Library of Congress Cataloging-in-Publication Data**

The arts of ministry : feminist-womanist approaches / Christie Cozad Neuger, editor. — 1st ed.
　　p.　cm.
　ISBN 0-664-25593-0 (alk. paper)
　1. Pastoral theology—Handbooks, manuals, etc.  2. Feminist theology. 3. Womanist theology.  I. Neuger, Christie Cozad, 1952–
BV4016.A78　1996
253'.082—dc20
　　　　　　　　　　　　　　　　　　　　　　　　　95-46683

For my mother, Shirley Cozad,
and for my amazing family, Win, Dan, and Cathy

# CONTENTS

# PREFACE

Much has changed in the past thirty years about how we understand and interpret the world in which we live. There have been radical shifts in the ways we go about the process of seeking "truth." We have learned, in the midst of the various liberation movements, that much of what has been assumed to be reality has rather been a perspective on reality that shifts as the perspective shifts. Feminist thought has been especially helpful in articulating that "the partial has paraded as the whole" and in engaging in a process of deconstruction that has helped to dethrone elitist, oppressive, and destructive assumptions. And, what is especially remarkable is that this epistemological shift has affected all aspects of our culture. There is widespread awareness that perspective impacts truth and that interpretations of reality are based in large part on a set of assumptions that are deeply influenced by our gender, race, class, sexual orientation, able-bodiedness, and ethnicity. Whether we are developing new theoretical perspectives, participating in healthy work relationships with colleagues, or trying to understand the members of our families, we are all affected by these shifts in the way we think about the world.

One of the most obvious ways we are all affected is that we have lost the certainty about much of our lives. In the past there were clearer roles for us to follow, clearer rules to govern our decisions, and clearer expectations about how to be. Today, we are more aware of what is not true than what is. We are without real markers on how to behave and what to believe. We are in transition and the uncertainty makes us all a bit anxious even as many of us are hopeful for what the shifts might mean for our future.

This book emerges in the midst of these shifts. We, as authors, have been aware that there are significant gaps between new feminist and womanist theories and the practices that need to emerge from those theories for the work of ministry. As ministers and religious leaders, we are often left without vehicles to take our new awarenesses and understandings into the day-to-day work of the Church. It was this experience of the gaps between liberation theory *x*

and liberating practice that motivated this book. It is our hope that these chapters can be useful in building new ways to understand and engage in ministry that reflect the transformations in knowledge that feminist and womanist thought has offered to us in the Church.

The book is designed to help religious leaders in two ways. First, we hope that it helps the reader to minister to women and men in this time of cultural upheaval, uncertainty, and expectation. The focus is on helping people to participate in the transformative processes at work in the culture and to find ways of joining in that process of creating a new world that is just and compassionate. Second, we hope that these ideas give religious leaders new ways of thinking about their work and engaging in ministry praxis that helps to renew the Church. This is an exciting time to be in ministry and we hope that these chapters will be helpful in opening up new possibilities and directions for the work of the church.

As editor, I would like to thank Tim Staveteig for both his support and his editorial expertise. I would also like to thank Alexa Smith for her initial encouragement of this book. It has been a pleasure to do this project with Westminster John Knox Press.

I would also like to thank the contributors for their commitment to this text and to their collaborative and collegial approach to the work.

In addition, I would like to thank United Theological Seminary of the Twin Cities for being the type of place where liberating theory and practice are nurtured, encouraged, and empowered at every level of institutional life.

Finally, I would like to thank my family, especially my husband, Win, for all of his active interest and support through the work of this book and in all the various aspects of our lives together.

CHRISTIE COZAD NEUGER

# CONTRIBUTORS

KATHLEEN D. BILLMAN, Associate Professor of Pastoral Care and Counseling, Lutheran School of Theology at Chicago, Chicago, Illinois

CAROL LAKEY HESS, Assistant Professor of Christian Education, Princeton Theological Seminary, Princeton, New Jersey

PAMELA HOLLIMAN, Executive Director, Samaritan Counseling Center, Ambler, Pennsylvania

CHRISTIE COZAD NEUGER, Associate Professor of Pastoral Counseling and Pastoral Theology, United Theological Seminary of the Twin Cities, New Brighton, Minnesota

JUDITH ORR, Academic Dean and Associate Professor of Pastoral Care, St. Paul School of Theology Methodist, Kansas City, Missouri

CHRISTINE M. SMITH, Associate Professor of Preaching and Worship, United Theological Seminary of the Twin Cities, New Brighton, Minnesota

EMILIE M. TOWNES, Associate Professor of Christian Social Ethics, St. Paul School of Theology Methodist, Kansas City, Missouri

# INTRODUCTION: BUILDING BRIDGES BETWEEN THEORY AND PRACTICE FOR THE ARTS OF MINISTRY

A few years ago a group of sixty women and a few men were participating in a working group on pastoral counseling from a feminist perspective. As we identified the core ingredients to a feminist theory, theology, and practice of pastoral counseling, we began to ask ourselves some key questions. First, we asked how many of us were in general agreement with the core principles named as feminist pastoral counseling. Second, we asked how many of us operated out of a philosophical commitment to feminist theory and theology in our clinical work. And third, we asked how many of us consistently put into practice the three or four primary principles for feminist pastoral counseling. The vast majority of the group were able to answer positively to the first two questions. However, when we got to the third question, there were at most a handful of agreements that we consistently were able to make the move from feminist theory to practice in our clinical work.

The reasons given for that gap between theory and practice were several. People said that they had never had supervision or mentoring in feminist practice. Many said that they had never even had a course in feminist perspectives in pastoral counseling—only in feminist theory and theology in a larger sense. There was no integration in their education between feminist theory and the work of ministry. Consistently people said that their clinical training had never offered a critique of traditional counseling practices from feminist perspectives—only from new theory in the psychological sciences themselves. This left these practitioners in pastoral counseling, all of whom were committed to transformative and liberating themes in feminist theory and theology, without access to thorough and effective practical knowledge for their work and without adequate methodology to make those shifts for themselves.

This story is not unique among clergy and pastoral practitioners. Many religious leaders have been to conferences and seminars on feminist topics only to find that the educational practices of the seminars themselves were contradictory to feminist thought. There have been many sermons given where the messages of liberation that were spoken were denied in the structure, exegesis, or illustrations of the work. And there are many examples where clergy who were working from a feminist orientation were unable to find styles of leadership, curriculum, and support networks to carry that orientation consistently into the ministry. Many religious leaders search for ways to take their core beliefs about the world, relationships, and God and create from them new and liberating ministry practice. I have been deeply motivated in the development of this text by the haunting and powerful questions from the students and clergy in feminist-oriented classes when they ask things like: "What about the rural women in my parish who don't believe in sharing their experiences with anyone?" "What about the people in my church who aren't even sure a woman should be in the pulpit—I don't want to come across as a radical." "I don't know how to help my parishioners move from their personal struggles to seeing the larger picture in which their lives are based." Religious leaders have been left with a lot of good ideas about theology and a lot of questions about ministry.

This book is intended to speak to the practice of ministry from feminist and womanist perspectives. No book can substitute for consultation, supervision, mentoring, and other hands-on learning techniques by feminist practitioners. Much of what is done in ministry is best learned in the apprentice models of theological education that have proven themselves so effective. However, most of the apprenticeship opportunities in ministry have not yet developed thorough and congruent practice that is informed by feminist and womanist thought. Theological education is still at the front end of creating new and transformative ministry theory/practice from which to teach those women and men now entering and engaging in ministry. Consequently, the chapters in this text offer a look at the practices of ministry from feminist and womanist orientations in ways designed to invite the reader to bridge existing gaps between feminist and womanist theory/theology and feminist and womanist practice in concrete ministry contexts. The authors help the reader to do this bridging work by sharing their own experiences, by their generous use of illustrations and conversations, by their careful and systematic explication of their theories of practice, and through their clear identification of method. These issues will be addressed again in the conclusion.

## Defining Terms

This text clearly locates itself in feminist and womanist claims. There are a number of ways to define feminism and womanism, and each author in this book shapes her definition around a variety of factors including social location, field of interest, training, and other, more idiosyncratic, particularities. The authors have been influenced by various feminist and womanist theories and perspectives, and those influences shape the way they understand feminism and womanism.

Most often the term *feminism* in the context of this book means the following commitments:

> the privileging of women's experiences, voices, and perspectives in the building of theory and practice

> the critiquing of theories, theologies, practices, and structures that exclusively or primarily reflect a dominant cultural exclusivistic point of view and that operate against the best interests of those marginalized by virtue of race, class, gender, sexual orientation, or able-bodiedness

> the operating from a self-conscious standpoint of gender as a social construction, and understanding the implications of that construction for the development of theory and practice

Most often the term *womanism* in the context of these chapters means the following commitments:

> a privileging of African-American women's experiences, voices, and perspectives in the building of theory, theology, and practice

> a critiquing of theories, theologies, practices, and structures from the combined standpoint of race and gender. The juxtaposition of race and gender forms a radically different standpoint than either of these categories alone.

> a focus on the harm that a fundamentally racist, sexist, and classist culture does to those who are marginalized by those particularities

> a belief in the necessity of racial solidarity between men and women, with appropriate gender critiques, for the dismantling of destructive racist structures

Both feminism and womanism share many things in common. For example, both have commitments to the following:

> the transforming of all lives, relationships, systems, and cultures so that they are inclusive, life-affirming, and just

> the belief that each individual life must be understood in the context of the power arrangements and rules of the

4

dominant culture *and* that the construction of theory
and practice must also listen carefully to each individual marginalized voice

the certainty that theories and practices based on feminist
and womanist perspectives are always inescapably and
intentionally political

a non-neutral stance on the goals and practices of ministry. As
Rebecca Chopp says, "Women and men engaged in feminist practices of theological education use feminist theory
to persuade, to change, to open up, and to transform.[1]

There are a variety of ways to define and nuance these terms.[2]
However, from the point of view of the agenda of this text, these definitions adequately capture the primary meanings. It is important
for us to avoid generalizations. One of the most significant problems
for feminist thought between the 1960s and the 1980s was its tendency to repeat the errors of patriarchal thinking and overgeneral-
ize its conclusions from the perspective of mostly white, middle-
class, educated women. As many of the following chapters point out,
voices from women who had been left out of feminist-theory building, especially the voices of African-American women, older women,
and, to a certain extent, lesbian women, helped call white feminists
to task for their exclusionary perspectives. In the last ten years, feminist thought has attempted to be much more attentive to the diversity of perspectives of women's experiences and the particular contexts from which women speak.

Since that twenty-year period, feminist thought has also encoun-
tered postmodernism with its intense focus on the social location of
the theorist as well as on errors about assumptions of truth in theories. The importance of standpoint and particularity in postmodernism has reinforced feminists' commitment to listening to diverse
voices and to building theory that is truly inclusive as well as just.

However, there are some difficulties with these commitments to
avoid generalization and the universalizing of particular conclusions when feminists seek to (1) claim the political and advocacy nature of feminist thought and (2) develop an adequate set of agreed-
upon principles so that the theories of ministry praxis can be
developed.[3] There have been three approaches to this dilemma,
which are discussed in the chapters that follow. The first has been
to claim the particularity of both the author and, to a certain extent,
the audience for the chapter. A second approach has been to acknowledge where theory is built on some generalizations and to
note the need for contextualization of the theory. The third ap-

proach has been to work at the meta-theory level—creating ways to guide the development of a theory of practice that takes seriously the diversity of people and the importance of particularity in this work. In order to build practice, there must be some basic agreement about worthwhile goals and about the meanings of transformation, liberation, and justice. Each of the authors struggle with these challenges to be both diverse and multicultural as well as to have an adequate set of theoretical conclusions upon which to build a theory of ministry praxis.

Another important set of terms to define comes from the title of this text—the "arts of ministry." Again, there are complications in an attempt to define why certain activities have been chosen for inclusion and other dimensions of ministry have not. There were two decision factors in making choices about chapter topics. The first was based on those arenas of theological education that are most often grouped under the rubric of "practical theology." Those fields include pastoral care, preaching and worship, Christian education, pastoral counseling, and administration. The first five chapters of this text deal with these dimensions of ministry. The second decision factor was more ambiguous and had to do with which ministry practices were crucial for an understanding of ministry from feminist and womanist perspectives. Several additional fields could have been added here, but I have chosen two that seem to be core to feminist practice—the discipline of ethics and the practice of mentoring. Because one key element to the work of ministry from feminist and womanist perspectives has to do with cultural analysis and prophetic themes, it seemed necessary to also include discussion about the practice of ethics in ministry. And, as Chopp suggests, "feminist theology is itself a type of ethical and moral practice aimed at survival and flourishing. As such, its very nature is to produce discourses of emancipation that are self-conscious and reflective of their own cultural-political location and, as far as possible, of their emancipatory potential."[4] Ethics is a primary practice in doing ministry from feminist and womanist perspectives.

The chapter on mentoring was born out of the awareness that, for many, the gap between theory and ministry praxis is based on a lack of mentors, models, supervisors, and consultants who work out of feminist/womanist orientations. Where there has been appropriate and helpful mentoring for women and men attempting to work out of feminist/womanist perspectives, the gap has been narrowed effectively. Mentoring is a necessary ministry praxis, to be offered and to be received for the sake of developing ministries of empowerment and liberation. For reasons that will become clear throughout the text, mentoring is also necessary for the development and maintenance of health for those who do ministry from feminist/womanist orientations.

The arts of ministry consist of those theories, theologies, methods, and practices that make up the everyday life of the pastoral practitioner. The focus for this book is on the practitioner working in the context of the parish, although the insights will be equally useful to those who are engaged in other forms of ministry. The reader will not find this book to be a "how-to" handbook, but rather a text that invites the practitioner to explore how certain assumptions about power, privilege, justice, and transformation might intentionally inform the work of ministry. The book is typical of a work in both practical theology and feminist theory in that the primary method grounds the theory in the lives of people who are in relationship with the pastor. The method moves from the issues that emerge in pastoral relationships to the work of conceptualizing theory and theology that is relevant to those issues. Part of the conceptualizing work involves drawing on the secular and theological traditions in a critical fashion, using feminist and womanist criteria as vehicles for the critique. Certainly a major force in this critique comes from thorough social analyses of the patriarchal culture in which we live and the implications of the cultural power arrangements for doing ministry. The method proceeds by building theories of practice from the deconstructed traditions and from the experiences of those whose perspectives have been left out of the traditional theories and theologies. The method then moves back to engagement with these reconstructed practices in order to provide relevant and transformative ministry and in order to test the practices that have been created. Out of that dialogue, the methodological spiral begins again.

These chapters on the arts of ministry use this method in feminist/womanist practical theology as they attempt to communicate new possibilities for ministries of personal, relational, ecclesial, and cultural empowerment.

## Goals for the Book

This book is first and foremost about relevant, effective, and transformative ministry praxis. The theories and practices proposed and described in the following chapters guide the reader toward enhancing her or his own work in ways that speak to the very core of ministry. The purpose of this text is primarily to assist pastors and church leaders to engage in the most helpful and transformative approaches to ministry as possible for all of the people within their care. The chapters are invitational, informative, and conversational. It is important to note here that, for the most part, these chapters are not exclusive; they are not primarily about women doing ministry with women. They are about the doing of ministry by all people, for all people, in response to God's ever-present invitation toward the fullness and wholeness of life. Ministry is to comfort and confront, to validate and to challenge, to support and transform. These chapters are written to speak to these tasks for ministry.

The second purpose or goal for this text is to provide the reader with cutting-edge research in feminist and womanist theory, theology, and practice. These seven chapters build upon the transformation of thought that has emerged from the past thirty years of feminist and womanist theory and make that accessible to the reader. Each chapter, in its own way, invites the reader to understand the importance of the kinds of social analyses, multicultural perspectives, and multivalent meanings, central to feminist and womanist starting places, that undergird the ministry praxis under discussion. Through the use of illustrations, cases, and examples, the rich, multidisciplinary strands of feminist and womanist theory and theology are woven into clear and usable ministry practice.

The third goal of this text is to try to draw together some of the implications from these chapters on ministry about the field of practical theology. If, indeed, these chapters do represent cutting-edge theory and theology undergirding a feminist/womanist orientation toward ministry, then what is it that they have in common? What does this revolution in thought and meaning, generated by the feminist and womanist movements, mean for the work of practical theology? How might the frames, foci, and conclusions of practical theology be transformed when viewed from the sociopolitical theological perspective of women? These questions will be revisited in the conclusion.

## Approaching This Text

There are a variety of ways to approach this book. Each chapter is a full presentation of the discipline in and of itself, so a reader interested in a particular topic, such as Christian education, might start by looking at that chapter alone. Or one might move systematically through the chapters in order. The chapters traditionally assigned to practical theology are arranged in such a way that the topics move from the more general to the more specific—from pastoral care to administration, with ethics and mentoring at the end. Reading the chapters straight through gives the reader a feel for the whole enterprise of ministry and how feminist and womanist starting points transform some of the traditional thinking about these practices.

## An Introduction to the Chapters

The chapter on pastoral care, by Kathleen D. Billman, uses four creative tensions to explore the deepest meanings of pastoral care today. Operating out of an understanding that pastoral care, perhaps more than any other dimension of ministry, is "a communal art, bringing together laity and clergy to offer ministries of care to one another and to those outside the boundaries of their congregations," Billman challenges congregations to look at how they might collaborate and conspire together.

In her chapter on preaching, Christine M. Smith picks up the theme of ministry extending both within and outside of the congregation. Using a primary metaphor of "resistance" to understand the mission of preaching, Smith makes a strong case that "feminist preachers find the impetus of their preaching emerging from the larger social context of our individual and collective lives." Smith builds a strong theological foundation for the work of preaching as both resistance and liberation.

In "Education as an Art of Getting Dirty with Dignity," Carol Lakey Hess offers a powerful and creative proposal for the ministry of Christian education. Hess suggests that, in moving between the margins and the center, the church may find a means to be renewed and transformed. In a celebration of both pluralism and diversity, she helps the educator to explore the creative tension between "hard dialogue" and "deep connection."

My chapter on pastoral counseling explores how a feminist approach might move through four processes in helping women, men, and relationships in times of distress. Using scriptural themes to help articulate the meaning of these processes, I discuss the tasks of coming to voice, gaining clarity, making choices, and staying healthy. The focus is on the work of pastoral counseling in the parish—a work that is too often and too quickly abdicated to secular mental health resources.

Judith Orr, using primarily an empirical method of research, explores what leadership and administration in the church looks like when done by women pastors. As she discusses the results of her many interviews, new styles and forms of administration emerge that enrich the leadership possibilities for all of us. Her well-developed theological foundations serve as a rich resource for understanding the ministry of administration and leadership as a key way that the people of God give shape to the covenants they have made.

Emilie M. Townes speaks to the central work of ethics in pastoral ministry today. Operating from a womanist starting place, Townes helps the reader to understand the importance of both the prophetic and the pastoral in the work of ministry. Townes uses as her focus point the concept of justice and builds, through a careful social analysis, a vision of the community of faith as both liberating and reconciling. She calls us to an ongoing confrontation with the structures of evil and an ongoing hope in the power of God's love.

The last topical chapter is written by Pamela Holliman. She explores, via conversations and illustrations, the meanings and possibilities of mentoring one another as a part of ministry. Holliman suggests that mentoring is the intentional sharing of wisdom with another and suggests that, especially for women, mentoring is important for testing new ideas and developing increasing confidence for going about the work of ministry.

The text ends with an exploration of how feminist and womanist perspectives on the practice of ministry are working to transform traditional understandings of practical theology, especially as it articulates the shared goals of inclusivity, radical social analysis, the transformation of destructive power arrangements, and the healing and empowerment of the church.

I am deeply appreciative of the commitments and the competencies of these authors. It is their hope that this book will be helpful to all people, clergy and lay, who are engaged in the transformative work of ministry in the church and in the world.

## NOTES

1. Rebecca S. Chopp, *Saving Work: Feminist Practices of Theological Education* (Louisville, Ky.: Westminster John Knox Press, 1995), 86.
2. There are a multitude of texts that work to define feminist and womanist thought. For examples of the discussions about definition, see Paula Rothenberg, *Race, Class and Gender in the United States*, 2d ed. (New York: St. Martin's Press, 1992); Hunter College Women's Studies Collective, *Women's Realities: Women's Choices*, 2d ed. (New York: Oxford University Press, 1995); Patricia Hill Collins, *Black Feminist Thought* (New York: Routledge & Kegan Paul, 1990); and Helen Tierney, ed., *Women's Studies Encyclopedia*, vol. 1 (New York: Peter Bedrick Books, 1991).
3. For a thorough discussion of some of the problems in bringing together feminist thought with postmodernism, see Linda J. Nicholson, ed., *Feminism/Postmodernism* (New York: Routledge & Kegan Paul, 1990).
4. See Chopp, *Saving Work*, 83.

# 1

## PASTORAL CARE AS AN ART OF COMMUNITY

*Kathleen D. Billman*

### Introduction

My mother recently became a Stephens Minister,[1] and a whole new discourse has now opened up between us about the joys and dilemmas of pastoral care. As I reflect on the kinds of questions that come up in our conversations from time to time (When is it appropriate to offer a word of challenge to someone whose behaviors appear to be self-defeating? How deeply involved do we allow ourselves to become in the lives of others? When and how is prayer offered in the context of a pastoral care ministry?), I am reminded that of all the arts of ministry, the art of pastoral care is perhaps the most far-flung activity. In addition to pastoral care ministries within congregations, there are wide-ranging ministries of care in all kinds of other places, such as hospitals, children's homes, youth correctional centers, hospice programs, retirement and nursing homes, campuses, military bases, and prisons. Although I am writing this chapter primarily for those who practice the art of pastoral care as parish pastors, I recognize that all these pastoral care ministries are related.

This recognition of relatedness leads me to voice two initial convictions about the pastor as caregiver. The first conviction, widely shared in contemporary pastoral care literature, is that pastoral care is a communal art, bringing together laity and clergy to offer ministries of care to one another and to those outside the boundaries of their congregations. There is increasing literature about the importance of such an understanding of care. There is also much practical help in training church leaders to offer care in many aspects of congregational life, from visitation to committee meetings, and to engage in pastoral care visits with people who are outside congregational settings.[2] An important task of the pastor as caregiver is to inspire participation in such ministries of care; to communicate a vision of pastoral care that has at its heart the *creation of communities of care*.

Another important task of the pastor as caregiver has to do with the role of the pastor as theologian. The pastor is called to exercise leadership in asking such systemic questions as these: (1) In what kind of *world* do I engage in pastoral care relationships? (2) *Where do I stand* as a caregiver in relation to the contexts of the people with whom I engage in care? (3) What *vision* of wholeness or health guides my ministry of care, that is, what kinds of persons and communities do I hope to help form? (4) *How* do I offer care; what *goals and methods* are appropriate? The pastor as caregiver should continually reflect upon and critique the assumptions that guide her or his own ministry of care, as well as help congregational colleagues to engage in this kind of reflection on the caring ministries of the community of faith.

My focus will be primarily on this latter dimension of the practice of pastoral care. I will begin where feminists typically begin, in the complex and messy soil of experience, where these questions emerge not merely as intellectual exercises but as struggles of the whole self; that is to say, we experience them in our bodies, our hearts, and our minds. It will be necessary to keep reminding myself that all the questions I have just raised—about the world in which care is practiced, the social location of the caregiver, the vision that guides care, and the methodology one uses in the practice of care—are inseparably related. Even as I try to tease them apart in order to probe each more deeply, I discover that the threads are interwoven and refuse to stay disconnected. It is, after all, whole cloth I am trying to examine.

I am indebted to feminist and womanist discourses in theology and psychology for helping me to name what I have learned in my own ministry as a pastor and as a teacher of pastoral care—and not only to name it but to value it and offer it as a contribution to a larger pastoral-theological conversation that includes many voices and perspectives. Throughout this chapter I will draw from the deepening well of feminist and womanist writings in Bible, theology, and psychology. These writings serve as dialogue partners in describing and analyzing my experience.

I begin with four creative tensions I have experienced as a pastor and teacher in North American, urban, and multicultural contexts, and the issues these creative tensions raise for articulating the context, role, vision, and methodology of the pastor as caregiver. From the interplay of these tensions emerges an image of the pastor as caregiver as *one who conspires and collaborates with others in the struggle to bring forth new life and hope from the creative tensions on the "boundary."* The next section of this chapter is an effort to engage a scripture text imaginatively—to "play" with the images of care as collaborating and conspiring that I find in that text as a way of exploring their possibilities and pitfalls. What follows is an exploration of some of the implications of these images for the theology and practice of pastoral care. I will then conclude by saying a word about how the movement of this chapter mirrors the process of pastoral care as I envision it.

## Four Creative Tensions in the Practice of Pastoral Care

I grew up in a tiny rural Lutheran parish. My fifteen years of parish pastoral experience took place in two struggling urban United Methodist congregations. I now teach pastoral care in a Lutheran theological school on the south side of Chicago. These contexts have indelibly shaped me. Although most of what I will say grows out of my urban experience, there is a strong thread that connects my urban and rural experiences. That connection has to do with struggle. When I think about who I am writing this chapter for, I have in my mind's eye pastors and congregations who are struggling both for survival and for significant ministry in their contexts, wherever those contexts might be.

From the early 1970s until today, I have struggled and rejoiced, given and received care in multicultural, North American, urban contexts. My first congregation, which everyone called "Greenwood," was situated on a boundary street (Greenwood Avenue) that almost literally divided predominantly Caucasian and predominantly African-American populations in the "Wilbur section" of Trenton, New Jersey. Greenwood's worshiping congregation was mostly peopled with elderly whites and African-American children and youth.

During the years when I ministered in Trenton, I watched the Greenwood neighborhood decline economically. I mourned with young mothers in our neighborhood who lost their babies (the high rate of infant mortality in urban America was no distant statistic), and I saw young lives of teenagers I knew destroyed by drugs and unemployment. In the course of eight years I buried roughly 25 percent of our small congregation (most of whom were elderly whites) and experienced with the survivors the death of a declining congregation. I also participated in the joy of a vital neighborhood ministry, saw young lives blossom and grow, experienced the talent, creativity, and vision that is present in urban America, tried to learn to dance, and learned vital lessons about the power of mutual respect, partnership, and reciprocity. This first context, amidst just such contradictions, taught me about the complexities of people's lives and communities, and about the wondrous ambiguities of pastoral care.

In the second context, while a graduate student, I worked part-time in a staff ministry in another urban congregation. One of the West-African members of St. Paul once described the congregation as a quilt, full of different colors and shapes, providing warmth for everyone. It was a lovely image, capturing both what we indeed experienced, in rare and exciting moments, and what we hoped we might someday really become. There were deep struggles, as Caucasians, Liberian immigrants and refugees, Jamaicans, and African Americans tried to carve out a space that we could all call "church." This congregation also struggled (and still struggles) with issues of survival and flourishing. I am always eager to hear news of the joy and struggle, the quilt-in-progress, that is St. Paul.[3]

At the urban seminary where I teach, it is becoming common to speak of ourselves as a "community of communities." Some communities within the community are seriously underrepresented, and we struggle with what it means to care for one another amidst critical differences, some of which involve personal preferences and needs, others of which reveal the systemic patterns of racism, classism, sexism, and heterosexism that are part of the fabric of our civic and ecclesial life in the United States. It is also a place of rich and stimulating encounter, with all the delights and opportunities that diversity has to offer—opportunities that many prospective seminarians will not experience because of their fears and stereotypes of the city. In these important ways, the seminary is much like the parishes in which I have ministered.

These are the contexts that have formed and shaped my understanding of pastoral care. When I speak of the importance and the limitation of my perspective, I acknowledge what is true for every theologian: our work is "standpoint dependent."[4] We write to address the problems with which we have struggled and to articulate the "joy set before us" (Heb. 12:2) in the journey of ministry. I suspect that readers will glimpse in the images I use a sense of urgency, of the struggle of life against death, of pastoral care as inseparably connected with prophetic witness.

Within all the differences I could name in these three ministry situations there are important commonalities. In each ministry context I have found myself wrestling with at least four creative tensions. I experience this "wrestling" as both exhausting and exhilarating; like Jacob, I emerge from these struggles both limping and blessed.

### Anxiety and Possibility

Trenton's most famous bridge contains huge letters that span almost the width of the Delaware; they are a remnant from Trenton's industrial glory days. The letters spell "Trenton Makes, The World

Takes." For several years the sign was not lit at night. It costs money to keep a huge sign lit throughout the night; besides, many of the industries that made Trenton famous are now closed.

In the midst of severe economic struggle, however, a decision was made to repair and relight the bridge. One of the desires that the "Trenton Makes" bridge symbolizes is the desire to make a contribution, to make a difference in the world—to give something that the world can take. Yet for many people, confidence that they can contribute and make a difference has been severely shaken.

This is not just an urban phenomenon, although the plight often seems most visible in urban America. In the movie "Grand Canyon," a hard-working African-American mechanic in Los Angeles begs his handsome nephew to break ties with a gang that he knows is involved in drug dealing. The uncle tries to kindle his nephew's hope for the future. His nephew responds that he does not expect to be alive when he is twenty-five. "Reality Bites," another 1990s movie, is about middle- and upper-class white college graduates, some of whom cannot find a job that is meaningful to them and others of whom have had no experience of lasting commitments that seem worth the effort. Although they do not live with the daily threat of violence, they are quietly desperate. Seventeen-year-old "Jake" has never known anything but life on his family's midwestern dairy farm, a business he expected to be passed on to him. Instead, the family faces foreclosure and bankruptcy.

In the above vignettes, economic forces create some of the anxiety and confusion that people face in contemplating the future (an anxiety that is not confined to the young). In diverse congregations, economic concerns intermingle with cultural and theological issues. The anxieties, pressures, confusion, and disappointments that individuals experience are often mirrored in the communal life of struggling congregations and those who try to lead them.

The first creative tension I have been attempting to convey has to do with how I experience the world of pastoral care in the United States at the turn of the century. I am using the term *world* in a particular way here, to refer to the ways the pastor as caregiver encounters global trends and ground shifts—images of past, present, and future life that fill newspapers and magazines, television and movie screens. In my own life and practice of ministry, my experience has been that the "center" (that is, dominant ways of understanding human relatedness and human accomplishment) is, to bend Yeats's familiar metaphor of the modern era, "not holding."[5] Many mainstream congregations and seminaries in the United States are struggling for survival.

This struggle for survival breeds enormous anxiety, yet it also harbors new possibility. Many churches, spurred not only by the struggle to survive but also by the struggle to recover the significance of the gospel in today's circumstances, are exploring their traditions in fresh and critical ways and opening their doors to new ministries. One congregation, located on the same street as an Islamic mosque, collaborated with their neighbors to create an interfaith dialogue that is bringing new possibilities for mutual ministries of care in their area.

This tension between anxiety and possibility shapes the practice of pastoral care. What issues does this tension raise for pastoral care? First, pastoral care in many congregations will take place amidst unprecedented opportunities for new kinds of relationships across boundaries that have previously separated people. It will also take place amidst communities' struggles for survival and confusion about foundational values and commitments. These struggles will take many forms. The pastor as caregiver in many congregations will face the challenge of helping persons engage difference creatively. This task is especially critical when survival is at stake, because when difference becomes too much of a threat there will be strong moves to silence voices that have criticized the status quo. Nearly every mainstream Protestant denomination in the United States is now experiencing a strong backlash toward feminists, womanists, and other minority voices—male and female. There are several powerful dynamics in this reaction. One has to do with resistance to the increased freedom of those who are claiming their right to speak and press for change. A related dynamic is the pain and anger of lost privilege on the part of those who were always looked to for leadership in the past. Another dynamic has to do with the terror caused by massive social upheaval and with the distance that exists within and among ecclesial academies, on the one hand, and local faith communities, on the other, in identifying and exploring the roots of this upheaval.

Rebecca Chopp writes, "The center is, in modernity, cracking, its fissures are widening, and in these fissures and cracks, discourses of emancipatory transformation may be formed."[6] For those who exist on the margins of established order, the upheaval in the "center" is filled not only with danger but with possibility as well. New ventures in life together may be negotiated precisely *because* of these fissures and cracks. Here, I believe, the pastoral caregiver has a critical role to play, as one who will explore with persons and groups the precarious and promising intersection between their need for boundaries, order, safety, and control, *and* their need for freedom, playfulness, imagination, and sacred mystery. But where does the pastor as caregiver stand in relation to the center and the margin?

## Oppressed and Oppressor

I have consistently ministered in contexts where I have experienced both privilege and marginalization. Thus the second creative tension with which I struggle is that of being simultaneously oppressed and oppressor,[7] and what that means for the practice of pastoral care.

Responding to the critique of white feminism by bell hooks and others, Chopp recognizes that "the place of a white middle-class feminist is, on the one hand, forever marginal to the center of the order as related to patriarchal relations . . . but it is also part of the center as related to economic and racial realities."[8] Rather than see this dual identity as paralyzing, however, Chopp images it as a place of energy and action.

> Yet precisely from this center/margin viewpoint, I see that the order works for no one, and thus any discourse of freedom and God from my place has the role of making co-present the suffering of the margins with the psychic destructiveness of the center. This is where I stand, with both blindness and insight, in a place from which I must listen and speak.[9]

In recent years, it has been the theologies of women of color, the responses of white feminists who have taken those critiques seriously, and the women of color and white women friends in my life who have helped me to name and face the challenges of being "both/and."[10] It is helpful to have this language to describe some of the most challenging experiences in my ministry. In every ministry story in this chapter, something of that tension can be found. But the following vignette offers an illustration of what is, in diverse forms, a common ministry dilemma.

A neighborhood woman comes to talk with me. She is a lesbian woman in a committed relationship with her partner. She wants me to do pre-union work with her and her partner and to lead a service that will enable them to speak public words of commitment and to seek God's blessing for their commitment in the presence of a community. I am aware of two realities simultaneously. The first is that I minister within an ecclesial context in which charges may be brought against me if I officiate at such a service; indeed, my very presence as an ordained woman in the church is perceived by some to be a threat to the moral order they perceive as absolute. The second reality I experience is that I participate and benefit from a world that is ordered in such a way as to sanction and support my heterosexual orientation and make it normative, casting countless women and men outside all the privileges I take for granted—not the least of which is the privilege to have a committed relationship celebrated and blessed. With this privilege, however, comes substantial loss—the loss of the presence and perspective of those who have been cast outside in this way and all the richness they could offer the community.

Pastors as caregivers exist in all kinds of social locations in relation to members of their congregations and communities. What my own experience of being on the boundary, of having a foot in more than one world, has given me is a keen sense of how important it is to be aware of our "place" in relation to those for whom we care—the delicate dynamics of power. Another complicating factor is the symbolic role of the pastor that in many circumstances evokes familiar images of authority, including religious or ritual authority. These power dynamics are exacerbated by the particular vulnerabilities of people in personal crisis, with whom the pastor as caregiver is often called to minister.

This experience of the boundary, of living simultaneously as oppressed and oppressor, raises important issues for the pastor as caregiver. How can pastors imagine and conduct their ministries of care in such a way that the strength, responsibility, and agency of others are enhanced? How can the experience of being "both/and" lend critical insight to what empowering help and care mean? How can the symbolic and institutional aspects of the pastoral role be used in a liberating way in the practice of pastoral care? What is the role of the pastor who lives "on the boundary"?

## Systemic Sin and Eschatological Hope

My first congregation was predominantly white, and in its efforts to build bridges with the African-American community had followed a rather typical (and problematic) ecclesial practice for mainstream inner-city congregations: it offered an After School Program for neighborhood children and youth, hoping to attract neighborhood families to its congregational life through offering a ministry in which most of its members were not involved. At the time that I became involved with this ministry, the program was in transition from one that had whites as leaders to one led by African-American teenagers, supported financially by the judicatory and several suburban congregations, and supported personally by the pastoral staff and occasional volunteers from the church. Several teenagers became active leaders of a ministry with elementary school children, and a few of them did become involved with the congregation. One of them was "Sheena."

It was clear from the first day I met her that sixteen-year-old Sheena was an extraordinary young woman. She bore many adult responsibilities in her family; she was articulate in her analysis of what was going on in her community; she was self-aware; and she was a person of imagination and vision. Sheena hoped to become a writer, but a guidance counselor at her inner-city high school had told her that this was not a realistic goal and had tried to interest Sheena in a trade. Sheena still hung on to her dream. With the support of the church, she and the other teenagers in the neighborhood program developed a community newsletter.

I noticed two things about Sheena's poems and editorials: first, that the ideas and images in her writing were imaginative and insightful; second, that she had not learned sufficient grammar and spelling skills to enable her to fulfill the dream she had of becoming a professional writer. Only long after the fact did I get a sense of the bind that may have developed for Sheena. On the one hand, she received lots of praise and affirmation from her church and community for her intelligence, creativity, and passion. On the other hand, Sheena also received negative messages about herself as an African-American woman and about her potential and abilities. Some of these messages came from her teachers, who did not challenge and assist her to learn what she needed to know to realize her own dream for herself. Others came from media and advertisements, from diminishing and shameful experiences (like being followed around in a department store by white store clerks, who acted as if Sheena was a thief), and from the limited number of doors that were open for her.

Mary Ballou and Nancy Gabalac describe a process whereby women learn to adapt to the dominant culture in ways that help them to survive, yet are harmful and costly to themselves. This process, which they call "harmful adaptation,"[11] is useful in describing the process through which whole groups of persons learn to believe negative messages about themselves. Their analysis has important implications for pastoral care. First, the adaptations people make to powerful social messages are framed as survival strategies rather than as individual pathology. To be able to adapt and survive is a strength, but it carries a tremendous psychic cost. Second, coming to perceive new possibilities for oneself involves both *analyzing* the social sources of the messages and *correcting* the distortions. Third, this kind of "corrective action and health maintenance"[12] requires an ongoing support community, because the structures and messages that engender harmful adaptation will continue to exert powerful pressure. In Christian terms, sin is systemic and an ongoing condition of our lives and cannot simply be understood in terms of individual responsibility, although taking responsibility is important in the face of sin.

Ballou and Gabalac's framework provides one way of understanding the dynamics of sin and hope. In the next paragraphs I will
reflect further on ministry with Sheena and other members of her
community. But at this juncture, these are the pastoral care questions that emerge from the relationship with Sheena that I have described thus far: In what ways may a pastor and congregation join
persons in keeping hope alive for a future in which they and their
communities would flourish? At the same time, how may pastors
and congregations also confront the depth of the damage done to a
person's/community's self image, as well as the concrete roadblocks
to the survival and flourishing of persons and communities? What
kind of pastoral care approach takes each of these with equal seri-
ousness?

## Empathy and Sociopolitical Analysis

As a pastor, part of my care for Sheena involved trying to listen
to and attend to her perceptions of her world, her struggles, her
dreams. Another part of that care involved experiencing, side by
side, some particular joys and sorrows of shared life in the same
neighborhood—common work in the neighborhood of ministry,
table companionship, moments of shared laughter and tears. A
world was created on the boundary of our different experiences, a
world that had a language of its own. This listening, this attempt to
become familiar with the sights, sounds, tastes, textures, and smells
of another's world, is one way of making more concrete the much-
misunderstood term *empathy* that some people confuse with sym-
pathy and others presume suggests that we can know exactly what
another's world is like. (Later in this chapter I will explore more fully
the place of this concept in conceiving the ministry of pastoral care.)

It is debatable how successfully I or other caregivers understood
Sheena's world or perceived the dilemmas with which she struggled.
But even if it were true that we had an accurate portrait of how
Sheena perceived her struggles, it is clear that we lacked a sociopolitical analysis of the situation she faced as an African-American
woman, as well as an analysis of our own social location in relation
to her. In an albeit unintentional way, I believe we may have exacerbated the pain of Sheena's oppression: we reminded her over and
over that she was valuable and talented, but we left her alone to figure out how to employ those talents in a dominant culture that did
not seek them. When she expressed concern or self-blame about
missing skills, we did not help her explore the systemic roots of her
lack of confidence, assist her in acquiring the skills, or collaborate
on communal challenges to the institutions that undermined her life
and the lives of people in the neighborhood—people to whom she

was deeply loyal.[13] Many of Sheena's friends were in a similar situation. They found a temporary haven in the church, a place of affirmation and care, a place where their stories could be respectfully heard and valued; but the church did not provide the tools for addressing the ongoing dilemma of being African American in a racist culture—a culture in which we (congregation and pastor) were implicated. We offered care, but we offered care in ways that supported rather than subverted the status quo.

While experiencing privilege in interracial relationships, I felt on the margin when it came to affecting the arenas of decision making that most influenced our life as a congregation. That experience of powerlessness challenged me to examine the kinds of assumptions about ministry and effectiveness that helped to determine the fate of congregations like my own and helped to constrain my life as an ordained woman. I began to examine the roots of my own lack of confidence in my perceptions and my voice—what constrained my own ability to bring about change. In at least one respect, my needs paralleled Sheena's. I, too, needed help in examining the systemic roots of my own lack of confidence, help in acquiring some needed skills, and access to an ongoing community of reflection and struggle.

In this and many other pastoral care situations I have experienced the creative tension between the need to immerse myself in the lives of others and the need to employ the tools of sociopolitical analysis in order to understand pastoral care situations. Without immersion in the lives of others, our analyses are distant and people become objectified; people can scarcely recognize themselves in our descriptions if they are devoid of the colors and textures, the sounds, smells, and tastes of their daily lives. Yet without sociopolitical analysis, our immersions may overwhelm us and cause us to lose sight of the larger systems in which our relationships and lives are embedded. How can we deeply enter into others' worlds in such a way that they feel understood and companioned? At the same time, how can we practice care in such a way that invites people to join with us in examining the structures and beliefs that shape our lives?

## An Image for Pastoral Caregiving

The creative tensions I have just described challenge some of the familiar images of pastoral care that have pervaded pastoral care approaches in both the classical and modern era. In the classical era, the image of the pastor as shepherd was (and continues to be for many) an important image for pastoral care. It suggests strength, courage, and leadership—all essential qualities for pastoral caregivers. But it does not suggest a common vulnerability or a mutual struggle to survive and flourish in a tumultuous world. (The shepherd is a different species type than the sheep and is somehow able to see dangers and possibilities for green pasture that the sheep cannot see.) In the modern era, the image of the pastor as "wounded healer" arose in part to address this concern. Yet that image may suggest a certain passivity in the pastoral role—an understanding of the cross that is focused on God's suffering love and the call to "suffer with," but not on another dimension of the cross, that is, God's resounding No to human suffering and the forces of death and destruction.[14]

What ways of imagining our role call us to live deeply within and amidst the creative tensions of our lives and ministries, neither being totally overwhelmed by them nor needing to appear totally in control of them? What images capture the ambiguity of pastoral life itself—the ways we are both deeply implicated in systemic sin and yet called forward to a life together that is beyond our imagining? What understandings of human action, lived in the greater sweep of God's movement in the world, free us for courageous action and keep us humble about our own motivations or the power of our own deeds? What way of understanding pastoral care does not divorce priestly and prophetic roles?

The image that has helped me to wrestle with these tensions is that of the pastoral caregiver as one who conspires and collaborates with people in the very midst of these boundary experiences. This image has biblical roots, to which I now turn. The exploration of a particular text can yield insight into the nature of collaborating and conspiring on the boundary.

## The Art of Conspiring and Collaborating: An Engagement with a Text

My fascination with Exodus 1:8–22, the story of the midwives who refused to comply with Pharaoh's command to kill Hebrew boys at birth, began when I was an urban pastor. I was invited to be part of a team of United Methodists who were visiting four major cities in southern New Jersey in order to listen to urban pastors and laity share their experiences of ministry in these cities. I was asked to present a Bible study that had "something to do with urban ministry," and this was the text I chose. I chose it because I was drawn to the image of pastoral ministry as midwifery, as a process of co-laboring with people to bring forth new life.[15] I was also drawn to the text because it depicted both the risk taking and the exercise of savvy and wit that urban ministry seems constantly to require. Finally, I was drawn to it because the circumstances of the Hebrews were so overwhelmingly negative and the power of the midwives so limited; yet they acted nonetheless, and their actions had hopeful consequences that surely would have been hard to foresee at the time that they were performed.

What does this text suggest about the tensions I have just elaborated? What does it suggest about the role of conspiring and collaborating as a way of responding to these tensions?

### Anxiety and Possibility

The first part of the text (Ex. 1:8–16) conveys enormous anxiety for Pharaoh and a hint of possibility for the Israelites, which Pharaoh aims to extinguish. What spells advantage in one context spells danger in another. The sheer growth of the Israelite people suggests a growing strength in one nation and a potential threat to another.

The first image of conspiring in this text is a frightening one, reminding us that great care must be taken in developing the images of conspiring and collaborating for pastoral care. Indeed, the first meaning of "conspire" in dictionaries is usually "to join in a secret agreement to do an unlawful or wrongful act" (Webster 10th ed.).[16] Pharaoh sends for Shiphrah and Puah and enlists them in a conspiracy to limit population growth among the Hebrews. His instructions are simple and grim: "When you act as midwives to the Hebrew women, and see them on the birthstool, if it is a boy, kill him." Viewed from the perspective of Pharaoh, the end justifies the means. The elimination of boy babies will, in his logic, eliminate the threat to established order that the Israelites pose to his realm.

There are almost no glimmers of possibility in this text, save two. One is suggested by Pharaoh's fear itself. That is, the text suggests that there is something tenuous about the established order. The greater the fear, the more tenuous the order seems, and the more tenuous the order seems, the harsher the measures taken to secure it will be. But the fear itself points to the human inability ultimately to control life. The second glimmer of possibility is suggested in verse 20b and has to do with the Hebrews continuing to multiply and to become very strong. The verse suggests, however subtly, that there is a process of life that will not easily be sabotaged, and God is involved in the struggle in behalf of the vulnerable.

### Oppressed and Oppressor

Because of the ambiguous language in the Hebrew text, it is unclear whether Shiphrah and Puah are themselves Hebrews or midwives to the Hebrews;[17] the NRSV identifies them as "Hebrew midwives" (1:15). One modern midrash on the text portrays them as

Egyptian women.[18] Shiphrah and Puah are "the only women in Exodus to act in an overtly political sphere, having direct contact with the Pharaoh (1:15, 18–19)."[19]

Regardless of their nationality, the power of the midwives is severely limited. They had to have known that Pharaoh's determination to carry out his plan did not ultimately depend on their cooperation. Indeed, the text ends with Pharaoh's "people" carrying out his grim plan (1:22). But it is undeniable that in relation to Hebrew women in the process of giving birth, the midwives wield an enormous (yet temporary) power and must choose how to use it. They decide to use it in behalf of the Hebrew women, even though the ultimate success of their actions to preserve life cannot be guaranteed and they have put themselves at risk in choosing as they have.

It is at this point in the text that the images of conspiring and collaborating are most visceral. Conspiring literally means "breathing together" (the second meaning in dictionaries often has to do with "working together toward the same result or goal"). Anyone who has participated in natural childbirth classes (or watched television or movie portrayals of natural childbirth) knows that regulated breathing is an essential part of the birth process. Childbirth coaches often join the laboring woman in breathing exercises that become more intense as labor moves into the transition stage, the prelude to birth. The act of coaching a woman in childbirth often involves sweat on the part of the coach as well as the laboring mother (though obviously not to the same degree!). But "co-labor" is indeed what happens in a delivery room. It is this activity that marks the participation of the midwives. Whatever co-laboring and conspiring went on between midwives and Hebrew families after the births is not known to us. It is not unreasonable to assume that the midwives may have conspired with the families to keep their boy babies hidden as long as possible.

## Systemic Sin and Eschatological Hope

Shiphrah and Puah's decision not to comply with Pharaoh's order entails consequences. Eventually Pharaoh will learn the truth, and the midwives will have to account for the number of Hebrew boy babies still alive. Here again there is a strong hint of collaborating and conspiring. When Pharaoh at last summons them and asks them why they have allowed the boys to live, the midwives speak as one: "The midwives said to Pharaoh, 'Because the Hebrew women are not like the Egyptian women; for they are vigorous and give birth before the midwife comes to them'" (1:19).

The first response in the face of systemic sin and evil was not to comply with Pharaoh's command and to continue to do their job, which was to help bring new life to birth. As they "breathed with" the women in childbirth, they conspired to thwart Pharaoh's plan. In preparing to face Pharaoh, they "breathed together" a story that was marvelously ironic. Because Pharaoh was already somewhat amazed and threatened by the prolific nature of Hebrew life, it is altogether imaginable that the midwives conspired to use Pharaoh's stereotype of the Hebrews against him. Did Pharaoh believe them? We do not know.

Although the historicity of such tales is the subject of ongoing debate, the *purpose* of them seems wonderfully clear. Phyllis Trible suggests something of the subversive fun this story may have had for Israel.

> What delight Israel must have had in telling the story! The mighty king of Egypt, Pharaoh of the Two Lands, male god incarnate, deigned to speak directly to females. Moreover, memory preserved their names, Shiphrah and Puah, while obliterating the identity of the monarch so completely that he has become the burden of innumerable doctoral dissertations.[20]

It is through such stories that imaginative vision is conveyed. Something beyond the drudgery of oppression and the hopelessness of tyranny is suggested through this text. God's name is mentioned in two ways: as the reason why the midwives would not comply with Pharaoh's instructions ("But the midwives feared God"—1:17a) and as a source of blessing in the wake of their risk (1:20).

### Empathy and Sociopolotical Analysis

In this area, we are especially limited to conjecture. We have absolutely no information on the interior lives of the midwives or how they felt about anything save that God did not want them to comply with Pharaoh's request. There seems to be enough sociopolitical analysis about Pharaoh to lead them to hatch the story they did about the Hebrew women who are "not like the Egyptian women" and still have a fighting chance to survive. A modern Jewish midrash on the text speculates that the women counted on two things: Pharaoh's stereotype of the Hebrew women and his ignorance about matters of childbirth.[21]

Christie Neuger has proposed the image of the Exodus as a central biblical image for pastoral care and counseling, particularly with marginalized people. I agree that it is not only a helpful image but it is obviously a *foundational* biblical image, not a peripheral one. At the same time, as Neuger points out, the Exodus image is not without its difficulties. No image is without limitations. We seek to identify the ones that can help us with particular struggles in particular moments of history.[22]

The Exodus image captures the thrill involved in moments of deliverance; the courage it takes to leave behind familiar tyranny and venture toward a land of promise; the risk and danger and loss of the journey; the precarious vision of a new world. On the negative side, one of the difficulties with the Exodus image is that it has sometimes been used to argue for a nation's divinely given right to a desired land (for example, Manifest Destiny in the United States, the Boer claim on South Africa's land, Israel's control of Jerusalem) and the notion that God plunders one nation for the benefit of another (even the "firstborn children" in that nation). Another difficulty is that exodus may not always be possible, even when it is fervently desired. Exodus may suggest journeys too incredible and huge for most people to attempt.

Thus I propose the portrait of the collaborating and conspiring midwives as a supplement to this exodus image, a story that itself is part of the Exodus tradition and acts as a kind of prelude to the great event. It is useful for times when small acts of faith, courage, and resistance are all that appear to be possible. Yet the text suggests that these acts of conspiracy and collaboration make a difference in people's lives and are woven together in a larger drama of God's saving activity in the world. Although there is much that is unpromising and unchangeable, even tragic, in their world, the midwives' behavior portrays just enough subversive play to suggest that *perhaps* all will not be lost in the long run. And where there is the sting of powerlessness, there is a stubborn noncompliance to the inexorable movement of systems of power—a refusal to give in even when adjustments need to be made. What would such conspiracy and collaboration look like in the actual practice of pastoral care? It is the task of the following section to paint some portraits.

### Pastoral Care as Conspiring and Collaborating

At the beginning of this chapter, I spoke about four creative tensions that I experienced as a pastor, and I lifted up the image of the caregiver as one who conspires and collaborates with people in the midst of these tensions. Then, returning to these tensions, I explored how the image of the caregiver as conspirator and collaborator is fleshed out in relation to a particular biblical text.

These four creative tensions are related to the four questions with which I began this chapter: (1) In what kind of *world* do I engage in pastoral care relationships? (2) *Where do I stand* as a caregiver in relation to the contexts of the people with whom I engage in care? (3) What *vision* of wholeness or health guides my ministry of care, that is, what kinds of persons and communities do I hope to help form? (4) *How* do I offer care; what *goals and methods* are appropriate? I will now return full circle to these questions and offer some responses, together with some of the implications I see for pastoral care practice. These "implications" are meant to be suggestive and evocative; they are, of course, in no way comprehensive or exhaustive.

### The World of Pastoral Care

> I believe that we are in a season of transition, when we are watching the collapse of the world as we have known it. The political forms and economic modes of the past are increasingly ineffective. The value system and shapes of knowledge through which we have controlled life are now in great jeopardy. One can paint the picture in very large scope, but the issues do not present themselves to pastors as global issues. They appear as local, even personal issues, but they are nonetheless pieces of a very big picture. When the fear and anger are immediate and acute, we do not stop to notice how much our own crisis is part of the larger one, but it is.[23]

I spoke of the world of pastoral care as a world characterized by anxiety and possibility, a world in which many persons, pastors, and congregations are experiencing that "the center is not holding" and are struggling to survive economically, culturally, psychologically, and spiritually. In such a world, pastors can play a critical role by exploring, with persons and congregations, ways to face the upheaval and grief of change, to engage difference creatively, to respond to fear, and to help define boundaries and create safe spaces while at the same nurturing freedom, playfulness, and imagination.

#### Conspiring and Collaborating in Such a World

One of the chief opportunities for pastoral care is the worship life of the congregation. In her helpful book *Ritual and Pastoral Care*,[24] Elaine Ramshaw explores the relationship between ritual and care for faith communities, individuals, and the world. With regard to addressing anxiety and possibility, the following observations are especially helpful.

The first has to do with the human need for order. Ramshaw's first premise about ritual is that ritual orders human experience. A healthy ritual provides the "stability of a dependable context within which variance can delight."[25] Closely allied with the need for order is the need to reaffirm meaning and the need to handle ambivalence, especially when people are confronted with situations that threaten meaning and stir chaotic feelings. The two ways that ritualization helps us to handle conflicting feelings are to reinforce the preferred emotion and to provide a safe mode of expression for the unwanted, conflicting emotion.[26]

Ramshaw believes, and I concur, that most churches are far more adept at reinforcing preferred emotions than offering opportunities to express such emotions as anger, fear, and profound sadness.[27] "Breathing with" people involves creating ritual space for lament and protest, as well as thanksgiving and supplication. If Walter Brueggemann is right that "only grief permits newness,"[28] then a crucial aspect of pastoral care is to encourage the fullest possible experience of that grief.[29]

There are a variety of levels at which this ministry for and with others takes place. A West-side Chicago congregation recently held a day-long vigil of lament and prayer for the scores of Chicago children who have been killed because of drug abuse and drug-related violence. Parishioners joined bereaved families in printing the children's names on crosses and bearing these crosses down neighborhood streets. The procession stopped to pray and sing at known drug houses. In a rural church in southern New Jersey, the pastor knew several women who were quietly grieving miscarriages alone. She invited them to come together to share their stories and their grief. The group became a source of new life for many of these women. In both of these ministries, pastors entered into the personal grief of persons and families and co-labored with them to bring that grief to full expression in ways that left the door ajar for newness.

Earlier I noted the struggles for survival that are occurring in my own and many others' ministry contexts today. What is behind these struggles for survival? There are complex factors that vary from context to context, of course, but I believe it is important to help congregations explore some global trends, "the larger crisis," that shape our lives and ministries. Sometimes pastors and congregations are browbeaten by their judicatories for not "caring enough" to attract new members, without being offered help in analyzing what is happening in the world and how our care for others might truly touch the real wounds of people's lives.

Globalization is a complex phenomenon, bringing both wonders and terrors. Writers on globalization point out that globalization "is creating a world-wide, uniform reality" that "can be seen in greater or lesser degrees in . . . global systems: the economy, science and technology, medicine, and to some extent education and the media."[30] The world is growing smaller and increasingly interdependent; opportunities abound for plumbing together the varied roots of our faiths and worldviews. Exciting possibilities for global relationships multiply as the process of becoming "one world" continues. In many arenas of life (for example, scientific and medical research, ecology, religion), the opportunity is there to create global strategies for global dilemmas.

In order to become one world, globalization "must relativize everything in its wake," except for the expansion and generation of wealth, which are its desired ends. Although there is much that is beneficial about this process, as I have just described, it also carries enormous dangers. Its homogenization of the world is disruptive and corrosive of particular cultures and communities; its unifying center is a web of market-driven values and goals. Some cultures and communities respond by withering, others by revitalizing and redefining themselves in light of the globalization challenge.[31]

The effect of these larger social forces at the congregational level is quite staggering. Along with all the new opportunities that come with globalization—multicultural communities and congregations, widespread exposure to a plethora of different values and assumptions about life together that challenge us to both critique and more clearly define and affirm our Christian assumptions—come dangers. From the "megachurch" movement, which harnesses conservative theology to the most sophisticated communication and pastoral care "technologies" available (that is, sophisticated training in how to lead groups of all kinds, a highly effective system for the delivery of care to individuals in need), to smaller "resistance" communities of all types, religious communities are struggling to respond to sweeping changes, set in motion by a globalization process that is more complex than I have described here, one that is largely driven by the expansion and generation of wealth. Some communities are literally shattering. In an essay reflecting on the nihilistic threat to African-American communities, Cornel West writes, "The recent market-driven shattering of black civil society—black families, neighborhoods, schools, churches, mosques—leaves more and more black people vulnerable to daily lives endured with little sense of self and fragile existential moorings."[32]

An important and urgent dimension of pastoral care is to help people "link personal life to the places where God is at work in larger contexts of dismantling. There are no personal issues that are not of a piece with the great public issues. To divide things up into prophetic and pastoral is to betray both."[33] Through preaching and Bible studies on the experience of exile and through liturgies that take seriously the link between personal and social pain, pastors encourage a larger, more communal understanding of what is shaping our lives.

## Where We Stand as Caregivers

I propose that one way to envision *where we stand* as pastoral caregivers is to claim the dual identity of being both oppressed and oppressor. This dual identity will look different depending on our social location. For "Cara," a Hispanic student, life in a mainstream seminary is often agonizing. She must constantly read and converse in a language that is not her familiar language, conform to worship and social patterns that are not nourishing for her, and cope with the anger she feels when confronted with racist attitudes. When she goes to her field education church and neighborhood, she must struggle also with the relative advantage that her education gives her over many of the people who live in her church's neighborhood and with the freedom she now has to drive away from that neighborhood. She speaks passionately about being "pulled apart"—not fully at home in either world, living on the boundary.

"Paul," a white pastor from a well-educated and affluent community, is now serving a working-class congregation. As a single man openly recovering from a drug addiction, he knows that he has lost his place on the ecclesial ladder that leads "upward." Yet Paul wants very much to love the people he serves. It is difficult for him because the sensibilities of the people are not his. Life in his town centers for many people in the tavern, a risky place for him. He now lives on the boundary, between worlds, and is trying to find ways to enter deeply into his new world and still retain his own passions and perspective. He struggles with his pastoral authority, because he knows that the people in his town have suffered "the hidden injuries of class"[34] and have been shamed by other pastors in the past.

To explore this dual identity is to reflect on the delicate dynamics of power—to ponder how ritual authority and institutional authority can be recognized and used in ways that are empowering for others, and to plumb our own experiences of marginalization for insights about what is helpful and healing.

### Conspiring and Collaborating from Such a Position

What can one do, on such a boundary, to enhance the freedom and flourishing of others, while not neglecting one's own? I will offer three illustrations. The first focuses on congregational life, the second on pastoral care with a couple, and the third on pastoral care with an individual.

The first illustration has to do with how persons come to *name* themselves and their location in the world. Many times pastors see the task of naming as their responsibility and feel inadequate if they cannot name a community's situations and issues in a way that inspires a community to action. The pastor as collaborator and conspirator, however, hopes to help birth the names, symbols, and language that people give to their own experiences—and to claim the power of naming for themselves.

I saw this naming process unfold in an early community organizing process in Trenton several years ago. The process began with listening—long and careful listening to scores of church leaders. People were encouraged to tell the parts of their stories they wanted to share; to share what drew them to their own congregations and what motivated them to stay there. They were invited to share their views on what was happening around them and why. Only after that long process of listening did the organizers invite the church leaders to come together to discuss a particular community issue. Even in that meeting, the role of the organizers was to ask questions that facilitated the church leaders' own naming and analysis of the community issue. For example: How did this situation come to be this way? Who would be affected if things were to change? Who would be helped if things were to change? What information would be needed to decide how to address this situation? Who stands the best chance of getting to various sources of information?

The group that gathered that night began with a sense of pessimism about what could be done to make a change in a situation that seemed inevitable and immovable. By the end of the evening, energy was high, tasks were divided up, and there was a spirit of hope. Skillful leadership was exercised, but exercised in such a way that the power of the community was enhanced. Such investment in co-laboring with people to name their needs, hopes, and strategies is an important element in pastoral care with couples and families, especially when the power differential is substantial.

Earlier in this chapter I described the power differential between the pastor and the lesbian couple who sought pastoral care and ritual blessing. Care that attempts to enhance the power of the couple will include genuine respect for these women as individuals and for their relationship, a willingness to learn from the couple about the ways they conceive commitment (not only to one another but to their families and other significant relationships), and a capacity to put issues of power and integrity on the table so that all partners in the conversation can engage the issues together. Care will also involve becoming knowledgeable about the theological and psychological issues this couple faces and the ritual options that exist, and making resources available to the couple, to their families, and to the congregation.[35]

Pastoral care at the individual level is rich with possibility and complexity. The individual who lies dying in a hospital bed may name himself or herself in many ways—in relation to his or her family, religious tradition, work, or friends. But in moments of extreme human limitation and fragility, he or she may struggle in new ways with words that have never yet been spoken, seeking to share the holy mystery that he or she encounters or the profound silence and abyss that is terrifying. The first step in helping people to voice their experience, "to hear into speech" that which has never been articulated, begins with the gracious commitment to listen past the borders of our categories, to communicate our valuing of what is waiting to be voiced, to learn a language that may be quite "other" from our own, and to be deeply aware of the language spoken through bodily expression as well as words.[36] Listening in such a way has always been an art and a mystery, the profoundest gesture of respect. To communicate, by eyes, face, voice, and posture, that one has something infinitely precious to learn from someone else is to offer back what often seems to be ebbing away—the capacity to touch or enrich another human being.

One pastor tells the story of an eighty-five-year-old man, "Ed," who was distressed when she was called to his congregation because "the Bible says women should not preach." Ed let it be known in the congregation that he would finish out the year and then leave the congregation. The new pastor visited Ed, listened to his concerns, and said that although she did not see things in the same way that he did, she respected how important his biblical convictions were to him. She shared some of the biblical passages that had been important in claiming her call to ministry. She told Ed that she would miss him when he left, that she was challenged by the depth of the theological struggles they had shared. Ed responded that he might reconsider his decision.

Shortly thereafter, Ed's cancer, which had long been in remission, recurred. This time the disease advanced rapidly. The visits between Ed and the pastor took on a particular ritual shape, which included visiting, hymn singing, and prayer, in which Ed would always have the last word. One night, in the hospital, Ed was too weak for much visiting and too weak to sing. After a long time of sitting with him and holding his hand, the pastor prayed softly about how much Ed had meant to her and taught her. Ed then followed the last element of their familiar ritual—concluding the prayer. His prayer was simply that God would bless her ministry. He died later that night.

Up to the end, the pastor had respected and marveled at Ed's capacity to grow, sensing in him a resilience that was worth exploring and valuing. In spite of a thorny beginning, he did not disappoint her. In wrestling with him, she attempted to learn his language of faith and to offer hers. She sensed his desire to hold on to his church and his faith. The metaphors of holding on and letting go permeated their conversations, as they struggled with what was essential and what one, in faith, could let go and trust to God. In letting go of life, Ed claimed the power to choose that the pastor had respected in him. In relinquishing his own life, he chose to offer blessing.

## The Vision that Guides Care

In their book, *A Feminist Position on Mental Health,* Mary Ballou and Nancy Gabalac identify several operating assumptions about what mental health means for women. I think these assumptions are helpful in probing our theological assumptions about what health and wholeness mean.[37]

Being healthy involves being at home with one's sexual, racial, and cultural identity, and being able to celebrate links with others who share that identity. Being healthy involves the capability of *receiving* data about oneself—from one's own self, from others, and from the environment—and *processing* that data in a way that recognizes that some data one receives are contaminated (for example, the data that women receive from the culture and the media that their value is measured primarily by their appearance). Being healthy involves being able to make decisions and judgments that promote survival growth for self and positive relationships with others and the natural environment. Being healthy involves being able to use power and knowledge to deal with self and environment in ways that promote one's own and others' development. Being healthy involves challenging and changing what can be changed in self and society and in learning to survive what cannot be changed. It involves engaging the contradictions between victim and agent, negotiating social constraints and individual responsibility.[38]

Each of the above assumptions is congruent with my theological assumptions. To be able to see oneself as a child of God, just as one was created or has come to be, is at the heart of the Christian understanding of grace. Other assumptions contain an implicit awareness that we live in a world where systemic sin and injustice mars self and relationships, yet there is still goodness and grace. Ballou and Gabalac offer a vision of health that includes ongoing struggle and limitation, yet hopes and works for change. I would add, however, that as a Christian I understand the struggle for wholeness for all people as God's saving work in the world, in which we are called to participate. Our hope is rooted in God's activity in our midst, but our eyes are also open to the depths of human tragedy and the cries of absence that are often deeply part of the Christian life.

*Conspiring and Collaborating in Light of That Vision*

Imagination is central to vision. Strategizing to overcome the real obstacles is an important dimension of attempting to realize a vision. How may care nourish and stretch the imagination and help people address the real and painful limits they face?

One important avenue for nourishing and stretching the imagination is to help persons explore the images that are important for them. Sometimes people offer these images to us by sharing their experiences and their dreams. In her article "Imagination in Pastoral Counseling," Christie Neuger tells the story of her pastoral counseling with Anna, a seminarian who suffered from depression.[39] In the process of constructing a history of her experience, Anna brought a series of drawings depicting herself in a fetal position within a cavelike room without doors or windows. As Neuger and Anna explored this image together, Anna realized that she felt trapped and helpless but also comfortable and safe in this womblike space.

Neuger describes how she and Anna worked with the womb image in a variety of ways. A turning point in Anna's relationship with God occurred when Neuger asked her to locate God in the image of herself in the womb. "To her complete surprise, she found that the womb was in God and that her image of God's will for her was to be enclosed in this restricting womb. It was important for her to see both the positive and negative ramifications of 'resting in God' so literally."[40]

Neuger worked creatively with Anna's image of herself and God. By not prematurely attempting to resolve the problems inherent in the image, but rather respecting and exploring it, Neuger collaborated with Anna to explore gradual modifications in the image and her behaviors in the world. Anna was not counseled to let go of her image, but gradually to place other images alongside it. In doing so, Anna expanded her range of choices and possibilities, even her ways of perceiving and experiencing God.

I once asked a group of teenagers in the Greenwood Program what they thought of when they heard the word *heaven*. A sixteen-year-old replied: "It would just be a really beautiful place . . . where you could go, lie down. Like they describe the Garden of Eden. No sadness, no starving babies, no sick people, no old people not wanted. . . . No needs or wants that you can't get because you're too poor."[41] We went on to explore how the teenagers imaged sin. Many of these images had to do with being constricted, or compelled to act in certain ways. Pastors have wonderful opportunities to explore people's images of their situations and even of what theological terms connote. The first step in conspiring, I suspect, is to know what pictures and dreams may yet be alive in people's hearts and what fears lie there as well.

Imaginative vision can also be nourished in worship. The eucharistic meal itself provides an "alternative vision . . . where the distribution of food is so different from the normal process in our world: not more for the rich and less for the poor, but an equal amount for all. . . . This ritual statement of hope is essential, even if all it can do is to awaken the hunger for a different way of being human; for when that hunger is awakened we stand in solidarity with all the truly hungry of our world."[42]

## The Goals and Methods of Care

When the hands that hold the host
Have plunged fingers, with seeds into damp soil,
Or swung an axe in sweat-soaked toil,
There's blessing in the cup.

When hands that break bread in remembrance
Have tenderly birthed a lamb
Or cradled an infant at midnight,
Life itself is elevated on the altar.

When the soul of a celebrant has known
The sweetness of friendship ripened on love's vine
Been duly crushed by heartbreak, flattened by aching loss,
The wine of the covenant is richly shared.

For the soot of the city,
The pain of the people.
The touch of another,
Stain the tablecoth, yet
Consecrate many hands.

By them, bread is blessed, and rises,
Thus, the corpus contains
Every grain of creation, broken
In bright conspiracy—transformed.[43]

This poem, written by a Roman Catholic laywoman and poet, Kathleen O'Toole, is dedicated to a parish priest named Michael Doyle "and all who 'conspire' in aspiring to a universal priesthood."[44] What goals and methods does this laywoman identify as "conspiratorial"?

The poem suggests that conspiring ministers immerse themselves in the lives of the people in their communities. Physical images dominate the opening lines—swinging arms, cradling arms, soil, sweat—*labor*. The minister labors with people in a variety of contexts.

Because the images are of the work of common people, the life that is "elevated" is ordinary life, lives of people whose stories are not usually told or celebrated beyond the bounds of their families. At the Church of the Sacred Heart in Camden, New Jersey, a book was published for its centennial celebration.[45] It was a huge book of stories—stories told of the various immigrant members who have lived and labored in that parish. It is a poignant and rather astonishing piece of work that includes not only the stories of leaders but even the story of a baby named Katie Cofsky, who "came on December 21, 1981 at the crucial time when the long night seems to win against the winter's tired light" and died "on the 51st day of her life." The stories are told with such poetic sensibility, respect, and tenderness that it is as if the reader is reading the story of royalty.

There are many ways to "elevate life." The spirit of the Greenwood Program was brought to life through the efforts of a professional photographer, who lovingly photographed the children, and a musician, who put the slide pictures to music so that the children, parents, and supporters might glimpse the holiness in their faces. Through quilts, banners, food, artistry of many kinds, people search for ways to express their lives. The task of care is to foster and support that expression.

Empathy is a crucial and much misunderstood term in pastoral care. In much common parlance it implies an easy ability to feel what others feel because we have experienced something similar. But empathy, which is so much a part of listening to forgotten stories and conspiring and collaborating with individuals and congregations, is that point where otherness captures our interest and attention, and where we seek to understand what we do not yet know. The parish gives us multiple opportunities to learn.

### A Concluding Word

When you write, it's like braiding your hair. Taking a handful of coarse unruly strands and attempting to bring them unity. Your fingers have still not perfected the task. Some of the braids are long, others are short. Some are thick, others are thin. Some are heavy. Others are light. Like the diverse women in your family. Those whose fables and metaphors, whose similes, and soliloquies, whose diction and *je ne sais quoi* daily slip into your survival soup, by way of their fingers.[46]

I agree with Edwidge Danticat: writing is like braiding your hair. I have been plaiting three strands of pastoral reflection together in this chapter: reflection on pastoral experience, reflection on feminist appropriations of the Judeo-Christian tradition and other sources of wisdom, and reflection on the implications of this interplay for pastoral practice. The strands are not even. Some are thick, others are thin. Some are heavy, others are light. Woven into the strands are the terrors and delights of ministry, the moments of clarity and ambiguity, the struggle with both survival and significance, gratitude for all that there is to draw on, fleeting frustration that the result is not as tidy as I would like. Braids do not stay fixed forever; they need to be plaited again and again. New patterns are always possible.

Pastoral care is like that.

## NOTES

1. Stephens Ministry is a lay pastoral care training program.
2. Some basic texts in pastoral care that discuss caregiving as a task of the community are John Patton, *Pastoral Care in Context: An Introduction to Pastoral Care* (Louisville, Ky.: Westminster/John Knox Press, 1993), 3–37; and Howard Clinebell, *Basic Types of Pastoral Care and Counseling* (Nashville: Abingdon Press, 1984), 394–415. There is a burgeoning literature in small-group ministries of care; there are also national training programs like Stephens Ministry for the training of lay pastoral caregivers.
3. For a wonderful glimpse of St. Paul, see Christine M. Smith, *Preaching as Weeping, Confession, and Resistance: Radical Responses to Radical Evil* (Louisville, Ky.: Westminster/John Knox Press, 1992), 176.
4. Letty M. Russell, *Household of Freedom: Authority in Feminist Perspective* (Philadelphia: Westminster Press, 1988), 14.
5. From William Butler Yeats, "The Second Coming," in *Selected Poems and Three Plays of William Butler Yeats*, 3d ed., ed. M. L. Rosenthal (New York: Macmillan, 1986), 89.
6. Rebecca S. Chopp, *The Power to Speak: Feminism, Language, and God* (New York: Crossroad, 1992), 16. Chopp makes reference to the work of Sharon Welch and Julia Kristeva. Her center/margin imagery is in dialogue with the womanist critique of bell hooks.
7. See Sharon Welch, *Communities of Resistance and Solidarity* (Maryknoll, N.Y.: Orbis Books, 1985), ix. Welch was the first feminist theologian I read who articulated this double identity for white women. Since then, I have become acquainted with many more feminist theologians who have made this dimension of experience a primary subject of investigation. Some of these will be named over the course of this chapter.
8. Chopp, *The Power to Speak*, 16.
9. Ibid.
10. I am grateful for the "Women of Color–White Women's Dialogue

Group" at LSTC, which has been a source of both tremendous challenge and blessing over the past three years.

11. Mary Ballou and Nancy Gabalac, *A Feminist Position on Mental Health* (Springfield, Ill.: Charles C. Thomas, 1985), 69–97.

12. Ibid., 98–129.

13. See Carol B. Stack, *All Our Kin: Strategies for Survival in a Black Community* (New York: Harper & Row, 1974) for a significant discussion of loyalty and reciprocity in one African-American inner-city community.

14. For a helpful exploration of these images, see Alastair Campbell, *Rediscovering Pastoral Care* (Philadelphia: Westminister Press, 1981); and Donald Capps, *Pastoral Care and Hermeneutics* (Philadelphia: Fortress Press, 1984), 76–121.

15. See Kathleen D. Billman, "Integrating Theology and Pastoral Care in Ministry," *Currents in Theology and Mission* 19, No. 3 (June 1992): 165–73.

16. As I was completing work on this manuscript, the bombing in Oklahoma City took place, catapulting the term *conspiracy* into daily use. For reasons that I will continue to try to make clear, I think the term is redeemable precisely because it provokes thought and is ambiguous—like ministry.

17. Drorah O'Donnell Setel, "Exodus," in *The Women's Bible Commentary*, ed. Carol A. Newsome and Sharon H. Ringe (Louisville, Ky.: Westminster/John Knox Press, 1992), 30.

18. Jane Sprague Zones, ed., *Taking the Fruit: Modern Women's Tales of the Bible* (San Diego: Women's Institute for Continuing Jewish Education, 1981), 42–43.

19. Ibid., 30.

20. Phyllis Trible, "The Pilgrim Bible on a Feminist Journey," *The Princeton Seminary Bulletin* vol. XI, No. 3 (New Series 1990): 237.

21. Zones, ed., *Taking the Fruit*, 43.

22. Christie Cozad Neuger, "Feminist Pastoral Theology and Pastoral Counseling: A Work in Progress," *Journal of Pastoral Theology* 2 (Summer 1992): 53–54; and "Shifting Context in Pastoral Care, Part II," unpublished lecture, Wesley Seminary, October 12, 1994.

23. Walter Brueggemann, *Hopeful Imagination: Prophetic Voices in Exile* (Philadelphia: Fortress Press, 1986), 45–46.

24. Elaine Ramshaw, *Ritual and Pastoral Care* (Philadelphia: Fortress Press, 1987).

25. Ibid., 24.

26. Ibid., 22–33.

27. Ibid., 32.

28. Brueggemann, *Hopeful Imagination*, 41.

29. A manuscript, tentatively titled *Rachel's Cry: The Prayer of Lament and Pastoral Ministry*, by Kathleen D. Billman and Daniel L. Migliore, is currently in progress that will develop themes presented in this section.

30. Robert J. Schreiter, "Globalization, Religion, and Theological Education," paper presented to the Chicago Center for Global Ministries, May 10, 1994, p. 3. Quoted with permission from the author.

31. Ibid.
32. Cornel West, *Race Matters* (Boston: Beacon Press, 1993), 16.
33. Brueggemann, *Hopeful Imagination*, 18.
34. See Richard Sennett and Jonathan Cobb, *The Hidden Injuries of Class* (New York: Vintage Books, 1973), for a helpful look at class dynamics.
35. See, for example, Kittredge Cherry and Zalmon Sherwood, eds., *Equal Rights: Lesbian and Gay Worship, Ceremonies, and Celebrations* (Louisville, Ky.: Westminster John Knox Press, 1995); and Smith, *Preaching as Weeping, Confession, and Resistance*, 87–109.
36. See Nelle Morton, *The Journey Is Home* (Boston: Beacon Press, 1985) for the origin of the much-used phrase "hearing into speech." See Donald Capps, *The Poet's Gift* (Louisville, Ky.: Westminster/John Knox Press, 1993), 39–73, for a helpful discussion of pastoral conversation as embodied language. See Neuger, "Feminist Pastoral Theology and Pastoral Counseling," 36ff., for the centrality of grace in listening to the stories of the marginalized.
37. Ballou and Gabalac, *A Feminist Position on Mental Health*, 76–77. I will widen these descriptions to include men as well as women.
38. Ibid.
39. Christie Cozad Neuger, "Imagination in Pastoral Counseling," in *Handbook for Basic Types of Pastoral Counseling*, ed. Howard W. Stone and William N. Clements (Nashville: Abingdon Press, 1991), 150–71.
40. Ibid., 163.
41. From a taped interview with members of the Greenwood Youth Staff, 1976.
42. Ramshaw, *Ritual and Pastoral Care*, 97–98.
43. Kathleen R. O'Toole, "Sacerdoces," from "Canticles in Ordinary Time," unpublished Masters thesis, p. 25, John Hopkins University. Copyright Kathleen O'Toole, 1991.
44. Ibid.
45. See "A Heart in Camden for a Hundred Years," a centennial booklet printed by Pine Industries, February 1987.
46. Edwidge Danticat, *Krik? Krak!* (New York: Soho Press, 1995), 220.

# 2

## PREACHING AS AN ART OF RESISTANCE

*Christine M. Smith*

Preaching is an act of ministry. It is done within particular social and religious contexts, and is thoroughly influenced by the
social location of the individual preacher. It is always contextual. It
is a public act of theological naming. What we have come to understand about language and naming is that those who *name* reality
ultimately create, shape, and control the world in which we live. Because it is a powerful interpretive act, preaching constructs personal, social, and ecclesiastical reality.

White, Western male Christian preaching often has taken the biblical text, the tradition, and the community of faith as the three primary starting places and points of focus for proclamation. For many
preachers of social, economic, and cultural privilege, unquestioned
authority is still given to scripture and tradition in the preaching act.
Individual nurture, inspiration, and personal salvation are often the
goals of such preaching. This homiletical focus and commitment
stands in real contrast to the particular witness of feminist preaching. Women who preach from various feminist perspectives and
men who embrace similar convictions and analysis share a belief
that this approach to preaching is no longer adequate.

In the United States there are also many women and men today
who understand that almost every category of religion, faith, theology, and life has been defined and proclaimed as universal truth by
white Euro-American males. With contemporary social and theological awareness, we know that such generalizations perpetuate
privilege and domination at the expense of human specificity and diversity. In the craft of preaching there also have been too many generalizations, universal claims, and assumed truths. We no longer
assume that any one methodology, style, or description can adequately name and articulate the vast array of differences among
preachers, nor do we find the effort to narrowly define desirable or
appropriate. In light of our growing awareness about social location
and contextuality, we know that any articulation about feminist
preaching will be significantly enriched and limited by the specificity of the author. What follows is the perspective of one woman's

voice—my own voice trying to give expression to the theological commitments, metaphors, and methodologies that inform my preaching and teaching. It is the voice of a white, economically privileged, North American, temporarily abled-bodied lesbian who is a clergywoman within the United Church of Christ in the United States.

Because I believe that social context and social analysis are primary focus points for preaching, my homiletical work stands in very real contrast to many of my colleagues in the field and to much of the contemporary homiletic's literature. I respect current homiletical work on the nature of narrative and its relationship to homiletical method and design, but I do not concentrate my work on form and design. I am grateful for the work presently being done in relation to biblical literary and rhetorical forms and the way those forms come to expression in the content and shape of the sermon, but I do not focus my work primarily on the movement from text to sermon. I appreciate and draw upon dimensions of an inductive method in relation to the preaching event, but want to make more specific and explicit claims upon my own life and the lives of the people in communities of faith than this method suggests or allows. I share a kinship with homiletical scholarship that focuses on the transformative power of language to reshape human consciousness and identity, but look to the fields of sociology and cultural anthropology to inform my social, homiletical, and theological analysis more than dimensions of linguistics. I find pedagogical commitments to develop a curriculum based on multicultural preaching to be absolutely crucial for the contemporary Christian church, but find myself moving beyond the celebration of cultural differences in a hope to uncover and address the forms of systematic oppression that immerse some individuals and communities in privilege and others in violence and genocide. The boldest critique I bring to the contemporary field of homiletics is that much of the literature seems more concerned with form and style, textual analysis, and linguistics than with significant social analysis and the kind of theological interpretation that flows from it.

I join my voice to the critical and constructive voices of preachers who are forging new homiletical perspectives and methodologies. These voices promise to influence and shape our preaching ministries. Rather than beginning with scripture and tradition, feminist preachers find the impetus of their preaching emerging from the larger social context of our individual and collective lives. Understanding the contemporary context of preaching is not just a means of more fully understanding the faith community; rather, context is understood as the arena in which the church lives out its ministry and mission in the world. The feminist preacher will attend to the particular issues, social systems, pervasive cultural values and ethics that structure the larger social and cultural world. Text, tradition, and faith community are important, but a hermeneutics of social context claims the agenda and commitments of the feminist preacher.

Feminist preaching as a ministry of resistance understands the magnitude of human oppression and injustice in the world and seeks to address it. The evil produced by interlocking systems of oppression and the injustice sustained by acts of individual and collective violence give rise to an urgent and distinctive homiletic. The methodologies and theological convictions that inform this understanding of preaching are utterly rooted in the commitments of liberation theology. Liberation theologians seek to shape theology and the practice of ministry in response to the concrete realities of human suffering and oppression, and toward a vision of liberation and restoration. The primary and ultimate agenda of resistance and liberation forms the ground out of which a ministry of resistance emerges.

## Theological Commitments Lead to Homiletical Practices

Preaching flows forth from a person's larger understanding of the theology and practice of ministry. A theology of ministry will be operative in a preacher's life whether that preacher is consciously aware of it or not, and it will profoundly inform the craft and act of preaching. Feminist thought and theology challenge the preacher to bring to consciousness all aspects of one's theology, biblical hermeneutics, social analysis, and ethical action in the world. It seems crucial for a volume that is striving to articulate feminist approaches to the arts of ministry that I now claim several of the foundational understandings of ministry that give rise to my distinctive approach to the art of homiletics.

## Ministry

I understand Christian ministry to be the liberating and salvific movement and activity of the people of God, guided and shaped by the spirit of the Christ revealed to us in Jesus' life, death, and resurrection. This liberating and salvific activity has to do with eschatological vision and liberating praxis. As eschatological vision, the people of God seek to articulate, proclaim, and embody the hope of shalom, the promise of healing and restoration, the transforming reality of God's saving justice and love. As liberating praxis, the people of God place their lives in solidarity with the oppressed, transform structures of human injustice, confront and challenge powers of domination, identify with and stand alongside the marginalized and disenfranchised of our world.

Emilie Townes, in her book *In a Blaze of Glory: Womanist Spirituality as Social Witness,* speaks about this connection between hope and praxis when she suggests that two critical theological affirmations are at the heart of womanist spirituality: eschatological hope and apocalyptic vision.[1] Womanist spirituality as a form and expression of social witness holds these two concepts in absolute tension. Apocalyptic vision is rooted in the belief that suffering and injustice can be eradicated or at the very least resisted, and eschatological hope affirms that this is possible within the framework of human history.[2] They cannot be separated.

> However, unlike the eschatological beliefs in the prophetic writings of the Hebrew Bible, womanist spirituality does not eschew the prophetic for the apocalyptic, but holds them in tension. Where the people of Israel lost confidence in the hope of God working in history and through human agency and turned to an apocalyptic eschatology that was pointed primarily to the future, womanist spirituality holds the eschatological and the apocalyptic in tension.[3]

Whether preachers understand ministry as eschatological vision and liberating praxis or as eschatological hope and apocalyptic vision, it is always a ministry of resistance and transformation. "It seeks justice in the midst of evil, peace in the midst of violence, freedom as a counterbalance to oppression, and community rather than injustice."[4]

Because I embrace ministry as eschatological vision and liberating praxis, I clearly locate myself within the larger theory and practice of liberation theology. This foundational commitment informs every aspect of my theological reflection and homiletical practice. My own theological method places scripture and tradition in dialogue with experience. In that dialogue there is a privileging of the oppressed and marginalized voices of our world. In the theological task of reflection and practice, voices of women, people of color, the poor, those with disabilities, gay and lesbian people, disempowered children and older adults receive particular attention in both the deconstructive and constructive work of theology and ministry.

Central to the way I conceptualize Christian ministry as liberating and salvific activity are my understandings of God, Christology, and ecclesiology.

## God

I understand God to be sacred Spirit revealed as power and presence. I embrace Carter Heyward's understanding of God as the power of right relation—that which inspires, gives rise to, and creates mutuality among us; that which transforms, saves, and liberates.[5] I also understand God to be Presence—the sacred dimension that exists within us, around us, and beyond us, sustaining and calling forth life among us. I do not believe God is primarily transcendent holy other, but rather the matrix out of which creation takes shape. I believe that God is a living, breathing part of all creation, yet more than we can name, understand, or fully know. I believe that God is in intimate relation to all creation, as creating, sustaining, empowering Spirit. I do not believe in a God that is all powerful and controlling; rather, I believe that God's presence and expression is inextricably woven together with our human limitations and our human agency.

## Christology

In the ministry and life of Jesus, Christian women and men have seen the possibility, the power, and the expression of redemptive, saving activity in the world. I believe that the power of God was incarnate in Jesus' liberating work in the world and that the memory and vision of that work of liberation becomes normative for Christian lives. However, I do not believe that the historical Jesus exclusively embodies the Christ of faith. Wherever people live in the power of right relation, or enter into radical acts of love, or give witness to justice, there is the Christ. Wherever individuals are liberated, oppressive structures are transformed, and the power of evil is confronted, we stand in the presence of the Christ, God incarnate, God made manifest among us.

## Ecclesiology

I believe that the Christian church is the community of faithful persons who understand their vocation in the world to be ministries of redemption and liberation. I affirm Leonardo Boff's belief that there is a vast difference between the institutional church as many Christian people often experience it and the liberating praxis of the people of God. In an effort to clarify this distinction, Boff looks at two ecclesiastical models of the church.

> One is oriented to the church as grand institution, with all its services institutionally organized and oriented to the needs of the church universal, the dioceses, and the parishes. This model of the church generally finds its sociological and cultural center in society's affluent sectors, where it enjoys social power and constitutes the church's exclusive interlocutor with the powers of society. The other is centered in the network of the basic communities, deep within the popular sectors and the poor masses, on the margin of power

and influence over the media, living the horizontal relationships of coresponsibility and a communion of brothers and
sisters more deeply.[6]

Communities of faith struggling to participate in God's liberating
activity of ministry often stand in stark contrast to the witness of institutional churches. If preachers and congregations were to accept
Boff's challenge to be more fully in communion with the masses,
then churches by definition would have to be involved in ministries
of resistance.

## Feminist Theology and Feminist Preaching

Preaching from a feminist perspective relies on feminist theology
because creating theological, social, and ecclesiastical change is
feminist theology's primary agenda. Feminist theology begins its
work with critical reflection on women's experiences of oppression
and marginality. The feminist theologian then draws upon those experiences in order to critique and reshape theological categories,
ethical paradigms, biblical hermeneutics, church history, and the
practices of ministry. Similar commitments and work face those
who embrace preaching from a feminist perspective.

In an effort to shape a new homiletic, preachers will place the traditional discipline and craft of homiletics in constant dialogue with
the critique and vision of lesbian women, women who have disabilities, poor women, older marginalized women, and women of diverse ethnic and cultural heritage. Understanding and attending to
the distinctive theological voices of feminist, womanist, mujerista,
Asian, and First Nation women will become an assumed part of
one's homiletic. Feminist preaching as a ministry of resistance inte-
grates and weaves women's critical and constructive theological
thought together with homiletical practice. It seeks theological, pastoral, biblical, and ethical language that will reflect the diversity of
all human experience. It compels us to make struggle, survival, and
resistance primary points of focus within our sermons and demands
that we shift the social, theological, pastoral, and ecclesiastical priorities of our lives.

## A Ministry of Resistance

In my own work I have been searching for metaphors that adequately describe and inform the nature and shape of preaching as a
ministry of resistance, deeply informed by a profound feminist
analysis. In my second book I turned to *weeping, confession,* and *resistance* as metaphors that might create a distinctive homiletical
methodology. How might preachers craft sermons that would pas-

sionately connect individuals and congregations to the pain and suffering of injustice and violence? When this effectively happens in
our preaching ministries, preaching becomes an act of weeping.

In an essay entitled "Theory as Liberatory Practice," bell hooks
speaks about a similar starting place for the practice and art of
teaching and the theory that undergirds it.

> It is not easy to name our pain, to theorize from that loca-
> tion. . . . I am grateful to the many women and men who dare
> to create theory from the location of pain and struggle, who
> courageously expose wounds to give us their experience to
> teach and guide, as a means to chart new theoretical jour-
> neys. Their work is liberatory. It not only enables us to re-
> member and recover ourselves, it charges and challenges us
> to renew our commitment to an active, inclusive feminist
> struggle.[7]

For preachers to theologize from the location of people's pain and
oppression is equally courageous and necessary. This is not an act
of despair; rather, it is an act of hope. It invites individuals and
whole congregations to remember and recover every remnant of
creation, and it challenges religious people to renew their commitment to the liberatory work of the gospel. Speaking as a womanist
theologian, Shawn Copeland speaks about this religious faithfulness as "Wading Through Many Sorrows."[8]

Confession as another primary metaphor for a new homiletic
suggests that truth telling is absolutely essential in a preaching ministry that seeks to resist oppression and move toward liberation. If
feminist preaching takes as its starting point systemic evil and oppression, the preacher's honest social analysis may be indicative of
how seriously that preacher embraces our human need for confession. When the truth of our human condition is proclaimed with
courage, preaching becomes an act of confession. Nelson Mandela,
in an endorsement of a collection of poems that seek to address social and political change, spoke about the power of poetry in a way
that opens up the meaning of confessional truth telling. He said,
"poetry cannot block a bullet or still a *sjambok* (whip), but it can
bear witness to brutality—thereby cultivating a flower in a grave-
yard."[9] Preaching as an act of confession, by the sheer force and possibility of its honesty, begins to cultivate life in the midst of a multitude of social and cultural graveyards.

Feminist preaching as a ministry of resistance builds upon the
foundations of weeping and confession. A preaching ministry that
is deeply rooted in a commitment to bear up justice in the world in
the face of what appears to be insurmountable evil is an act of resistance. It is crucial to name this kind of preaching *a ministry of*

46   *resistance* rather than a ministry of transformation. Though a transformed world is the ultimate hope that undergirds such a ministry, if preachers listen carefully to the oppressed voices surrounding them, they will discern that the language of survival, struggle, and resistance is what permeates these messages of indictment and hope, not the language of transformation. Transformative language assumes a certain measure of privilege and power that neither accurately describes nor reflects the lived realities of oppressed people. Henry Mitchell, in *Black Preaching: The Recovery of a Powerful Art*, says, "There is a radical difference between listening to an essay designed to enlighten and listening to a Word desperately needed to sustain life."[10] Resistance language and resistance preaching are about this kind of survival. For women preachers, who minister from within communities that are struggling to sustain life, survival may be a central reality of human experience that is deeply acknowledged and understood. This is the starting place for relevant and vital preaching. For women preachers, who minister from within communities of social and economic privilege, struggle and survival become compelling categories of human experience that have the power to reshape our proclamations.

    Eleazar S. Fernandez, in his book *Toward a Theology of Struggle*, makes an important claim for the necessity of theological work that focuses on the struggle rather than the result of liberation.

> Liberation, as I perceive it, is still the direction of the theology of struggle, but the focus of the theology of struggle is on the struggle. The struggle is still long and protracted before the dawn of the new day may fully come.[11]

Even though feminist preaching as a ministry of resistance may ultimately move us toward liberation, it accents resistance because it takes the concrete reality of human struggle seriously. Whatever our social location, resistance language has a concreteness and a specificity that connects, enlivens, and fuels acts of justice.

    Speaking about feminist preaching as a ministry of resistance rather than a ministry of transformation is not making an assertion that minimizes or trivializes the craft and ministry of preaching. Naming feminist preaching as a ministry of resistance is an attempt to honor the struggle that is involved in bringing about individual and collective change. Thus it is an affirmation that makes hopeful and crucial claims of power. William Sloane Coffin, in his book *A Passion for the Possible*, says, "Hope resists, hopelessness adapts."[12] Resistance is an act of individual and collective hope. When preaching is a ministry of resistance, it participates in the shaping and forming of a people. A ministry of resistance informs and helps create whole communities of resistance.

In her book titled *A Poetics of Resistance: Women Writing in El Salvador, South Africa, and the United States,* Mary K. DeShazer attempts to articulate *how* poems actually participate in resistance.

> First, they refuse the pretense of objectivity, instead asserting polemically the terms of their engagement with the topic at hand. In so doing, they claim as their own the task of historiographic reconstruction. Second, they violate poetic decorum in order to invite conflict and confrontation. They express anger stylistically via capital letters, exclamations, profanity, and arguments ad hominem; they hammer readers with aggressive catalogs, lengthy repetitions, and fierce rhetorical questions designed to evoke discomfort. For the reader's initial resistance will contribute ultimately to the success of the resistance poem. Finally, and simultaneously, they call forth from their audience an alternative complicity, a willingness to participate in a re-visionary project—ethical, political, literary—that could actually make a difference in the lives of the marginalized.[13]

Feminist preachers need to evaluate the quality and power of their rhetorical and homiletical strategies to discern whether they could actually help reconstruct history and make a difference in the lives of those who are oppressed. Just as a poetics of resistance understands the necessity and importance of sometimes violating poetic decorum and using fierce rhetorical strategies in its justice work, preachers need to create new homiletical strategies that call forth an "alternative complicity."

## The Liberating Practice of Feminist Preaching

Many demands face feminist preachers engaged in a ministry of resistance. I want to explore three primary challenges: (1) to reflect critically upon every aspect of one's own theology in order to discern the ways it perpetuates and undergirds the oppression of women; (2) to probe the connections between women's oppression and all other forms of oppression; and (3) to listen constantly to voices of critique and struggle outside one's cultural and social reality in order to expand and transform one's own homiletical agenda and one's preaching voice.

### Reflecting Critically on One's Own Theology

Beverly Wildung Harrison describes the breadth of the feminist theological critique and vision with challenging words.

> The critique we feminists make of Christianity involves a long agenda for theological change. It requires an extended and profound rethinking of all the language, images, and

metaphors central to Christian theology, a re-visioning that will surely not be exhausted soon.[14]

Feminist preachers engaged in a ministry of resistance commit themselves to rethinking the entire preaching task in relation to gender justice. God language, biblical interpretation, christological doctrine, and all theological categories need to reflect an awareness of women's distinctive experience and oppression. Special attention will be given to gender-inclusive God language in scripture, and images of God that emerge from within women's experience.

A critical and constructive kind of biblical hermeneutics is needed in feminist preaching. Preachers will interpret the scriptures by developing a keen eye toward women's invisibility (Sarah and Hagar in the Sarah, Abraham, and Hagar story in Genesis), subtle and blatant expressions of violence against women found within the texts (Jephthah's daughter in Judges), accounts of women's leadership (the Samaritan woman and her apostolic witness in John), and stories of women's strength and wisdom.

Ethical paradigms and theological assumptions that have gone unquestioned must be evaluated and a critique waged as to their impact upon the real lives of women. Joanne Carlson Brown and Carole R. Bohn confront us with the heart of this challenge in a book that addresses the relationship between Christianity and abuse.

> The central image of Christ on the cross as the savior of the world communicates the message that suffering is redemptive. If the best person who ever lived gave his life for others, then, to be of value we should likewise sacrifice ourselves. Any sense that we have a right to care for our own needs is in conflict with being a faithful follower of Jesus. Our suffering for others will save the world.[15]

Feminist preaching as a ministry of resistance will critically examine ways that traditional theological assumptions perpetuate women's suffering and oppression, and then will seek to construct theological understandings that liberate.

Feminist preachers in particular need to consider carefully the implications of their Christologies—how beliefs and doctrine about the historical Jesus and the Christ of faith fundamentally shape our collective understandings about normative humanity and divine possibility. Carter Heyward names what is ultimately at stake for us as we approach the topic of Christology.

> It is my thesis here that the historical doctrinal pull between Jesus of Nazareth and Jesus Christ, the human Jesus and his divine meaning, is no longer, if it ever was, a place of creative christological inquiry. Worse, it is a distraction from the

daily praxis of liberation, which is the root and purpose of Christian faith.[16]

Will our preaching distract us from the concrete, material realities of injustice, or will our preaching *reveal* what liberating Christo-praxis looks like in the world?

In shifting from a focus on Christology to Christo-praxis, two challenges face us: (1) One part of this movement involves the systematic critique of every aspect of sacrificial theology that has formed a Christian faith that idealizes crucifixions, suffering, and crosses. Preachers are key religious interpreters who can begin to help religious communities identify and condemn the contemporary crucifixions of our day, and harness their collective power in efforts to stop them. (2) A second part of the movement from Christology to Christo-praxis involves identifying, naming, and participating in those activities in life that are truly redemptive. Heyward describes this part of the work when she says, "In this praxis theological knowing would cease to be a matter of discovering the Christ and would become instead a matter of generating together images of what is redemptive or liberating in particular situations."[17] Some of the most creative theological work being done today comes from within oppressed communities, communities of resistance, communities of hope, where people are giving clear voice to specific expressions of Christo-praxis in our world.

Dismantling sacrificial theology is as painful as proclaiming redemptive activity is celebrative, and both are needed from preachers who accept a ministry of resistance. Preachers do this theological work knowing that nothing less than people's lives are at stake when we strive to move from Christology to Christo-praxis.

## Probing Connections of Oppression

Because a feminist preaching ministry of resistance assumes a very broad social and theological agenda, in addition to the explicit deconstructive and constructive theological task, preachers will understand that women's oppression cannot be understood or addressed apart from all other forms of human oppression and injustice. Sexism is fundamentally linked to classism, North American imperialism, ageism, ableism, racism, heterosexism, and militarism. Feminist preachers will examine economic realities and assumptions that pervade our common life. Preachers will strive to understand the global impact of North American imperialism. Sermon illustrations will draw upon the distinctive worldviews and theological understandings of people with disabilities. The relational commitments and prophetic gender realities embodied in the lives of lesbians and gay men will be acknowledged and honored. White supremacy will be exposed as an ongoing expression of violence and evil in our contemporary lives.

In order to ground our preaching in social and theological specificity, preachers will need to cultivate a methodology that enables them to name the connections between systems of oppression and to probe the particulars of each oppression. In *Preaching as Weeping, Confession, and Resistance: Radical Responses to Radical Evil,* there were four steps that I developed in an attempt to move from social analysis to theological reflection: (1) Six forms of systemic oppression were specifically named—handicappism, ageism, sexism, heterosexism, white racism, and classism. (2) Selected radicalizing moments that I had experienced with each expression of evil were shared. This step helped me clarify and understand how my own life had been challenged and changed by concrete encounters with dimensions of each form of oppression. (3) Specific human "faces" of each form of oppression were identified, such as white racism and its economic violence and cultural imperialism; sexism with its resultant rape, battery, and incest; classism and the realities of homelessness, poverty, and unemployment. This is a crucial step in moving our preaching ministries from universal abstractions into the specificity and concreteness of human injustice. (4) Finally, key theological affirmations that continue to justify and perpetuate each form of systemic oppression were identified and named. In some cases, new theological constructs were also articulated as examples of the kind of theological work needed to help eradicate each expression of oppression. This step challenges feminist preachers to clarify both the deconstructive, critical theological work that needs to permeate our preaching ministries, and the new, constructive theological thinking that might participate in shaping a new social reality.[18]

Feminist preaching proclaims a vision that assumes the fundamental interrelatedness of all creation and seeks to nurture and inspire a deep sense of religious accountability. It is a kind of preaching that is predicated on the belief that social analysis is as crucial to the art of homiletics as theology and exegesis.

### Listening to Diverse Voices

I want to lift up several women's voices that can be particularly formative for contemporary feminist preachers. Women's voices of resistance and struggle can be found today within the academy of theological scholars. They can be found working among us in churches and communities immersed in everyday life. They are found as exiled voices driven from their own homeland. They are found walking our city streets and in the intimacy of our living rooms. These women's voices are found in the midst of protest marches and in the celebration of the Eucharist in mainline churches. Women's voices of resistance are appearing wherever people are violated and oppressed, wherever people hurt and suffer, and wherever people are longing for new life. These formative voices are claiming new truths, justice, passionate life, for individuals and whole communities. Any feminist homiletic of resistance will seek to acknowledge and affirm the reality that countless preachers are being transformed by these radically diverse, sometimes indicting, voices.

Justo and Catherine Gonzalez, in *The Liberating Pulpit*, speak to the particularity of these voices and how each has its own point of departure.

> It is for this reason that Third World theologies often begin from the perspective of the poor, and emphasize economic oppression and its structures—both international and domestic. Theologies of liberation that reflect the struggle of culturally suppressed minorities often begin from the experience of cultural identity and its recovery. Likewise, feminist, womanist and mujerista theologies tend to center their attention on issues related to gender oppression—although womanist theology also places issues of race at the center of its concern, and mujerista theology adds the dimension of culture.[19]

Remembering that all voices of struggle and resistance are rooted in particular social contexts and specific cultural communities is essential. Each preacher will be uniquely changed by these voices depending upon that person's social location. How a preacher experiences a voice of resistance will depend on whether that preacher stands within the community of resistance out of which the voice arises, or is listening as an outsider. There are serious ethical issues involved as preachers listen to different voices and struggle to understand the impact of those voices upon one's own preaching ministry. Appropriation is the act of using another's voice as if it were one's own. This is not an appropriate homiletical strategy. A more appropriate homiletical strategy might be to listen to voices different from one's own in order to move more fully into the complex human distinctions that exist among us. For example, instead of using a Guatemalan poet's work as if we experience what that artist describes and proclaims, we invite the poet to expose the classism and imperialism that permeates our own lives. Instead of white women preachers using African-American women's theological critique and constructs as if we could speak *for* them or *with* them, we welcome their indictment of the limitations and violence of our own white racism. Differences are not what divide the human community. It is our unwillingness to deal with the specific ramifications of those differences in our life together that divides. Listening to voices distinctly different from one's own in order to move more fully and faithfully into what those differences actually can mean for all of us is an act required of the feminist preacher. It is to some of these voices that I now want to turn.

In September of 1993, the Association of Practical Theology held its annual meeting in Los Angeles. The Association went there to engage in an urban immersion experience. During our weekend, two women social workers, Veronica and Vickie, spoke to our group about their work with women who are at high risk for contracting AIDS. They informed us that every five minutes someone is infected, and every fifteen minutes someone dies. With absolute clarity they said, "AIDS is not a moral issue; it is a health issue."[20] There was some resistance to this statement from within our group. For some in our group, *how* people contract AIDS was the central issue. After all the questions and comments, these two social workers simply replied, "If some of you feel the need to dwell on the moral question and to debate the issue, that is where you must be. For us, AIDS is not a moral issue; it is a health issue, and people are dying."[21]

Vickie and Veronica's voices will deeply inform a feminist homiletic. Preventing this death is the primary ethical paradigm out of which faithful decisions about AIDS are made. Evaluating and judging individual morality are exposed as tenacious opponents to redemptive activity. Christo-praxis becomes the urgent and unswerving commitment, not another discussion of theology absolutely abstracted from the concrete realities of people's lives. These are voices of resistance, voices that take survival, struggle, and injustice as their starting place. How do we listen more fully to these voices?

In a book that came out in the fall of 1994 we find a prophetic critique of Christianity in relation to the lives of people with disabilities. Nancy Eiesland, in *The Disabled God: Toward a Liberatory Theology of Disability*, suggests that there are two primary tasks that must be a part of a liberatory theology of disability: political action and resymbolization.[22] A part of the resymbolization involves imaging God as disabled and imaging the Eucharist as a primary ritual place where the disabled God meets us all. During this central feast of the Christian faith, the disabled God particularly meets people with disabilities in moments of radical empowerment and affirmation.

> "Do this in remembrance of me." Who is the one we remember in the Eucharist? It is the disabled God who is present at the Eucharist table—the God who was physically tor-

tured, arose from the dead and is present in heaven and on earth, disabled and whole.[23]

Not only does Eiesland invite us to transform our theological understandings of God and the Eucharist; she also invites us to think about and proclaim resurrection in new ways.

> Resurrection is not about the negation or erasure of our disabled bodies in hopes of perfect images, untouched by physical disability; rather Christ's resurrection offers hope that our nonconventional, and sometimes difficult, bodies participate fully in the imago Dei and that God whose nature is love and who is on the side of justice and solidarity is touched by our experience.[24]

These theological assertions are challenging and compelling. In recent years Christian preachers have been asked to image God as female, Asian, African American, and poor. We are now being asked to think of God as limited, disabled, changed by the experience of being incarnate in a disabled body. Feminist preachers are asked to struggle with the indicting and transformative truths Eiesland expresses. Preachers who have a disability will surely respond to Eiesland's voice in radically different ways than preachers who are temporarily abled-bodied. Regardless of where we stand, it is true that the lived experiences of people with disabilities have been absolutely silenced, marginalized, and rendered invisible in our human history and religious practices. As preachers engaged in a ministry of resistance, seeking to uncover the silenced voices of people with disabilities, we will be asked to rethink and resymbolize every aspect of Christian theology and faith.

Our theologizing and preaching today are also profoundly stretched by the distinctive voices of lesbian women. Episcopal priest Carter Heyward has waged a systematic critique of heterosexism and homophobia as that which enforces and maintains male supremacy. In her book *Touching Our Strength: The Erotic as Power and the Love of God*, she names the power of life among us as erotic energy and forges a new sexual theology.[25] Heyward's words remind us in a poignant way that lesbian women's presence and critique within the institutional church are shaking the foundations in ways we cannot yet fully discern.

> If we are to live with our feet on the ground, in touch with reality, we must help one another accept the fact that we who are christian are heirs to a body-despising, woman-fearing, sexually repressive religious tradition. If we are to continue as members of the church, we must challenge and transform it at the root.[26]

Lesbian women are some of the voices from within our culture that are challenging preachers to dismantle much of the body-despising, woman-fearing, sexually repressive theology of the Christian church. They are asking that preachers take seriously the chronic sense of exile and homelessness that permeate the lives of lesbian women and gay men. They are urging preachers to stop denying the rising number of teenage suicides among gay and lesbian youth. Their voices are probing the theological and religious dimensions of "coming out," the haunting distortions of selective biblical hermeneutics, and the powerful connections between erotic power and God's redemptive activity. For lesbian women preachers, discovering and drawing upon these lesbian voices will be like coming home. For many heterosexual preachers, these voices will demand honesty about heterosexual privilege and the church's complicity in the oppression of lesbian and gay people.

Finally, I want to turn to two African-American womanist theologians whose work promises to transform the biblical hermeneutics of feminist preachers, as well our understandings of human ethical activity.

Many Euro-American women preachers, particularly those who are economically privileged, find it nearly impossible to understand or comprehend the fundamental issue of survival that permeates and forms the social reality of many people of color in this nation and throughout the world. If white preachers of privilege cannot begin to grasp more fully this issue of survival, then we will never be able to understand the ultimate dividing lines and violent implications of white supremacy, cultural and economic imperialism, militarism, and class oppression that influence all of our lives. Survival is a profound religious and theological category for contemporary preaching.

Katie Cannon, in *Black Womanist Ethics,* urges us to see that Black women make their moral and ethical decisions out of an environment of survival, not freedom. She confronts us with the notion that freedom as the starting point of ethical decision making is a white, dominant construct having little relevance for Black women's lives. It only serves to minimize, trivialize, and reduce the real moral and ethical agency of Black women's lives.[27] To understand the moral agency of Black women's lives one would need to understand fully the concrete expressions of *invisible dignity, quiet grace,* and *unshouted courage.*[28] For many African-American women preachers, I can only suppose that Cannon's ethical and moral assertions are known and assumed as a part of the foundational fabric of daily life. For white preachers, who have been profoundly influenced by dominant thinking that idealizes personal freedom as the source of human action and choice, Cannon's words provide a crucial challenge. A part of Cannon's challenge to the preacher is to stop making universalizing ethical statements and to deepen the ways we contextualize issues of moral and ethical agency and action.

In a similar radical vein, Delores Williams, in *Sisters in the Wilderness: The Challenge of Womanist God-Talk,* shifts our biblical and theological thinking. With a clear and persistent focus on the Egyptian slave woman Hagar, whose oppression and moral agency is recorded in Genesis, Williams invites us into a multilayered conversion experience. She challenges all of us who use liberation language and analyze our social, political, and ecclesiastical lives out of liberation categories, suggesting that those liberation categories and constructs are inadequate. She writes, "The Hagar-Sarah texts in Genesis and Galatians, however, demonstrate that the oppressed and abused do not always experience God's liberating power."[29] Williams refuses to be convinced that Hagar's story is one of liberation, and she presses us to consider it a story of survival. Hagar, and African-American women after her, have lived their lives much more out of a survival/quality-of-life ethics than out of a liberationist ethical position.[30] At the very least she is suggesting that there is a fundamental tension between liberation ethics and survival/quality-of-life ethics. In response to the ethical shift, she goes on to invite us to reconsider the nature of God and God's saving activity, the nature of human existence, and the nature of moral and ethical activity. She finally suggests that perhaps *wilderness* is a more appropriate description of the lived experience of African-American women and the locus of God's activity than *exodus.*[31]

Any preacher today needs to take seriously the voices of African-American womanist theologians. These womanist theologians raise critical issues for preaching within the African-American church experience, and they demand biblical and theological transformation from those of us who are listening from the outside. Not only are they demanding that we take survival as a starting point for theology and preaching seriously; they promise to shift all our ethical categories and understandings, and deepen and change our assertions about God's saving, redemptive activity. Shifting from liberation to wilderness as a locus of God's presence and a primary place of human moral agency is a monumental challenge to the language and theology of feminist preaching.

Other women speak about survival in ways that are instructive for our theological and homiletical lives. Donna Kate Rushin talks about this reality as "this bridge called my back."[32] Gloria Anzaldua describes her life as lesbian and Chicana as living in the "border-lands."[33] She says, "Tension grips the inhabitants of the borderlands like a virus. Ambivalence and unrest reside there and death is no stranger."[34] Chung Hyun Kyung speaks about Asian women's lived experience when she says, "Colonialism, neo-colonialism, militarism and dictatorship are everyday reality for most Asian women. . . . They create food for life out of nothing. Their bodies take and carry all the burdens for survival."[35]

All of these different worlds of humanness are confrontive for preachers committed to a preaching ministry of resistance. If we allow ourselves to encounter all these passionate women's voices—their critique, their visions, their distinctive worldviews, their theological constructions, and their lived faithfulness—our preaching ministries will change. Many of these women's voices speak from within a collective, community identity that gives rise to a radically different context for preaching than does a middle-class, Euro-American context of comfortable privilege and isolated individualism. The voices that emerge from women's diverse lives are filled with confrontation and hope. There are indeed holy places of difference among us that both challenge and terrify any conscientious preacher. A preaching ministry of resistance urges us to listen well and speak boldly.

### Feminist Preaching: Voice and Action

Karen Baker-Fletcher, in a powerful essay about Anna Julia Cooper's writing and speaking as a Black woman in post–Reconstruction America, suggests that *voice* was the key metaphor that informed her work. For Cooper, voice was something much larger than speaking; it was a way of life, an expression of resistance, "speech in action."[36] Speaking at a time in history when the silencing of Black women's voices was the customary violence of the day, Cooper lived with full, courageous voice. The risk each one of us assumes and the costs each one of us bears when we come to voice are significantly different depending on the amount of privilege we hold within our culture and world. Even so, the fullness and challenge of Cooper's understanding of voice may well direct us toward preaching as an art of resistance.

> Voice calls attention to pain and suffering. Voice criticizes oppression. Voice offers and demands solutions to problems. Voice cries out in passion, anger, and outrage. Voice motivates others to follow. Voice shocks and touches people to respond. Voice challenges attitudes, social customs, and

practice. Voice motivates reform. Voice calls people out for radical, revolutionary action. Voice resists systems of injustice.[37]

As we find voice and as we persist within the demands and challenges of this ministry, contemporary preachers might discover and embody once again the radical nature of God's mandates for our lives and the ultimate life-giving power of resistance.

## NOTES

1. Emilie M. Townes, *In a Blaze of Glory: Womanist Spirituality as Social Witness* (Nashville: Abingdon Press, 1995).
2. Ibid., 121–23.
3. Ibid., 123.
4. Ibid.
5. Isabel Carter Heyward, *The Redemption of God: A Theology of Mutual Relation* (Washington D.C.: University Press of America, 1982). In this book Heyward begins in a more systematic way to develop a theology of mutual relation, a theological project that permeates all her subsequent work.
6. Leonardo Boff, *Ecclesiogenesis: The Base Communities Reinvent the Church* (Maryknoll, N.Y.: Orbis Books, 1986), 7–8.
7. bell hooks [Gloria Watkins], *Teaching to Transgress: Education as the Practice of Freedom* (New York: Routledge & Kegan Paul, 1994), 74.
8. M. Shawn Copeland, "Wading Through Many Sorrows: Toward a Theology of Suffering in Womanist Perspective," in *A Troubling in My Soul: Womanist Perspectives on Evil and Suffering,* ed. Emilie M. Townes (Maryknoll, N.Y.: Orbis Books, 1993), 109–29. See these pages for her fuller exploration of a theology of suffering from a womanist perspective.
9. Mary K. DeShazer, *A Poetics of Resistance: Women Writing in El Salvador, South Africa, and the United States* (Ann Arbor: University of Michigan Press, 1994), 311. DeShazer quotes Nelson Mandela's comments on the book jacket of Carolyn Forche's book *Against Forgetting.*
10. Henry H. Mitchell, *Black Preaching: The Recovery of a Powerful Art* (Nashville: Abingdon Press, 1990), 21.
11. Eleazar S. Fernandez, *Toward a Theology of Struggle* (Maryknoll, N.Y.: Orbis Books, 1994), 23.
12. William Sloane Coffin, *A Passion for the Possible: A Message to U.S. Churches* (Louisville, Ky.: Westminster/John Knox Press, 1993), 88.
13. DeShazer, *A Poetics of Resistance,* 271.
14. Beverly Wildung Harrison, "Keeping Faith in a Sexist Church," in *Making the Connections: Essays in Feminist Social Ethics,* ed. Carol Robb (Boston: Beacon Press, 1985), 227.

15. Joanne Carlson Brown and Carole R. Bohn, "For God So Loved the World," in *Christianity, Patriarchy, and Abuse: A Feminist Critique*, ed. Joanne Carlson Brown and Carole R. Bohn (New York: Pilgrim Press, 1989), 2.

16. Carter Heyward, *Speaking of Christ: A Lesbian Feminist Voice* (New York: Pilgrim Press, 1989), 13.

17. Ibid., 20.

18. Christine M. Smith, *Preaching as Weeping, Confession, and Resistance: Radical Responses to Radical Evil* (Louisville, Ky.: Westminster/John Knox Press, 1992).

19. Justo L. Gonzalez and Catherine G. Gonzalez, *The Liberating Pulpit* (Nashville: Abingdon Press, 1994), 22–23.

20. This conversation with two women named Vicki and Veronica took place at a meeting of the Association of Practical Theology, September 1993.

21. These are not the words exactly, but they are very close to what was said during our visit with these two women.

22. Nancy L. Eiesland, *The Disabled God: Toward a Liberatory Theology of Disability* (Nashville: Abingdon Press, 1994). She discusses political action and resymbolization particularly in chapter 3.

23. Ibid., 107.

24. Ibid.

25. Carter Heyward, *Touching Our Strength: The Erotic as Power and the Love of God* (San Francisco: Harper & Row, 1989).

26. Ibid., 47.

27. Katie G. Cannon, *Black Womanist Ethics* (Atlanta: Scholars Press, 1988). The entire book develops this basic ethical assertion, shifting from freedom to survival as the locus of ethical activity.

28. Ibid., 105–57. Within these pages invisible dignity, quiet grace, and un-shouted courage are explored as dimensions of Black women's ethical agency in the world.

29. Delores S. Williams, *Sisters in the Wilderness: The Challenge of Womanist God-Talk* (Maryknoll, N.Y.: Orbis Books, 1993), 144.

30. Williams, *Sisters in the Wilderness*. This is one of the fundamental tenets that undergirds the entire book.

31. Ibid. Throughout the book Williams builds new theological and ethical understandings and ultimately invites the reader to consider wilderness as a more adequate description for the locus of God's activity than exodus.

32. Donna Kate Rushin, "The Bridge Poem," in *This Bridge Called My Back: Writings by Radical Women of Color*, eds. Cherrie Moraga and Gloria Anzaldua (New York: Kitchen Table, 1984).

33. Gloria Anzaldua, *Borderlands: The New Mestiza* (San Francisco: Spinsters/Aunt Lute, 1987). Anzaldua uses the image of borderlands to describe the lived reality of Chicana women who exist within both Mexican and Anglo worlds.

34. Ibid., 4.

35. Chung Hyun Kyung, *Struggle to Be the Sun Again: Introducing Asian Women's Theology* (Maryknoll, N.Y.: Orbis Books, 1990), 23.

36. Karen Baker-Fletcher, "Soprano Obligato," in *A Troubling in My Soul,* ed. Townes, 184.

37. Ibid.

# 3

## EDUCATION AS AN ART
## OF GETTING DIRTY WITH DIGNITY

*Carol Lakey Hess*

### Of Dirty Dresses and Girls Who Are Much

When one of my sons, Paul, was a toddler, he was stocky, assertive, and invariably disheveled from hard play. I wish I had a dollar for every time someone said to me with admiration, "He's a real boy," or, even more poignantly, "He's *all* boy." Emblazoned in my memory is a day when my daughter, too, was a toddler. A group of children were playing on a playground, their parents chatting on the side. Marie, my daughter, was frolicking about in a blue-smocked dress. Her cheeks were smudged with dirt, her knees and bare toes were stained green with grass, and her dress was a glorious and dirty collage of all the places she had been; the sheer joy of unself-conscious play emanated from her. I recall that I was beaming, both in vicarious enjoyment and in quiet pride; my daughter was engaging this world with confidence—getting dirty with great dignity! My contentment was disrupted as another mother commented disapprovingly, "She's not much of a girl, is she?"

My response, "It depends on what you mean by girl," was an important step in the development of my feminist approach to education. When we educate children, we explicitly and implicitly shape their gender identities. The prevailing pattern is clear: boys are supposed to engage the world with aggression and transform the dirt into dream worlds; girls who do so are scorned. Recent studies indicate that by adolescence, if not before, girls get the message: only boys inherit the earth.[1] That day on the playground flashed in my mind on another occasion when, after preaching, I was handed a small slip of paper. On one side were two verse citations: 1 Cor. 14:34 and 1 Tim. 2:11–15, which prohibit women from teaching and command their silence in church and their subordination to men. On the other side were the words of Prov. 3:5 printed in bold: "TRUST IN THE LORD WITH ALL THINE HEART; AND LEAN NOT UNTO THINE OWN UNDERSTANDING." A double whammy; I was not supposed to teach in church, and I was not to have confidence in my own understandings. The message I understood was,

"You're not much of a woman, are you?" Men can engage the world and transform it; women who do so will be scorned. Marge Piercy, a "strong woman," has been where my daughter and I have been, and then some:

> A strong woman is a woman in whose head
> a voice is repeating, I told you so,
> ugly, bad girl, bitch, nag, shrill, witch,
> ballbuster, nobody will ever love you back,
> why aren't you feminine, why aren't
> you soft, why aren't you quiet, why
> aren't you dead?[2]

Gender training begins early, and it is pervasive. Studies show that gender coding has a significant influence on how parents treat their children, beginning in early infancy.[3] The explicit instances of selective gender socialization are only the tip of the iceberg. I shudder to think of the subtle looks and implicit body language that have unconsciously shaped my children's understanding of themselves as "real boy" or "real girl." Although I think the consequences for girls are more oppressive than the consequences for boys, I am quite sure that both boys and girls are harmed by gender training. Boys are reared to be autonomous, controlling, and assertive; girls are reared to be connected, submissive, and caring. The fact that women most often do the primary caretaking and men are rather distant fathers intensifies boys' growth in separateness (and loss of connection) and girls' growth in connection (and avoidance of separation).[4] Transgressing these expected patterns of behavior will cause difficulties for either gender. In fact, it may be the case that those who exhibit a combination of traits have the most difficulty. Think about it. To say admiringly that Paul is "all boy" is to say that he is no part girl. Had he toted a doll with him in his exploits, he no doubt would not have earned his "all boy" accolades.[5] On the other hand, if my daughter had dressed like a boy and acted like a boy, perhaps she would have been dismissed as a "tomboy" without further thought. But, she was a dirty girl in a pretty dress. She wasn't "much of a girl" because she was a girl who, *as a girl,* grasped much from life.

Dirty Marie in her pretty blue dress is an ambiguous image for many. I pose this as a symbol for balanced gender identity: with autonomy *and* connectedness, with control *and* flexibility,[6] with assertiveness *and* care. For girls, balanced gender nurture requires that we both critique the social restrictions that have been placed on girls (allow them to get dirty with "boys" activities) while at the same time recover and appreciate those ways of knowing and doing that have been preserved by girls and women (not insist that they have to act or look just like what we would expect boys to act and look like in order to get dirty in the boys' arena). Accomplishing this balance will not be easy. According to the American Psychological Association, social norms are still conventional: "Females who display 'womanly' traits and males who display 'manly' traits are more favorably evaluated and judged more psychologically healthy than those who do not. Conversely, those who engage in what is perceived to be cross-sex behavior can be the victim of social sanctions."[7] For girls and women this creates an intractable double bind; wombs and brains, competency and femininity are perceived to be incompatible. If women are successful, they are unfeminine. If they are feminine, they are perceived as incompetent. My words to the woman who betrayed my daughter were more true than I realized, for a lot, indeed, depends on what we mean by girl.

## What Do You Mean by Girl?
## A Feminist Approach

To write "a feminist approach to Christian education" is in many ways to "get dirty." Feminism itself, in its recognition of the differences in human experience, is a necessarily diverse, shifting, messy, and creative movement. In its variety of forms, feminism recognizes that there has been a long-standing injustice toward women and advocates for the full humanity of women. Thus feminism is assertive; it is self-consciously political in that it "has to do with the working out of visions about the just order of social life."[8] In being for the full humanity of women, feminism calls for changes in the lives of both men and women, ultimately aiming toward liberation from all forms of dehumanization.[9]

A feminist approach to Christian education proclaims and works to bring about the good news that girls and women, as well as boys and men, shall inherit the church along with the earth. For this to happen, communities of faith need to give girls and women a voice and need to learn from the particular gifts and experiences of girls and women. This is not simply for the well-being of girls and women, it is for the full humanity of all in communities of faith.

## Toward the Full Humanity of the Church:
## Voices from the Margin

A community of faith that knows its center in Christ will increasingly move toward the stranger on the margin, contends Letty Russell.[10] This center in Christ makes the movement outward possible, and the movement toward the margins continually renews the central practices and convictions of the community of faith. Reclaiming our center and moving toward the margin are both essential for the future of the church; neither can be done without the partnership of women.

Lois M. Wilson has recently invoked Mark 5:21–43 for our efforts to reimagine community life. In this wonderfully complex narrative, Jesus is called upon by Jairus, an important and pious man, to heal his sick daughter. As Jesus sets out to heed Jairus' plea, an outcast woman with a flow of blood appears, and she interrupts Jesus as he travels. While Jesus apparently digresses from his task and allows the "unclean" woman to be healed, the little girl dies. It is as if, in the course of Mark's narrative, "the first story of Jairus' daughter cannot be told until the story of the woman at the edge is told, until she is made free and made safe," observes Wilson.[11] Healing at the periphery is connected with death at the center. And yet, after the woman is healed, Jesus revives the important man's daughter. According to Wilson, Mark seems to be announcing that "the healing of one of the edges takes place, and the healing of the center is then made possible."

In our time, daughter church as we know her is dying. The important leaders are calling out to God for healing. Outcast daughters on the margin, women who have been neglected and pushed aside, are taking the initiative to seek healing from the one who came to heal. It even seems as if God has to be nudged and awakened to their cries. Perhaps, however, it is only after Christ has called to the ones on the margins, "Daughter, your faith has made you well; go in peace, and be healed of your disease" that Christ can call to the church, "Talitha cum, little girl get up." The healing of the one follows the healing of the other; furthermore, as with the little girl, healing does not come without a dying and resurrecting.

The churches of Jesus Christ are in the process of dying to what was and rising to something new. Especially for North American Christianity, life is messier these days. No longer do the churches enjoy privileged status and unquestioned religious hegemony; Christendom has been rent by pluralism and secularism. Although this has seriously demoralized many, it is deemed by others to be an opportunity for the church to really be the church.[12] I'm with the latter group; I don't lament pluralism the way some do. I think it *exposes* a problem rather than poses one. When the nation was considered a Christian nation, the church learned neither how to discourse with the "other" (including the "other" in its midst, women) nor how to separate gospel from dominant patriarchal worldviews.[13] No longer enjoying religious hegemony, the church doesn't know what to do without the former kinds of power structures and authority. We are now having to learn to "speak as one without authority," to use Søren Kierkegaard's phrase, and we are having to learn to speak in ways that don't presuppose the compliance, obedience, and submission of others around us. "Peace" and stability are often obtained at the great cost of subduing and suppressing voices who call for justice. The unleashing of the voices of the oppressed, who previously paid that price, has led to unrest, confusion, and both old and new forms of orthodoxy, to be sure. But the unleashing of these voices has also led to new visions, revitalization, repentance, and a renewed concern for justice.

Communities of faith are in disarray, but the solution is not to revert to repressive forms of "harmony" and authoritarian uniformity. The disestablishment of the church means that the church now is in a position to listen to and converse with others in a more just manner. For the healing of the church in general, those who have been dehumanized on the margins must be healed first.

My daughter was dehumanized on the playground by the mother who sought to exclude her from being a girl because she got dirty. I was dehumanized in the church by the man who sought to exclude me from being a preacher because I was a woman. My son, too, was dehumanized by those who selectively reinforced his stereotypic male behavior, to the point of implicitly expunging "feminine" traits.[14]

How can our healing take place? I think healing will take place when communities of faith engage seriously in the hard dialogue and deep connections of honest conversation. Women at the edges are teaching us this.

## Conversational Education: Hard Dialogue and Deep Connections

I said earlier that a feminist approach to Christian education needs to give girls and women a voice and that we can learn how to do this from examining women's experience. Although I do not think there is any single "essence" to either women or women's experience, and I certainly do not believe men and women should function in different spheres, I do think that women have been the bearers and keepers of certain distinctive types of experience.

In their important work *Women's Ways of Knowing*, the collaborative authors suggest that women develop their "voice" and best flourish in environments that are "connected" rather than "separate." As opposed to separate environments that presume the ignorance of the learner, connected environments presuppose that all those who come together bring something important and have something important to contribute to the educational situation. Connected environments are those in which "real-talk" takes place.

Real-talk is a type of conversation that "includes discourse and exploration, talking and listening, questions, argument, speculation, and sharing."[15] The authors contrast this with didactic talk in which the speaker's intention is to "hold forth rather than share ideas." Real talk is cooperative, mutual, and deeply interpersonal. In such conversations, speaking with and listening to others includes speaking with and listening to oneself. Real talk is empathetic, nonjudgmental, and receptive; yet it is also passionate, honest, and self-disclosing. The authors argue that "connected teaching," indebted to but also stretching women's experience, ought to characterize education.

I pose "real-talk" as the goal of a feminist Christian education. Rather than use the term *connected education,* I would like to speak of *conversational education,* which is characterized by "hard dialogue and deep connections."[16] For genuine connection to occur in communities of faith, honest and deep dialogue needs to occur. Hard dialogue presumes and fosters genuine relationality; it is dialogue that allows participants to ask difficult and ofttimes painful questions. Deep and authentic connections can result only when we have argued, dialogued, and conversed in such a manner with one another. Such connection requires listening to the voices of those on the margins of community life.

Conversational education is particularly appropriate—though strikingly squelched—in Christian communities. The Christian understanding of the triune God is inherently relational and conversational. The Trinity points to a God who is a dynamic and mysterious conversation between distinctive but inextricably related divine "persons." More than that, trinity represents a God who is separate from and "other" to, but inextricably connected with creation. Our connections to one another are grounded in our deep connection to this God who is "for us." Theologian Catherine La Cugna notes that relationality is "at the heart of God's essence." She further contends that the doctrine of the Trinity, which describes this relationality, "is ultimately a practical doctrine with radical implications for Christian life." Relationality, it is important to emphasize, is not simple connectedness. It requires both particularity and communion; it affirms differentness as well as connectedness. Thus La Cugna suggests that "diversity among divine persons is a principle for affirmation of the diversity within creation."[17]

In addition to speaking of the conversation within God and between God and humanity, we can look at the tradition of conversation that communities of faith have had concerning their relationship to God. Our sacred texts represent humanity's conversation with God, including instances of extreme chutzpah where human beings questioned and wrestled with God. Furthermore, these texts and the traditions that emerged from them witness to the long, deep, and often painful conversation that our forerunners in the faith had with each other. Dorothy Bass seeks to remind communities of faith of the conversational nature of traditioning. She calls congregations to "see their tradition as something that is not alien but theirs, something to be argued with and within, something whose meaning is not yet fully understood, something that can live only as they themselves, in all their particularity, bear it into the future that is still in the making."[18]

A conversational understanding of community life requires more than just authentic dialogue within the community. In order for a community of faith to make ethical decisions, conversation is required between communities. As Sharon Welch has recently argued, individual Christians and individual communities "cannot be moral alone."[19] The discernment of truth and true practice requires the interaction of those whose experiences, interests, and backgrounds are different. Because all of our views are partial and because our social locations influence our theologies, we cannot be moral unless we are in engagement with those who are different. Thus, as Welch observes, "pluralism is required, not for its own sake, but for the sake of enlarging our moral vision."[20] Though it does not end there, faithful moral deliberation begins with including women in the process of moral discernment.

For much of church history, however, women have been marginalized or excluded from the conversation. Though their voices could not be fully contained and though they have made remarkable contributions despite attempts to silence their voices, they have not been full partners. Like the woman with the flow of blood, women of faith have had to come up from behind and find their own healing (Mark 5); like the Syrophoenician woman, women have had to call God to task (Mark 7); like Mary Magdalene, women have told others of their experience of God's resurrecting power and have not been believed (Mark 16:9–11). We need to make women full partners in the conversation of faith—for the well-being and healing of the entire community. Unfortunately the teaching of the church, in its variety of forms, works against this.

### The Teaching of the Church

Teaching involves more than just what our printed curriculum tells us to do during that hour we designate "church school." The life we live together in communities of faith constitutes the curriculum of education. We can evaluate the teaching of our communities in light of the "three curricula" that all educational institutions teach: the explicit, the implicit, and the null curriculum. The explicit curriculum refers to those messages we convey to girls and boys, men and women, intentionally and explicitly—usually the content of our teaching. The implicit curriculum includes what we teach indirectly because of the cultural milieu of our life together: the structure of patterns of interaction, the tacit values, and the habitual processes. The null curriculum is that which teaches by virtue of its absence. With regard to the null teachings, educator Elliot Eisner contends that "schools have consequences not only by virtue of what they teach, but also by virtue of what they neglect to teach. What students cannot consider, what they don't know, processes they are unable to use, have consequences for the kinds of lives they lead."[21]

What are we saying to girls and women in our explicit teachings? What kinds of interactions are we allowing, and how does this implicitly influence the development of girls and women? What are we leaving out, and how does this neglect impact girls and women? These are the questions we need to ask. I believe that communities of faith ought to (1) explicitly teach women to claim and appropriately assert themselves in communities of faith; (2) engage in "real-talk," a form of honest conversation that emerges from women's experience; and (3) incorporate women's stories and concerns into our life together. A conversational understanding of the educational ministry advocates honest grappling with one another, with our tradition, and with God. This is not happening, however, and its consequences for women are troublesome.

We in the church need to face and correct a hard reality: being a girl in a community of faith shaped by certain theological teachings and educational processes can be hazardous to one's development. Although Christian communities are diverse, and it would be presumptuous to speak for all of them, I would like to unmask prevalent well-intentioned teachings that are inadvertently dangerous to women. We need to beware of current educational patterns that (1) *explicitly* teach girls and women to give themselves away by denouncing self-assertion as sin; (2) *implicitly* frustrate girl's and women's development by promoting attitudes and processes that avoid struggle and conflict; and (3) *neglect* the stories of assertive women and *evade* stories that expose violence against girls and women.

## The Explicit Curriculum of Christian Education: What Are We Saying to Girls and Women?

I will begin with the explicit curriculum by looking at two main aspects of explicit teaching in communities of faith: theological anthropology and images of God. Girls and boys, men and women, are shaped significantly by theology and language.

## Christian Education and Theology: Giving Ourselves Away

Religious educators often ask the question, How can we teach our theology and tradition in a way that gets the theology across at the particular level of the learner's development? This is an important question, one that I myself have addressed. I would, however, like to pose a different question that is far more important educationally: How does our theology and tradition teach us—in both helpful and harmful ways—what it means to be a human being? More specifically, I would like to ask, How does our theology influence the development of voice in girls?[22]

Having read above about the man who tried to silence my preaching by quoting scripture, you might be expecting here a discussion on theologically sanctioned women's subordination. Although such theologies are more prevalent than we might think, and although folks like that man are plentiful, they will not be reading a book on feminist approaches to ministry. What I want to address here is a more subtle problem—the way in which communities that support the preaching and teaching of women undermine women's voices by conveying theological teachings that are biased toward powerful male experience.

When we think of theological anthropology, a systematic description of human nature in light of God, we think of abstract teachings that academic theologians transmit to the learned few. Certainly, academic theologians are a key source of theological teachings, and many of those teachings never cross the threshold of a church door. Some teachings, however, become very influential and even spawn simplified popular versions.

For example, Reinhold Niebuhr's impressive study *The Nature and Destiny of Man*[23] has been extremely influential; countless pastors have been shaped by his understandings of sin and grace. Niebuhr's anthropology, impelled by an understanding of human depravity, trades on the assumption that "man loves himself inordinately." Driven by the creative yet diabolical combustion of incredible possibility and monumental insecurity, "his" whole existence is tainted by inordinate self-interest, ideological narrow-mindedness, pride, and will-to-power. Though Niebuhr recognizes an alternative expression of sin, sensuality or evasion of the self, this is ultimately subsumed under self-centeredness. Grace addresses the reality of pride; it shatters the self, which alleviates self-interest and renews the capacity for self-sacrificial giving. Grace, the power of God in and over human beings, recenters the ego and produces the capacity to live "heedless of the self."

Niebuhr's theology, which in fact is rather nuanced in its development, has a popularized version, captured in the adage "let go, let God." It goes something like this: Because of human self-centeredness, human striving seems to get in the way of God's intentions. We sinful creatures ought to recognize our sin and stop trying to manage the world, because all we do is screw it up. We ought simply to allow God's will to take its course. Being the sinful, self-centered creatures that we are, it is best that we submit to those religious authorities who interpret for us what God is doing in the world.

Many feminist theologians, beginning with Valerie Saiving in 1960, have attacked pride-based anthropologies such as Niebuhr's. A representation of sin as self-assertion, self-centeredness, and pride speaks out of and to the experience of *powerful men*, feminists aver. Women are better indicted for such things as lack of self, self-abnegation, and irresponsibility—what Susan Nelson Dunfee refers to as "the sin of hiding."[24] When sin as pride is generalized, self-abnegation is rendered a virtue and is harmfully reinforced. A theology that emphasizes self-sacrifice as the human telos—and urges the faithful to "let go"—functions to enervate further women's struggle for self-assertion. For many women, and powerless men as well, humility, selflessness, and self-sacrifice are the *sin;* pride and self-assertion are the appropriate responses to "grace." Dunfee admonishes that "by encouraging woman to confess the wrong sin, and by failing to judge her in her actual sin, Christianity has both added to woman's guilt and failed to call her into her full humanity." [25] More than that, it fails to call *the church* into its full humanity.

For women, patterns of gender socialization and faith socialization reinforce one another; being female and being religiously faithful are equated with submission, dependence, obedience, and self-sacrifice. "One might expect of theologians that they at least not add to these pressures," charged Valerie Saiving, adding, "one might even expect them to support and encourage the woman who desires to be both a woman and an individual in her own right." However, she concluded, "theology, to the extent that it has defined the human condition on the basis of masculine experience continues to speak of such desires as sin or temptation to sin."[26]

Certainly there is a place for theological formulations that warn against what Reinhold Niebuhr called "the will-to-power" and its consequences; certainly there are times when we should let go. However, the emphasis on the sin of pride and grace-inspired self-sacrifice emerges out of and speaks most relevantly to the experience of powerful men. Sin as pride and grace as self-sacrifice are often irrelevant and even harmful to developing women whose sense of self is weak rather than strong. For many women, the self that they need to give up is the self-abnegating self; if we want to preserve Niebuhr's language, then we must make clear that for many women the sacrifice that they need to make is the sacrifice of their propensity to sacrifice.

The reality of the pride of the powerful makes the assertion of the humble even more needed. I do not reject the Reformed understanding of total depravity; I simply see implications that are opposite from what have been drawn. An awareness of total depravity does not imply submission to authority or giving up oneself; rather, it calls for a wide and inclusive conversation that is stretched by numerous voices. It calls us to question those in power; it points to the crucial responsibility of those on margins to inform those at the center. By making a virtue out of giving oneself away, current theology diminishes the conversation of community life and thereby enhances the pride of the powerful. Hard dialogue, which demands self-assertion, is deemed a sin, and deep connections are thus prevented.

We must correct this theologically driven betrayal of women; we need to encourage women to develop and assert their voices in the conversation of community life. We need to announce that women cannot "let go and let God" all the time; sometimes they must hold on and announce "here I stand, so help me God!" In fact, genuine relationality demands self-assertion. As Saiving noted, the promotion of a selfless human being leaves us with "a chameleon-like creature who responds to others but has no personal identity of his [sic] own."[27] A theology that reinforces women in their propensity to give themselves away does not promote authentic community; it rather promotes false relationality. As Carol Gilligan contends, "Making connections with others by excluding oneself is a strategy destined to fail," for "relationship implies the presence of both self and other."[28]

The educational implication is not that we stop teaching about the dangers of pride and self-assertion. Rather, the implication is that we hold in tension our tradition's tensive critiques toward both self-assertion and self-abnegation. The good news that binds the testaments of our cannon, normative for Christians in Jesus the Savior, is that the powerful are to be humbled and the humble are to be exalted. We need to acknowledge the presence of both positions in our midst, and we need especially to keep in mind the particular life situation of girls and women. Our theological teachings must encourage appropriate forms of self-assertion. Extolling the self-sacrifice of the powerful is a valid theological teaching; reinforcing the self-sacrifice of the lowly is an abomination of the gospel. Chances are, when we preach against the sin of pride, those who are already laid low will take the message to heart, and those who are currently exalted will miss the point.

One of the reasons that powerful men fail to get the point regarding the sin of pride is the countervailing image of God as a powerful, controlling, all-knowing *male*. In the case of women, the exclusive use of male images for God reinforces the disempowering effects of theological anthropology. Boys and men are taught to guard against pride and will-to-power while at the same time given the model of a God who is proud, powerful, and "all boy." Girls are taught to guard against pride and will-to-power while given the model of a God who is proud, powerful, and "no part girl." Thus, in addition to providing a balanced theological anthropology, we need to attend to the way in which prevailing images of God contribute to the dehumanization of women.

## Christian Education and Images of God

"I wish I could at least find a church using inclusive language/imagery so that my daughter wouldn't have to grow up with negative male imagery and feel the alienation and ambivalence that I feel," commented one mother in a recent study of women's spiritual lives.[29] This mother is painfully aware of the way in which language and imagery shape our self-understanding and view of reality. The language we use and the images we champion do not simply correspond with and reflect "reality"; language and images shape and determine particular constructions of reality.

In her book *Critical Caring*, Valerie De Marinis describes a kindergarten church school class session on the image of God. Mrs. Green, the church school teacher, asked the class to draw a picture of God. Six-year-old Heather drew a picture of God with two faces, one male and another female. Her shocked and dismayed teacher responded, "No, that's not what God looks like. God the Father is male. God doesn't have two faces," and proceeded to cross out Heather's drawing with a red pen. She then ordered Heather to do it again, "This time, the right way!"[30] Heather stared in silence at the blank sheet she was given. She left after class that morning with her defaced drawing, and when she got home she had her mother put the picture in the closet.

The damper this event put on Heather's emerging personality led the family into therapy and eventually into another church. The therapist worked gently to reactivate this little girl's spunk and theological imagination. Heather's therapy was completed when she produced a drawing of God as a dancing butterfly. "It's the same

God as in my other one, but God can dance now. I hate this red $X$ [pointing to the red mark made by Mrs. Green, the church school teacher, on her first drawing]. My butterfly won't ever have an $X$ on it. I wouldn't put an $X$ on her drawing. God doesn't like what she did. It was not good. God is free now, not staying in the closet anymore."[31] Not only was Heather's theological imagination revived, but her theological voice was activated. She was able to bring a prophetic judgment against a failed authority and declare, "God doesn't like what she did." Sadly, it took serious therapy to undo the damage this failed authority caused.

Heather's story could easily have ended differently. This girl who somehow managed to break out the cultural bonds of gender socialization and draw a male/female God was nearly reshackled through the theological teachings of the church, most pronounced in the church school setting.[32] For every young child, like Heather, that experiences the squelching of a creative imagination there are twenty-five children whose imagination is shaped by stereotypic images. The number of children who draw male gods and receive selective affirmation is as tragic as the number of children who experiment with nontraditional gods and are punished.

The power of our "pictures of God" to both liberate and hold us in bondage is immense, according to Jungian psychologist Ann Ulanov.[33] Many boys grow up with inadequate images of God, even though they feel a part of God's image. Many girls grow up feeling ambivalent about and alienated from a God that does not include them.

Feminist concerns about imaging God have recently touched tender nerves. Yet the critique of male images for God is in continuity with the Reformed legacy of iconoclasm and the Catholic heritage of mystery. All images of God are images; when we forget this, we create an idol. Elizabeth Johnson reminds us, "to speak rightly of God" involves recognizing the important "open-endedness to talk about God" who "is mystery beyond all imagining."[34] Genderizing God with exclusively male images deforms the imaginations of both boys and girls, leading to idolatry. Drawing the practical implications of Johnson's work, Mary Aquin O'Neill asserts, "When access to the mystery of God is limited by a hardening of the theological imagination, men as well as women and children of both sexes suffer deprivation."[35]

Recognizing that images of God are limited, partial, provisional, and open-ended does not mean that images for God are inappropriate. Rather, it means that any single image is seriously inadequate and when used exclusively leads to idolatry. One of the most important things a community of faith can do is to shape children's imaginations with a variety of images of God. This will not only serve gender identity more faithfully; it will promote theological development. As a seminary professor, I am finding that a number of students come to seminary with a fairly monolithic and rigid image of God. Indeed, in many cases the image of God has become exhaustively identified with God. When that particular image is challenged, the integrity of faith itself is threatened. This happens in churches as well, which is perhaps why so many youth leave the church. Like Celie, in *The Color Purple*, who had difficulty conjuring any image of God other than the white grandfather in flowing robes, replacing inadequate childhood images "is hard work, let me tell you." Celie felt that her only choice was to stop praying to that God; she was unable to trust in the old image and afraid to consider alternatives. "He been there so long, he don't want to budge. He threaten lightening, floods and earthquakes."[36] It is no doubt neater to present only one image of God; it sets children up, however, for idolatry—and the loss of faith when the inadequacy of the idol (monolithic image) is exposed. "To neglect God-images as images means that they are free to gather power to knock us over," warns Ulanov. "Only if we keep them as *images* of God do we have a chance to keep a foot in reality too."[37]

Feminist concern about imagery for God goes beyond whether or not God is called "he" or "she." God imaged as the Almighty, distant, unchangeable, and impassive Father/King is a God untouched and unsullied by human life. This God is a God of glory. To those for whom this image of God is foundational, female imagery can only seem dissonant. Ironically, though women are to be neat, pure, and clean in appearance, it is female experience that most actively engages the earthiness and dirtiness of life. Female imagery for God frequently evokes the dirtiness and messiness of birthing, the manual labor of baking and weaving, and the kind of creativity that makes something out of "the good for nothing" at hand rather than out of untouched nothingness.[38] Female imagery for God champions the God who gets dirty, and it announces to us that we must get dirty too.

## Recovering Male Images?

Originally, when images for God such as father, lord, and king were presented, they had the effect of provisionalizing all other male authorities.[39] Temporal fathers, lords, and kings were placed aside—sometimes leading to untoward civil and familial effects. Hebrew midwives Puah and Shiphrah, the initiators of the Exodus, disobeyed and lied to Pharaoh because they revered and served God (Exodus 1). Abigail, wife of Nabal, corrected her husband's foolish behavior because she trusted God and her own wisdom in discerning God's work (1 Sam. 25). "Indeed," asserts Alicia Ostriker, "wherever women's spirituality has arisen as an independent force, there we are typically reminded that we are to call no man father, master, or lord, and that 'whosoever shall exalt himself shall be abased; and he that humbleth himself shall be exalted' (Matt. 23:1–12)."[40]

In an interesting analysis of Pentecostal women who believe themselves subordinate to men, Mary McClintock Fulkerson observes that commitment to God the father leads otherwise submissive women to challenge temporal authorities when their call to preach is at stake. These women hold to the superiority of men and subject themselves to male authority in all matters—"except preaching the gospel." Says one about preaching: "I will not allow anybody to tell me what to preach or how to preach it except God."[41] Although I do not advocate the uncritical use of male imagery for God, I do believe that we need to recover and reinforce the subversive impulse of male language for God. Unfortunately, rather than leading to women's liberation from fathers, lords, and kings, male images for God have often had the reverse effect of turning fathers, lords, and kings into gods. Similarly, although the incarnation of God in the male person of Jesus of Nazareth represents divine rejection of patriarchal power, Jesus' maleness has been used to exalt men and to keep women out of positions of leadership in the church. The importance of Jesus' maleness is that he used the power that was granted to him as a means for empowering others. Implicitly, he turned patriarchy—and its consequences for men and women—upside down. But, like a spring that maintains its shape no matter how hard you try to straighten it, the church turned it back around. Most perversely, rather than see Jesus as the reinterpretation of what it means to be male and powerful, the church has often interpreted his maleness as the seal of male aggrandizement while promoting his servanthood as exemplary for female self-sacrifice.

At the very least, those who retain male images for God must teach against such patriarchal perversion of their intention. And, if they are to be faithful, those who use male imagery must take seriously the call to nurture women who will call no one father, lord, or king.

Alongside explicit theological teachings that thwart women's growth and self-development are implicit norms and attitudes that further prevent self-assertion and the development of voice.

## The Implicit Curriculum of Christian Education: What Kind of Talk Is Allowed?

The problems inherent in the explicit theological anthropology of the church become intensified in the educational processes of the church. Two prevailing patterns of education work against self-development: the banking approach and the small-group sharing approach.

## Don't "Bank" on Women's Flourishing

The "banking approach" to education was so-named by Paulo Freire, an educator who worked with oppressed peasants in Brazil. This approach presumes that it is the teacher's role "to 'fill' the students by making deposits of information which the teacher considers to constitute true knowledge."[42] Banking, in Freire's view, suffers from "narration sickness"; it is always telling and rarely listening. The teacher is the knower, and the learner is the receptacle for the teacher's knowledge. It is teacher- and content-focused, and it requires passive, compliant, and accommodating learners. Banking education, further, is orderly and systematic; the prized information is often presented in a coherent and polished manner that assumes its verity. In communities of faith, banking education is combined with a particular educational piety: there is an implicit assumption that God can be described in an orderly and coherent manner, and there is a corresponding expectation that the learner espouse the teacher's way of formulating God's order.

There is nothing wrong with the systematic presentation of tradition and belief, especially in a time when there is so little knowledge of the tradition. There is something drastically wrong, however, with approaches to teaching that do not foster the type of questioning and depth conversation that is necessary for growth in theological maturity. Questioning is not especially encouraged in presentational teaching styles; when questions do arise, they are answered from within the parameters of the system presented. As Freire puts it, this type of educational paradigm leads to the "castration of curiosity." "[T]oday teaching, knowledge, consists in giving answers and not asking questions."[43] This is a problem for men and women, but it is especially harmful to women. Because theology has been constructed and transmitted from a male-biased perspective, questions and creative assertions from the margins of women's experience, like Heather's picture of God, are often either dismissed as trivial or too quickly denounced as heretical.

Beautifully crafted and coherent lectures are not to be despised, but they do not stand alone as educational processes. I am reminded of George Eliot's discussion of beauty. Admiring pure and pretty conceptions of beauty, she also pointed to another type.

> But let us love that other beauty too, which lies in no secret of proportion, but is the secret of deep sympathy. Paint us an angel, if you can, with a floating violet robe, and a face

paled by the celestial light; paint us yet oftener a Madonna, turning her mild face upward and opening her arms to welcome the divine glory; but do not impose on us any aesthetic rules which shall banish from the region of Art those old women scraping carrots with their work-worn hands, those heavy clowns taking holiday in a dingy pot-house, those rounded backs and stupid weather-beaten faces that have bent over the spade and done the rough work of the world— those homes with their tin pans, their brown pitchers, their rough curs, and their clusters of onions.[44]

I invoke this image not to reinforce female servitude but to highlight the messy, dirty, earthy side of life. Life together in community, life lived in engagement with this world, is messy, conflicted, rough, dynamic, and weather-beaten. It is rarely smooth-flowing, celestial, mild, and unscathed. In fact, Eliot warns, "In this world there are so many of these common coarse people . . . it is so needful we should remember their existence, else we may happen to leave them quite out of our religion and philosophy and frame lofty theories which only fit a world of extremes."[45]

Feminists in their varieties have taught us that the process of discerning God's intentions and living out faithful lives is of that "other kind of beauty"—a mysterious, messy, and at times wearying endeavor. Christendom's repeated attempts to assert uniformity notwithstanding, Christian faith and practice are irreducibly contextual, provisional, and variable. A feminist approach to Christian education embraces the messiness and dirtiness of discerning what the Christian message and life mean at this time. It is like what Judith Plaskow refers to as "Godwrestling."[46] As Plaskow puts it, God's will does not come, à la Cecil B. DeMille as the boomings of a clear male voice. Rather, God's will is discerned and disclosed through communal wrestling, puzzling over, and conversing about our mysterious and complex traditions. We need to be taught how to engage in such wrestling, and we need to be brought into the community of others in order for such wrestling to properly occur.

I want to be careful that we do not too quickly denounce all forms of presentation as banking. There is a kind of presentational teaching—"back-talk"—that actually fosters rather than inhibits conversation.[47]

I was recently instructed by an African-American student in one of my classes. He gave a presentation to a group and was surprised by the lack of response. When he asked the group why they were not engaged, they said that he should have used a more dialogical style. He told the group that presentation was a typical style in his community, and the group retorted, "Well, you should try dialogue." As he and I reflected together on this experience, he commented, "You know, in the African-American church, people talk back when you present something. You don't just go in and say, "Let's dialogue"; you rather go in and say, "Here's what I think about this," and then they talk back to you." What may look on the surface like banking education is deeply dialogical; back-talk is a process that teaches people to listen, to question, to back-talk. In fact, it is especially important for women teachers, who frequently have difficulty asserting teaching authority, to realize that conversational education does not mean that the teacher disappears. Freire does take great pains to blur distinctions between teachers and students, for all are learners and all can teach one another. This doesn't mean that a teacher cannot speak her voice and offer her view. Teachers who speak and invite back-talk generate vital and dynamic classroom situations. It is important that the teacher really welcome back-talk, both providing honest responses to questions and allowing for questions to cast a new light on the material presented. Rather than train devotees, the teacher should nurture thinkers. If the teacher communicates to the learners that they are all in the process of learning together, then the teacher will provide an atmosphere that generates back-talk, for the benefit of all. Genuine teacher-talk and student back-talk can be far more conversational than some methods that claim to be dialogical.

## Sharing the Journey and Avoiding the Adventure

Dampening though banking education is, its opposite, small groups, is often no more helpful. The small-group movement is sweeping the nation, and it is significantly influencing educational paradigms in communities of faith. Although small groups appear to be places where people can really grapple with theological and life issues, this is turning out not to be the case. According to Robert Wuthnow, small groups avoid the mess and dirt of theological grappling every bit as much as banking paradigms. There is a decisive cultural milieu to small groups that emphasizes tolerance, comfort, and refraining from judgment.

> The social contract binding members together asserts only the weakest of obligations. Come if you have time. Talk if you feel like it. Respect everyone's opinion. Never criticize. Leave quietly if you become dissatisfied.[48]

> Emotional support is defined to mean encouragement rather than criticism or guidance. The group tells its members they are okay, but refrains from offering constructive advice.[49]

Although this seems like a great improvement over educational processes that are passive and teacher oriented, small groups like this inadvertently work against honesty and self-development.

"Rather than encouraging people to seek higher goals," says Wuthnow of the kind of spirituality that is encouraged, "it can inoculate
them against taking the risks that may be necessary for true
growth."[50] This is particularly true for women. Although tolerance
and comfort *are* important aspects of community life, they do not
stand alone. Feminists from a variety of different standpoints are
recognizing the danger that surface connectedness poses for girls
and women. Psychologist Carol Gilligan uncovers the "patina of
niceness and kindness" that prevents adolescent girls from differ-
entiating themselves and speaking their voice; political philosopher
Iris Young warns against the growing desire for community that
avoids difference and ends up reproducing homogeneity.[51] Unfortunately, the metaphor of "connected education" can contribute to
this problem if connection is understood to preclude disagreement
and judgment.

The small-group movement, with its norms of tolerance and loose
commitment, inadvertently thwarts conversational education and
stunts the development of women. It is not simply the growth of girls
and women that is at stake here; it is also the vitality of the community as a whole. If the voices of women are flattened by the patina
of niceness and kindness of small-group life, then an important
prophetic impulse will be lost. The good news of the gospel is not
simply that God has mercy on us; the good news is that God wants
to bring redemption and renewal to the groaning creation. Recognition of injustice calls for moments of prophetic critique and judgment. Women in small groups pressed by the implicit norms of
small-group life to accept everyone's way of being will withhold critiques of sexist forms of behavior. Not only are the women deprived
of voice; they are also withholding their *needed* social criticism.
Women's prophetic voices are needed in communities of faith for
the full humanity of all involved. Everyone's growth is stunted when
struggle and conflict are eliminated.

One of the normative practices of small-group life is the sharing
of personal stories. Although story sharing has potential for fostering deep connections, many groups develop an implicit story for-
mula replete with normative "theolingo" that reduces the conversational potential of story sharing. For storytelling to be real-talk, it
must break out of such patterning.

Sharing stories has been and continues to be a source of empowerment for women as they struggle psychologically and spiritually.
"The new stories that women tell each other in conversations with
each other, in consciousness raising, and in fiction, poetry, and
other literary forms are key sources for discovering the shape of
women's spiritual quest," suggests Carol Christ.[52] Story sharing that

is empowering (for example, that which took place in early feminist consciousness-raising groups) allows for differentness and disagreement. Furthermore, such story sharing should foster the emergence of tensive themes. No two stories are the same, and different stories describe God's activity differently. God's grace is evident in one; God's absence in another; God's convicting call to righteousness in another; God's comforting presence in still another. When storytelling happens freely and regularly, theology retains its rich messiness. And, as noted earlier, it contributes to a richer ethical life that has an enlarged moral vision.

To give an example close to home, some white feminists have had to repent of their early moves to quickly concentrate on and censure "father" language for God. For many African-American women, this is simply not the central issue.[53] It is the case that in a community of hard dialogue and deep connections, some women can share their stories of why "father" language is painful to them, whereas others can reclaim this language or deal with different concerns (such as the problem with God's assumed "whiteness").

Story sharing in communities of faith historically centers around biblical narratives. This remains important in a feminist perspective on Christian education. Yet feminists have recognized that important stories of women have been excluded in storytelling. In examining the third element of congregational curriculum, we will look at those teachings that are absent.

### The Null Curriculum of Christian Education: Whose Stories Are Missing?

A feminist perspective on the null curriculum of Christian education notices two things that are glaringly missing: the history of women of faith, and the confession of the sin of violence against women.

### Dangerous Memories: Who the Hell Is Vashti?

Can you name the judge of Israel who was also a prophet of God? This judge was a military commander who led the troops of Israel in battle against the Canaanites. This judge was a poet and musician. Still stumped? One final clue: this judge was remembered as "mother of Israel." Does Deborah ring a bell? Don't be too hard on yourself if you didn't answer this correctly. Most people have only a vague recollection of Deborah. I recently asked an eminent preacher if he had ever preached on her story, and he said he had not. Alas, he is not the only one. The story of Deborah is like a dirty secret; it languishes unread and untold. It was saddening but not surprising when a group of university women recently told me that they didn't know that such a narrative as Judges 4 and such a female hero as Deborah were in the Bible.

Deborah is not the only forgotten heroine. In the last few years I have written about and presented workshops on strong women in the Bible. My all-time favorite biblical woman is Queen Vashti, whose story is told in Esther 1.[54] I know off the bat that most Christians, including many Christian pastors, have never heard of Vashti. When I shared with one pastor, who prides himself on his biblical literacy, that I was writing on Vashti, he queried, "Who is she, an ancient near-eastern goddess?" When I told him who Vashti was, he complained, "Well you can't expect me to know all those obscure characters in the Bible." I include in the subtitle above one friend's comment that seems to sum up most people's response to my project on this biblical woman: Who the hell is Vashti?

It is no surprise that Deborah and Vashti are dis-remembered in our traditioning process. They are strong women who get dirty in men's business. Consider Vashti's story. Vashti is queen to king Ahasueras, and she is ordered by him to parade her beauty before his court of men. The men having partied for weeks and no doubt drunk, Vashti refuses to come. The king is enraged by her brazenness, and he deposes the assertive queen who took mastery over herself. Advised by his henchmen, he puts into motion a law that decrees that men shall be masters of their houses. A kingdomwide search is made for a new queen to crown in Vashti's stead. The pliant and submissive Esther finds favor and is crowned. Though the king achieves his goal of asserting his power over his plucky wife, his personal weakness is a glaring contrast to Vashti's courageous integrity. Ironically, his beautiful and deferent replacement wife finishes what Vashti began; she ends up the master of the story![55]

Most Christians can tell of Sarah's desire for a son, Miriam's nurturing protectiveness toward baby Moses, and Mary's sweet submissiveness toward God, but they have no idea that we have in our tradition a queen named Vashti who refused to obey her husband's command and a judge named Deborah who was first-in-command and who was perhaps remembered as "a woman of fire."[56] Although the presence of these women does not fully mitigate the patriarchy of the biblical texts, the absence of their stories in our traditioning exposes the way in which selective retelling influences the perpetuation of patriarchy and sexism.[57] Vashti and Deborah are subversive memories; if we tell their stories, the imaginations of girls and women will be dangerously unfettered.[58]

Christian history has by and large been told from the vantage point of theological victors—men who have held religious power. There are contained in our traditions subversive strands and hints, indicating that cracks in patriarchy have repeatedly opened. The views of most women, however, and of those who have been denounced as heretics have either been left out, distorted, or evidenced only in the reaction against them. Thanks to the work of such scholars as Elisabeth Schüssler Fiorenza, the Christian community is toiling to recover and remember the lost history of women in the church, including women leaders.[59] Telling the Christian Story means telling the stories of the women whose voices call out from the gaps and cracks in the patriarchy that could not fully contain them.

Recovering the memory of strong women, though bound to be met with resistance, is the easier side of activating the null curriculum.

## Texts of Terror: What Do We Do with Them?

There is another group of biblical narratives that is a part of the null curriculum, and these narratives are much harder to handle. Phyllis Trible describes them as "texts of terror";[60] stories in which women are absolutely dehumanized—through abuse, rape, murder, and dismemberment. Pastors and teachers ignore these texts because they do not know what to do with them. How does one teach on Sarah and Abraham's cruel treatment of Hagar (Genesis 16 and 21)? How does one tell the story of the Levite's concubine who was dismembered (Judges 19)? Where is the "good news" in the rape of Tamar (2 Sam. 12)? What does one do with Jephthah's vow to God that led him to sacrifice his young daughter (Judges 11)?

Ignore them is what we do, and it is precisely what we should not do. Surely, we are called to preach the "good news," and these texts are irredeemably "bad news." Yet, leaving them out makes the bad news worse. These texts reflect perennial attitudes toward women, and we need to tackle them directly. We need to talk about the way in which these stories mirror violence against women today. As the ancient rabbis sometimes did, but Christian writers failed to (Heb. 11:32), we need to judge the actions of such men as Jephthah; and we may even need to cry out to God in rage and sorrow for the reality of such events. What we cannot do is pretend that these stories don't exist! We in the church have something to say about violence against women, and it is time we started teaching and preaching against it—lest we continue to silently ignore and thereby sanction this appalling and pervasive violation of human rights. Here, precisely, is where women cannot "let go, and let God." Women cannot give themselves away to societal violence and passively expect God to rescue them; they must take back their bodies, take back their voices, take back themselves—for the full humanity of all.

By confronting texts of terror, we give women the freedom to bring their own terror to communal conversation, and we force ourselves to take that terror seriously. If our theology is woven into a cloth that is missing the threads of women's suffering, it is of an inadequate fiber. It is texts on women's suffering that allow the deepest kind of conversation with God; they move us to call God and one another to task. Franklin Littel, noting that Christians can learn a lot from Jewish chutzpah, which encourages wrestling with God, remarked that Christians "have not usually been trained to wrestle with the angel, to question what happens under God's sovereignty." Instead, many of our theologians, as indicated above, have "raised obedience, submission, and acceptance of one's fate . . . to religious virtues."[61]

In conjunction with confronting these stories, we need to take a fresh look at the way in which the reality of violence against women illumines our theology. For instance, one of the key theological themes of Christianity is forgiveness. This is an important theme, but it can be used in a way that is harmful to battered women and to other people who have been victimized. Facile teachings on forgiveness that suppress legitimate anger have prevented many women (and other victims) from raising their voices and taking stands against injustice, including the injustice of domestic abuse. Not only does this suppressed anger intensify the pain of the victims, but it also precludes repentance and restitution on the parts of the perpetrators. The full humanity of no one is being served by this shallow "patina" of forgiveness.

By balancing our anthropology, engaging in hard dialogue, and reincorporating neglected strands of our tradition back into the conversation, we can move toward theological "real-talk" in communities of faith.

Teaching people in communities of faith to engage in real-talk and conversation is a paradoxical endeavor; it transgresses gender barriers and stereotypes. It requires listening and speaking; tolerating and critiquing; connecting with and separating from; finding common ground and pointing out disagreements; wearing dresses but getting them dirty; living assertively while cradling a baby doll. It is messy stuff. Dynamic, conversationally alive communities are less unified, less organized, and less cohesive than monolithic and homogeneous communities. We cannot be afraid of this, and we cannot run away from such dynamism at the first sign of mess. Although destructive strife is certainly not our aim, unsettledness and creative rumbling are part of the renewal process. When we see these things happening, why do we "make a commotion and weep"? Do we not know that daughter church is not dead but is about to be raised (Mark 5:39–42)? As daughter on the margins is being healed, Christ is calling to daughter church, "Talitha cum." Let us get up!

## Getting Dirty with Dignity:
## Girls Who Are Still Much

The other day my daughter, now eleven, came home from school and excitedly told me about the music concert she was singing in that evening. Her bright demeanor changed as she complained, "One of our songs uses 'mankind.' I told my teacher that those words were sexist." "Did she change the words?" I asked. "No," she reported with a grimace. "She said it was too late to change it, that 'mankind' was meant to mean women and men, and that we should leave it as it is. I guess I'll just have to sing 'humankind' all by myself." "I'm sorry she wasn't willing to change the words, but I'm really proud you mentioned it to her," I said. "I know, I'm glad I did too," she smiled and trounced off. I looked at her and remembered the toddler with the smudged face and dirty toes; I beamed as I watched her go. "She is much girl," I mused. My daughter is not afraid of the messiness of life; she got dirty in her quest to inherit the earth, and things did not turn out perfectly. But she did not give up her place in the quest. Marie once again got dirty with dignity— and with voice. Yes, she had to sing "humankind" alone that night, but she was not afraid.

A lot depends on what we mean by girl.

## NOTES

1. Jane O'Reilly, "The Lost Girls," *Mirabella* (April 1994): 116.
2. Marge Piercy, "For Strong Women," in *The Moon Is Always Female* (New York: Alfred A. Knopf, 1980), 56.
3. See James A. Doyle, *Sex and Gender* (Dubuque, Iowa: William C. Brown, 1985). Adults interact differently with—and even see different qualities in—an infant *when the same infant* is designated as either boy or girl.
4. Nancy Chodorow, *The Reproduction of Mothering: Psychoanalysis and the Sociology of Gender* (Berkeley: University of California Press, 1978).
5. Although I had to chuckle, my older son, Nathan, was not amused when he and his male friend were given B's in cooking and the female members of their group were given A's "for the same work." His interpretation: Rather than concede that this "real boy," who excelled in math and sports, could also be accomplished in female-dominated spheres, the teacher perceived his work as less adequate than that of his female counterparts. Nathan did acknowledge, with a twinkle in his

eye, that no amount of reverse sexism would have enabled his teacher to give his mother anything as high as a "B" for her (mercifully infrequent) cooking.

6. Note that I want to replace the concept of submissiveness, which I think is part of female gender socialization, with flexibility. Submissiveness is a term that, for women, needs to be given a moratorium.

7. Kathleen Hall Jamieson, *Beyond the Double Bind: Women and Leadership* (New York: Oxford University Press, 1995), 138. See also the Bem Sex-role Inventory Professional Manual (Palo Alto, Calif.: Consulting Psychologists Press, 1981).

8. Claus Offe, quoted in Iris Young, *The Politics of Difference* (Princeton: Princeton University Press, 1990), 74.

9. Letty M. Russell, *Church in the Round: Feminist Interpretation of the Church* (Louisville, Ky.: Westminster/John Knox Press, 1993), 22.

10. Ibid., 176–78.

11. Lois M. Wilson, "Re-Imagining Community," *Church & Society* 84, no. 5 (May/June 1994): 64.

12. See Douglas John Hall for an in-depth treatment of the disestablishment of the church in a post-Constantinian era, in *Thinking the Faith* (Minneapolis: Augsburg Publishing House, 1989). Hall argues that we need a theology of the cross that embraces the conflicted, ambiguous, and painful nature of life instead of a theology of glory that understands faith in terms of triumph, progress, and (frequently) uniformity.

13. I define patriarchy as a worldview (conscious or subconscious) that assumes that women are subordinate to men and that separates women's spheres of activity from men's. Clearly, women as well as men can reflect a patriarchal worldview, as is evidenced in some of my illustrations.

14. I consider descriptions of "masculinity" and "femininity" to be social constructions rather than essential human differences. Although there *may* be some biologically determined differences between men and women, social expectations for gendered behavior are reinforced so early that it is hard to identify what, if any, are essential male/female differences. In fact, some deconstructivists argue that the division of human beings into the two opposing categories of male and female is a social construction. See Judith Butler, "Gender Trouble, Feminist Theory, and Psychoanalytic Discourse," in *Feminism/Postmodernism*, ed. Linda J. Nicholson (New York: Routledge & Kegan Paul, 1990).

15. Mary Belenky, Blythe Clinchy, Nancy Goldberger, and Jill Tarule, *Women's Ways of Knowing* (New York: Basic Books, 1986), 144.

16. See Carol Lakey Hess, *Caretakers of Our Common House: Women's Development in Communities of Faith* (Nashville: Abingdon Press, forthcoming).

17. Catherine La Cugna, *God For Us: The Trinity and Christian Life* (HarperSanFrancisco, 1991), 264.

18. Dorothy Bass, "Congregations and the Bearing of Traditions," in *American Congregations*, vol. 2, *New Perspectives in the Study of Congrega-*

*tions,* ed. James P. Wind and James W. Lewis (Chicago: University of Chicago Press, 1994), 188.

19. Sharon Welch, *A Feminist Ethic of Risk* (Minneapolis: Fortress Press, 1990), 38.

20. Ibid., 126.

21. Elliot W. Eisner, *The Educational Imagination: On the Design and Evaluation of School Programs,* 3d ed. (New York: Macmillan, 1994), 103. See also Maria Harris, *Fashion Me a People* (Louisville, Ky.: Westminster/John Knox Press, 1989).

22. This section is indebted to my article "Gender, Sin, and Learning: A Developmental Perspective on and Educational Response to the Theological Anthropology of Reinhold Niebuhr," *Religious Education* 88, no. 3 (Summer 1993): 350–76.

23. Reinhold Niebuhr, *The Nature and Destiny of Man,* vols. 1 and 2 (New York: Scribners, 1941, 1943).

24. Susan Nelson Dunfee, "The Sin of Hiding: A Feminist Critique of Reinhold Niebuhr's Account of the Sin of Pride," *Soundings* 65, no. 3 (Fall 1982): 323.

25. Ibid., 317.

26. Valerie Saiving, "The Human Situation: A Feminine View," in *WomanSpirit Rising: A Feminist Reader in Religion,* ed. Carol Christ and Judith Plaskow (San Francisco: Harper & Row, 1979), 39.

27. Ibid., 41.

28. Carol Gilligan, quoted in Lyn Mikel Brown, "A Problem of Vision: The Development of Voice and Relational Knowledge in Girls Ages Seven to Seventeen," *Women's Studies Quarterly* 19 nos. 1 and 2, (Spring/Summer 1991): 60.

29. Miriam Theresa Winter, Adair Lummis, and Allison Stokes, *Defecting in Place: Women Claiming Responsibility for Their Own Spiritual Lives* (New York: Crossroad, 1994), 157.

30. Valerie De Marinis, *Critical Caring: A Feminist Model for Pastoral Psychology* (Louisville, Ky.: Westminster/John Knox Press, 1993), 68.

31. Ibid., 79–80.

32. The teachings of the male pastor of the church were the same as those of Mrs. Green, and he supported her actions.

33. Ann Ulanov, *Picturing God* (Boston: Cowley Publications, 1986), esp. 164–84.

34. Elizabeth Johnson, *She Who Is: The Mystery of God in Feminist Theological Discourse* (New York: Crossroad, 1992), 7.

35. Mary Aquin O'Neill, review of *She Who Is* in *Religious Studies Review* 21, no. 1, (January 1995): 19.

36. Alice Walker, *The Color Purple* (New York: Harcourt Brace Jovanovich, 1982), 168.

37. Ulanov, *Picturing God,* 170.

38. See Elizabeth Bettenhausen, "Re-Imagining Creation: Gathering at the Table of Necessity," *Church & Society* 84, no. 5, (May/June 1994): 75–81.

39. Thomas Ogletree notes that exclusive attachment to Yahweh provided Israel with "resources for resisting any religious sanctification of what

might otherwise appear to be 'natural' hierarchies among human be-ings" (*The Use of the Bible in Christian Ethics* [Philadelphia: Fortress Press, 1983], 61).

40. Alicia Suskin Ostriker, *Feminist Revision and the Bible* (Cambridge, Mass.: Blackwell, 1993), 60.

41. Mary McClintock Fulkerson, *Changing the Subject: Women's Discourse and Feminist Theology* (Minneapolis: Fortress Press, 1994), 269.

42. Paulo Freire, *Pedagogy of the Oppressed* (New York: Seabury Press, 1970), 63.

43. Paulo Freire and Antonio Faundez, *Learning to Question: A Pedagogy of Liberation* (New York: Continuum, 1989), 35.

44. George Eliot, *Adam Bede* (New York: Signet Classics, 1961), 177.

45. Ibid.

46. Judith Plaskow, *Standing Again at Sinai: Judaism from a Feminist Perspective* (New York: HarperCollins, 1990), 31.

47. See also bell hooks [Gloria Watkins], *Talking Back: Thinking Feminist, Thinking Black* (Boston: South End Press, 1989).

48. Robert Wuthnow, *Sharing the Journey: Support Groups and America's New Quest for Community* (New York: Macmillan, 1994), 6.

49. Ibid., 14.

50. Ibid., 18.

51. Lyn Mikel Brown and Carol Gilligan, *Meeting at the Crossroads: Women's Psychology and Girls' Development* (Cambridge: Harvard University Press, 1992); Iris Young, "The Ideal of Community and the Politics of Difference," in *Feminism/Postmodernism*, ed. Nicholson.

52. Carol Christ, *Diving Deep and Surfacing: Women Writers on Spiritual Quest* (Boston: Beacon Press, 1980), 12.

53. Susan Thistlethwaite, *Sex, Race, and God: Christian Feminism in Black and White* (New York: Crossroad, 1991), 114–17.

54. Carol Lakey Hess, "Vashti" and "Deborah," in *Women in World History* (Yorkin Press, forthcoming).

55. Vashti's defiance was not missed on Marie. Recently, I used Esther 1 for a children's sermon. As I was preparing the sermon, I asked my daughter if she would wear a pretty dress and play Vashti. With a smirk, she said she did not want to look like a fool in front of all those people. Remembering the story's point, she refused to play the refuser; I was trumped!

56. The stereotypic interpretations of Mary and Miriam are another issue altogether; Mary's purity and Miriam's filial piety are theological constructions that further thwart women's growth and assertiveness. I sometimes wonder if those who describe Mary have read the Magnificat; these are not the words of a sweet maiden!

57. As the daughter of a Holocaust survivor, I am compelled to mention recent work by Jewish feminists who point out the way in which Christian scholars (including feminists) portray Judaism as hopelessly patriarchal and Christianity as a liberating contrast to Judaism. Such dualism not only perpetuates anti-Judaism; it also obscures the ambiguity of both traditions. Judaism and Christianity are both patriarchal,

and they both contain liberating moments. It seems to me that Christians have to come to grips with the fact that the most striking heroines are in the Hebrew Scriptures, and these narratives have been absent in Christian teaching. See Judith Plaskow "Christian Feminism and Anti-Judaism," *Cross Currents* (Fall 1978): 306–9; A. J. Levine, "Second Temple Judaism, Jesus, and Women: Yeast of Eden," *Biblical Interpretation* 2, no. 1 (1994): 8–33.

58. It has been my great joy to have students and colleagues tell me that my recovery of these stories is influencing their preaching and teaching. Vashti and Deborah will not remain silent!

59. Elisabeth Schüssler Fiorenza, *In Memory of Her: A Feminist Theological Reconstruction of Christian Origins* (New York: Crossroad, 1989).

60. Phyllis Trible, *Texts of Terror* (Philadelphia: Fortress Press, 1984).

61. Franklin Littel, *The Crucifixion of the Jews* (New York: Harper & Row, 1975), 127.

# 4

## PASTORAL COUNSELING AS AN ART
## OF PERSONAL POLITICAL ACTIVISM

### Christie Corad Neuger

Linda, a thirty-five-year-old, Euro-American, upper-middle-class woman, came to pastoral counseling with a strong sense of panic and desperation. Her marriage was in trouble. She felt out of control in her life. She was distracted, nervous, irritable, and worried. She had a deep Christian belief in the permanence of the marriage vow and the obligations of marriage. She had married in her late 20s, had a four-year-old son who was very close to his father, and had built her life around marriage and mothering. She worked part-time in a bookstore, although her Japanese husband, Peter, was pressuring her to quit her job. She wanted the pastoral counselor to "help her get her act together again" so she wouldn't "lose it all."

Margaret, a thirty-year-old, African-American woman, came to pastoral counseling having attempted suicide three times. She felt out of control of her life and unable to understand why she was having so much trouble. She lived in an all-white neighborhood, was married to a police officer, and had a twelve-year-old daughter and a six-year-old son. She wanted the pastoral counselor to help her stop being so unhappy.

Rebecca and Hyun Son, a Korean couple married for twenty years, had immigrated to the United States early in their marriage. Their daughter had been raised in this country. Rebecca initiated the visit to a pastoral counselor because she felt that their marriage was falling apart. She was very upset that Hyun Son no longer had any ambition to succeed, and her own desire to achieve seemed to be pulling her away from their life together. She said that she was losing her respect for him because she had become stronger than he was. When they arrived at the counseling appointment, it turned out that Hyun Son did not know where they were or why. Rebecca wanted the pastoral counselor to change her husband so she wouldn't feel so guilty.

Nathan, a thirty-year-old, white graduate student, came to pastoral counseling for help in understanding the dynamics in his relationships with women and for help in resolving the conflicts of his inner life. He felt powerless in his own being, and yet he also understood the challenges that the women in his life were making about his privileged place in the culture. He wanted the pastoral counselor to help him move forward and take responsibility for his future.

Terry, a Euro-American, middle-class lesbian woman, came to pastoral counseling because she felt alone. It wasn't that she didn't have friends; it was more that she didn't feel that there were any real connections between herself and the people in her life. She worried because her own self-perception was so different from the feedback she got from others about who she was. She knew that she had lots of feelings going on inside, but the people around her experienced her as distant and uninvolved. She wanted the pastoral counselor to help her try to make sense out of her loneliness.

These people came to a feminist pastoral counselor for help in the midst of their struggles and distress. They chose a pastoral counselor with a feminist perspective because they had a sense about what that perspective might mean for understanding the complex mix of factors going on in their lives and the need to understand, analyze, and give voice to that complexity before new and authentic resolutions could be found.

This chapter is about pastoral counseling, in the church or in specialty settings, that operates out of a clear radical feminist perspective. It is primarily a constructive effort in the theory and theology of pastoral counseling. It builds on theories of feminist social theory, feminist psychotherapy, feminist theology, and theories of contextual analysis. It is also reflective of my work as a pastoral counselor with the people introduced above and with many other women and men over the years.

I will first explore the definitions both of pastoral counseling and of feminist perspectives, knowing that there are many ways to articulate and nuance those definitions. I will move from there to four dimensions to the process of pastoral counseling that reflect the importance of cultural and power analysis as well as the importance of the individual and family stories that are brought to the pastor for care.

## Defining Pastoral Counseling

Pastoral counseling needs to be distinguished, on the one hand, from the larger ministry of pastoral care (see Chapter 1) and, on the other, from counseling that happens in secular contexts. Pastoral counseling is a focused form of pastoral care that is primarily geared toward caring for individuals, couples, and families who are in distress. It is time limited and oriented toward helping people to make choices or changes that will improve the quality of their life and relationships. It is different from pastoral care, which is a more informal and ongoing care relationship than is pastoral counseling. It is important to note that pastoral counseling consists of an agreement between the counselor and the counselee to work together for a limited period of time in order to address particular life problems. Thus it is considered a specialized subset of pastoral care.

In addition, pastoral counseling, like pastoral care, is offered by people who are trained and authorized by the church and is seen, even when carried out in specialized settings, as one dimension of ministry.[1] However, over the fifty years since the development of this specialty area, pastoral counseling has become more and more set apart from the general ministry as it has increasingly claimed the field of psychology as the primary informant to its theory. Integration of theology and spirituality into pastoral counseling has become problematic in much of the field. And, as the discipline of psychology has taken on particular shapes, pastoral counseling has tended to adopt those shapes somewhat uncritically. Therefore, along with the problem of theological disconnection, there has been a strong attitude of individualism and privatism that has been deeply woven into the practice of pastoral counseling.

There are other distinctions between pastoral counseling and secular counseling that will be important for this discussion, because the primary resources for feminist pastoral counseling have come from explorations in secular feminist psychology and psychotherapy.

First, pastoral counselors have generally attempted to see individuals in a more holistic fashion than have secular counselors. The pastor in a parish who does pastoral counseling often has the advantage of knowing the counselee in a larger context than just the counseling room. She or he may be very familiar with the counselee's family situation, work life, religious concerns, and so on. This greater focus on the larger picture of the counselee, although still quite individualistic in orientation, sets the stage for the counselor to be able to see the counselee in relationship to the world in which she or he lives—a crucial component to a feminist orientation.

A second distinction is that the pastoral counselor has often been trained as a generalist rather than as a specialist in psychology and clinical theory. Although specialists in pastoral counseling have gone through additional training in psychotherapy, all pastoral counselors have gained their initial exposure to the care of people in a more generalist frame. This frame has theological reflection at its core, even though the more specific education in pastoral counseling may well have de-emphasized the integration of theological/spiritual resources into the practice of counseling. This generalist training anchored in theology has some advantages for a feminist perspective on pastoral counseling. One advantage is that there is less deconstruction to do around the patriarchal assumptions of psychotherapy. Psychotherapeutic systems tend to weave very tight worldviews about health, dysfunction, and change that allow little dialogue about diversity, power analysis, and social location, and these are the very categories crucial to a feminist perspective.[2] Another advantage is that theological traditions become naturally available as resources for a feminist-based approach to pastoral counseling, for good and for ill. So, although theology requires considerable deconstruction in order for it to be useful for a feminist orientation, there are remarkably liberating and insightful themes in the theological traditions that can be used for the process of empowerment in pastoral counseling.

Third, pastoral counselors, especially those working in the parish context, cannot devote as much of their time and focus to doing counseling as do secular counselors. Counseling is one of many tasks in the parish. Because of that, the pastor must find ways to work that respect the multiplicity of ministry demands, that acknowledge the multiple roles that pastors generally have with parishioners, and that integrate the collaborative nature of ministry for counselor and counselee. Therefore, the pastoral counselor, especially in the parish, needs to find creative ways to engage in helpful pastoral counseling. Much of secular counseling has oriented itself around the assumption that people both needed and could afford (time and money) to engage in long-term processes for the sake of their increased mental health. More recent psychotherapeutic theory has begun to document that good counseling can (and indeed should) occur over a shorter period of time.[3] As I describe the processes that make up a feminist approach to pastoral counseling, it will be important to remember that those processes do not have to be limited to a traditional one-on-one counseling relationship. In fact, the more useful feminist counseling process will combine strategies of counselor/counselee(s) time with a mix of group work and education.[4] Consequently, the time-limited and multiple-role context of the parish-based pastoral counselor does not need to mean automatic referral to outside professionals, nor does it need to be seen as a disadvantage for a feminist orientation to pastoral counseling.

Finally, pastoral counselors are grounded in vocational, ecclesial, and theological metaphors that shape and ground the practice of counseling and the nature of the counseling relationships. There is a commitment on the part of pastoral counselors to see the image of God in the people with whom they work and to see God's active presence in the midst of every relationship. This commitment of openness to the power of God's love and possibility in the counseling work, and the consequent acknowledgment of God's lure toward justice guides the counseling process in every moment.

## Defining a Feminist Orientation

It is important to note that the meaning of the word *feminist* has been undergoing continual reappraisal and transformation as the women's movement has changed and grown over the past thirty or so years of this feminist wave. It has given priority to a variety of concerns over those years—from a focus on equality with men, to a commitment to knowing the contemporary and historical experience of women as guiding, to an analysis of gender and the social construction of gender, to a larger acknowledgment of the variety of power systems that organize the culture into systems of dominance and subordinance. A multicultural, multivalent analysis that includes the power dynamics around gender, class, race, sexual orientation, able-bodiedness, and age are now seen as central to the feminist project. What has not changed in the definition of radical feminism is its commitment to the analysis, subversion, and overthrow of cultural patriarchy.

Patriarchy, as Gerda Lerner has defined it, is "the manifestation and institutionalization of male dominance over women and children in the family and the extension of male dominance over women in society in general."[5] It takes all sorts of forms including the pervasive intimate violence against women, women's economic and contributive restrictions in the workforce, behavioral mandates for women in keeping with a subordinate status, women's exclusion from the meaning-making processes in the culture, and an exclusive understanding of God as male. However, the definition of patriarchy as solely oriented around gender has been extended by feminist theorists to include a broader understanding of the variety of systems of dominance and submission with the recognition that generally one is a member of several of those systems at any given time. As Rebecca Chopp notes, "Indeed, patriarchy is revealed not simply as a social arrangement nor as individual acts of cruelty toward women on the part of men but rather as a deep spiritual ordering that invades and spreads across the social order—through individual identity, to social practices, to lines of authority in institutions, to cultural images and representation."[6] This means that patriarchy has created a dis-order in all power arrangements, and simple categorizations of oppressor and oppressed cannot be made without an understanding of the power systems that are in operation.

The key to this set of definitions is the understanding that feminism, as currently understood, is a set of political assumptions and commitments that have to do with the transformation of a culture that disadvantages all women, women and men of color, gay men and lesbians, women and men who are disabled, children and the aged, and people who are poor or working class—those people who are not on the dominant or ruling side of the culturally determined, value-laden split. Feminism is a political and public enterprise built out of a commitment to the experience of those who are disadvantaged in the cultural power arrangements. It is very personal in that it is built out of the hearing and privileging of those disadvantaged and normally ignored perspectives, *and* it is always political.[7]

## A Feminist Orientation to Pastoral Counseling

The question that must be asked, one that is being asked in contemporary feminist psychotherapy, is, Can there ever be a true alliance or integration between something as individual and personal as counseling and something as deeply political and activist as feminism? This is an important question. Pastoral counseling cannot call itself feminist just because it agrees to listen carefully to women's experience and to support women as they strive toward self-realization and fulfillment. Pastoral counseling cannot call itself feminist just because it works with particular women's crises and experiences. Pastoral counseling cannot call itself feminist just because it tries to be nonsexist. Pastoral counseling cannot call itself feminist even when it focuses on the way the culture has done harm to women that must be undone. Pastoral counseling can be considered to be feminist only when its goal is not just personal transformation, but transformation of the culture—including the church—as a part of the counseling process. Is this possible?

My answer to that question is a resounding "yes." Not only is it possible but it is necessary, and it is in keeping with the nature of the ministry of which it is a part. A feminist-oriented pastoral counseling *is* for the benefit of individuals, and it is in keeping with the nature of ministry that claims that the care of people includes their empowerment to transform "principalities and powers" for the good of God's kin-dom. How to do that is not always clear, but the attempt to do that is what is required of us.

A feminist approach to pastoral counseling is held together by the warp of feminist social theory that includes feminist psychology/psychotherapy, and the woof of feminist theology. In the following four sections, the nature of that counseling process will be woven out of these two strands and will be built out of a foundational assumption that is articulated well by Laura Brown in her superb text titled *Subversive Dialogues.* She writes:

> What makes [counseling] practice feminist is not who the clients are but how the therapist thinks about what she does, her epistemologies and underlying theoretical models rather than her specific techniques, the kinds of problems she addresses, or the demographic makeup of the client population. . . . Feminist therapy aims to deprivatize the lives of both therapists and people with whom they work by asking, out loud and repeatedly, how each life and each pain are

manifestations of processes operating in a larger social context. At the same time, feminist therapy requires that each life experience be treated as valuable, unique, and authoritative, an expert source of knowledge regarding both the individual and the culture as a whole.[8]

## Four Dimensions of a Feminist Pastoral Counseling

As the opening vignettes demonstrate, this is not a chapter about counseling with women. This chapter is about the theoretical, theological, and clinical processes that resource pastoral counseling—a pastoral counseling that is about the business of transforming patriarchy. When people come to the pastor for counseling, it can be assumed that they are experiencing considerable distress, pain, anxiety, fear, or uncertainty. The counselee is there in order to explore what is causing the problems and to attempt to make changes in her or his life that will relieve the distress. Usually people do not come to counseling, especially pastoral counseling, unless they are experiencing this kind of distress. It is rarely a "frivolous" choice to seek help in this way.

Pastoral counseling from a feminist perspective, as noted earlier, seeks to investigate the pain of the counselee from the perspective of life in a toxic culture. The assumption is that the counselee and the counselor are engaged in a collaborative process of trying to name, understand, and transform the cultural harm that has been internalized and that continues to exist in relationships, in work settings, and in the culture at large. This assumption includes the belief that it takes a great deal of deconstructive work in the counseling process in order to get at, name, understand, and change those patriarchal structures that have done so much harm. The hope is also that this process of personal, systemic, and cultural transformation will further the king-dom of God.

I propose the following four dimensions to describe the movement of feminist-oriented pastoral counseling. Those processes are (1) coming to voice; (2) gaining clarity; (3) making choices; and (4) staying healthy. As described earlier, these four processes do not have to be fully accomplished in a one-to-one traditional counseling process but may helpfully occur through a combination of personal counseling, group counseling, and education.

### Coming to Voice

The issue of language and voice has long been a hallmark of the feminist movement. Not only have many key theoretical works been developed around the rubric of voice and speech, especially finding a different voice and language than that which has been provided out of a dominant culture, but a critique of male-dominated language has been around since before the first wave of feminism and the suffrage movement.[9] There has long been the clear understanding that language not only reflects reality but it also creates it. When the language of the culture does not carry the experience or perspective of women or others of nondominant cultural status, then the culture will not operate in the best interests of those groups. And not only are the people in these groups deprived of empowerment and full participation in the culture, but the culture is damaged, too. As Jean Baker Miller says, "What I do see is that our dominant society is a very imperfect one. It is a low-level, primitive organization built on an exceedingly restricted conception of the total human potential. It holds up narrow and ultimately destructive goals for the dominant groups and attempts to deny vast areas of life. The falsity and the full impact of this limited conception has been obscured."[10] There is a great deal at stake for both individuals and the culture in new language being developed and claimed by people who have been deprived of it.

Nondominant groups have not only been deprived of language but have also been denied voice.[11] Most works in feminist counseling have focused on the importance of helping girls and women to gain access to their own voice. Miriam Greenspan, in the first comprehensive text on feminist psychotherapy ever written, discusses the importance of what Nelle Morton called "Hearing into speech."[12] It is not just a matter of being able to tell one's story that is being emphasized here. It is the empowerment of hearing oneself speak and learning to believe in the truth of that long-denied voice, language, and narrative. Greenspan talks about her own experience:

> The simple process of women sitting and listening to each others' stories respectfully and with an ear to the shared strengths as well as the shared ordeals had some very powerful therapeutic effects. Our relationship to everything—our bodies, our work, our sexuality, the men and women and children in our lives—emerged in a thoroughly new light. Together we saw that the old terms used to describe politics, relationships, sexuality, power and language itself were an outgrowth of male experience and had to be reinvented from our own point of view as women. For many of us, the overwhelming sense was of seeing the world through our own eyes for the very first time.[13]

The process of losing voice may be a somewhat subtle one for girls and women, although there are many times and places where girls' voices are crushed explicitly through violence and other overt acts of harm. Lyn Brown and Carol Gilligan have documented that this loss of voice seems to happen to many girls in late childhood/ early adolescence. Gilligan and Brown did a longitudinal study of girls moving from age eight into their early teen years. They found that younger girls were in significant relationships with their peers and would speak directly and clearly about violations and injustices done to themselves or to their friends. By the age of eleven these same girls were moving away from their own knowledge, using the phrase "I don't know" much more frequently and expressing implicit and explicit knowledge of the rules they were to follow in order to be acceptable and "in relationship." Gilligan and Brown summarize their findings by saying:

> At the crossroads of adolescence, the girls in our study describe a relational impasse that is familiar to many women: a paradoxical or dizzying sense of having to give up relationship for the sake of "relationships." Because this taking of oneself out of relationship in order to protect oneself and have relationships forces an inner division or chasm, it makes a profound psychological shift. . . . Women's psychological development within patriarchal societies and male-voiced cultures is inherently traumatic.[14]

Mary Ballou and Nancy Gabalac talk about this experience of loss of voice through the language of harmful adaptation.[15] This is the developmental process in which women (and this can probably be extended to other nondominant groups; see Chapter 1) have been systematically taught from birth onward, in a repetitive, spiraling way, how to adapt to the culture's dangerous definition of being female. They describe the process through five stages: humiliation (being reduced in one's own and others' eyes), inculcation (learning the rules), retribution (punishment for breaking the rules), conversion (believing the dominant culture's definitions and limitations of women), and conscription (persuading our daughters and other women of the rightness of the cultural lie). These are the processes that insidiously strip women of voice and push them into accepting the loss of potential language and authentic story.

Women and other members of nondominant groups have thus learned to interpret their own stories and experiences, needs and goals, through the lenses of the other—those they have been taught to please and appease. Often they have lost access to their truths and their honest strengths. As Jean Baker Miller says:

> Tragic confusion arises because subordinates absorb a large part of the untruths created by the dominants; there are a great many blacks who feel inferior to whites, and women who still believe they are less important than men. This internalization of dominant beliefs is more likely to occur if

there are few alternative concepts at hand. On the other hand, it is also true that members of the subordinate group have certain experiences and perceptions that accurately reflect the truth about themselves and the injustice of their position. Their own more truthful concepts are bound to come into opposition with the mythology they have absorbed from the dominant group. An inner tension between the two sets of concepts and their derivatives is almost inevitable.[16]

With these descriptions of the power of lost language and denied voice, one can understand how feminist therapists can claim that this approach to counseling sees cultural pathology and harmful adaptation at the core of the distress that women and other marginalized groups bring into counseling. The focus is not on the intrapsychic or idiosyncratic formation of personal pathology; the focus is on internalized patriarchy and the damage that contextual patriarchy continues to do.

Laura Brown speaks of these issues with poignant insight when she talks about the counselee's loss of her or his "mother tongue." She says that the process of counseling is the work of counselor and counselee to

> come together to learn the client's emotional "mother tongue," the "native language" in which an undistorted image can be told through the freed voice of the client who is no longer silenced. There is not, in this metaphor, the necessity for an actual change of spoken language. It is more about how the client comes to rename experience, retell a narrative, in a way that no longer violates well-being, but rather empowers or liberates.[17]

In order to help a counselee move to a knowing and reclaiming of her or his "mother tongue," it is fundamental for the counselor to be present with the counselee as fully and respectfully as possible— validating her or his attempts to find language for realities that have been denied, minimized, and distorted by the dominant culture. The pastoral counselor and the counselee must work together, collaboratively and mutually, to find the language that will authentically express the nature and power of the narrative. It is in finding that language and claiming the right to speak it that empowerment for change is made possible.

Regaining language and voice for the power of naming one's self, one's environment, and one's God has been a primary agenda for feminist theology as well. If pastoral counseling is a weave of the social sciences with primary religious and theological resources, then it is important to note that both feminist theology and feminist psychology place the power of naming at the core of empowering people and cultures that have been disenfranchised. Mary Pellauer says, in *God's Fierce Whimsy*, "If there's anything worth calling theology, it is listening to people's stories—listening to them and honoring and cherishing them, and asking them to become even more brightly beautiful than they already are."[18]

One can see the centrality of language and naming to the theological traditions in the creation stories of Genesis. In the creation story represented in Genesis 1, the naming of each element of God's work is part of the essence of creation. As God creates day and night, the earth, and the sky, each is carefully named and evaluated. It is, in part, the naming that makes the creation real. In the creation story recorded in Genesis 2, God creates *'adam* and a pleasant environment and then realizes that *'adam* is isolated in the garden. As God attempts to create a companion for *'adam,* part of that relationship-building process is inviting *'adam* to name the new creations. As they are named, they take on meaning and, thus, enter into relationship with *'adam.* The one who names embues that which is named with meaning and enters into the relationship according to the meaning given in the naming.

Traditionally, *'adam* has been understood to be male (God later makes a female out of *'adam*'s rib). Although it is probably more accurate to understand that *'adam* signifies undifferentiated humanity and it is only through the splitting of *'adam,* which resulted in two human beings, that sexuality and gender were created, it is important at this juncture to recognize the attributed understanding of *'adam* as Adam. Thus, in the Judeo-Christian traditions, the right to name is traced back to Adam. Male privilege has been understood to include the right to name and give meaning to the significant dimensions of culture. Women have not had the opportunity, nor the authority, to participate in that naming process despite the centrality of naming for joining that which is named in relationship. However, as naming is the privilege granted by God to *'adam* = "humanity," it is important that women now accept the vocation of that process and learn to claim voice and language for that purpose. Women's naming of self, context, and creation is needed for the sake of the full participation of humanity in the ongoing co-creative process with God. Helping women, and all those who have been denied the right to voice and language, to name reality in their "mother tongue" is an important dimension to the personal and cultural transformation that is the purpose of feminist pastoral counseling.

As women take on the vocation of naming themselves, one another, their contexts, and God, they are creating revolutionary change. Those things that have been assumed to be true—where the "partial has paraded as the whole"[19]—are called into question. New perspectives and realities emerge that change the world. Mary Daly says that this is the primary theological task when she writes:

> There is a dynamism in the ontological affirmation of self that reaches out toward the nameless God. In hearing and naming ourselves out of the depths, women are naming toward God, which is what theology always should have been about. Unfortunately it tended to stop at fixing names upon God, which deafened us to our own potential for self-naming.[20]

Although pastoral counseling has always been about naming and storytelling, it has not understood that naming to involve a deconstructing of patriarchal, internalized, and constantly reinforced language for the sake of transformation. In this transforming process, not only is an individual empowered toward self-, other-, and God-knowledge, but a new language is created and passed on for ongoing transformation of the creation.

When Linda came to my office for counseling, she had lost a sense of herself. She was panicked and hopeless about her life. She framed her problem as having a need to get back to a good Christian attitude about marriage so that she would stop driving her husband away. She believed in the irrevocable nature of the marriage contract and yet felt as if she were being closed off and made numb in her family. She consistently spoke of herself as lacking something and of her behavior as inadequate. Linda had lost touch with her own "mother-tongue." She had internalized the language of patriarchy to understand her own "deficiencies." In order to work toward regaining language and voice, Linda joined a women's support group facilitated by a feminist pastoral counselor and she continued in pastoral counseling with me.

As Linda heard the other women around her fumbling to speak their true narratives, she began to develop hope that she, too, had a right to name her own experience as real. Very slowly and tentatively Linda shared similarities with the women in the group until she was able to tell some of her own story. She had never believed that her experience was important before. In the counseling relationship, she described a history of sexual abuse by her alcoholic father along with a deep belief that she was somehow causing her own pain. She and her four sisters were isolated from each other. Each of them had gone through painful divorces. Linda had felt very judgmental of their failures until she began to see what they probably had shared in common. Finally, she was able to articulate her pain in her husband's preoccupation with pornography and his insistence on her cooperation with his sexual choices. She was able to give voice to her pain and horror and helplessness at this pattern in her marriage. Through both the group experience and the individual counseling, Linda was able to confront her husband on his behavior and let him know that she would not be willing to participate in it with him. As he recognized her growing strength and her beginning development of boundaries, he became worried about losing the marriage relationship on which he very much relied. They entered counseling together to work on a more fulfilling marriage and to gain a deeper and more just understanding of what a "Christian" commitment meant. This helped Peter to articulate his Japanese understanding of sexuality and of relationships between men and women and how his sense of being a disenfranchised stranger in the United States (even after ten years of being there) caused him to cling even harder to power structures that were familiar to him. They began to gain the ability to question automatic assumptions each had about the other and the other's values, needs, and rights. Their mutual gaining of language and the ability to engage in cultural analysis greatly enhanced their ongoing ability to communicate and negotiate their future together. They passed on some of these skills to their son whose behavior at home and school began to improve radically.

### Gaining Clarity

In the story of Linda and Peter described above there was a sense that once voice and language began to be available, new clarity also was possible. These two processes do go together, but they are not a natural continuation. In fact, one of the things that is most helpful to know about a feminist perspective on pastoral counseling is that most of it is "counterintuitive." I use the term intuitive here cautiously because what is often called intuitive has been deeply distorted by internalized patriarchal biases and externalized reinforcement for following through with those biases. When counselors rely primarily on experience and intuition in pastoral counseling, they are very likely to collude with toxic value systems and exclusionary assumptions. When they gauge other people primarily by their own experiences, they find that they are able to work effectively and healthily only with people who are enough like themselves not to challenge their deeply held truths about life. Pastoral counseling that is hopeful of participating in personal, familial, and cultural transformation needs to be willing to question anything that seems to be a "truth" of the dominant culture.

Gaining clarity in the counseling process requires considerably more than telling/hearing the story. It requires seeing the story through a variety of important lenses and routinely asking the epistemological question, How do we know what we know? It means that, although gender is a crucial category around which life experience is organized and interpreted, it does not always have to be the starting place in a feminist approach to pastoral counseling. Sometimes the appropriate starting place is with race or class or sexual orientation as the dominant category of oppressive experience. The counselor must be well informed about the power dynamics within this culture around gender, race, class, age, sexual orientation, and able-bodiedness. This requires more than extrapolation from personal experience. Although various systems of dominance and subordinance in this culture have a great deal in common, they cannot be exchanged for one another in terms of assumptions about the ways they impact people's lives. Pastoral counselors who practice out of a feminist, multicultural, multiple-analysis context need to research multicultural perspectives, seek out colleagues and consultants with different racial, class, and sexual orientation experience than her or his own, and explore her or his own internalized and external contexts of privilege and disenfranchisement. They need to explore how they respond to their own experiences of privilege in the culture, knowing that they are probably in categories that make them both oppressed and oppressor in the variety of situations in which they live.

As Julia Boyd writes:

> In doing therapy with women of color, feminist therapists must recognize that they will again become students. . . . Making the assumption that prior mental health training or feminist politics will transcend the necessity to comprehend the ethnic and cultural lines of survival for women of color will place both the client and effective treatment in serious jeopardy.[21]

These issues are especially important for the egalitarian relationship required of a feminist perspective. In an egalitarian relationship, power differences are acknowledged and minimized to the extent possible for the counseling relationship to function. If power is shared to the degree possible, then it is important to be able to analyze and acknowledge the kinds of power and privilege that exist in that relationship. People who have experienced themselves as relatively powerless in many settings (and this may include many clergy in general) are often unable or unwilling to see the arenas in which they are granted power and the nature of the power they exercise. For many women, at least, power has such a negative connotation that they are unwilling to claim it. Consequently, the very real power that does exist is used in an indirect manner that makes accountability for it difficult.

In order to help explore narratives from the variety of cultural lenses that are necessary, the pastoral counselor needs to take responsibility for knowing the kinds of consequences that exist for those who are not part of the dominant power system. Pastoral counselors need to know, for example, the following:

> Approximately one out of two women are beaten in their intimate relationships.
>
> The suicide rate for gay and lesbian youth is at epidemic proportions.
>
> The average black woman college graduate in a full-time position receives less than 90 percent of her white counterpart's salary, which is equal to the earnings of a white male high-school dropout.
>
> Hispanic women who work full-time earn about 82 percent of what comparably employed white women earn.
>
> One third of all women homicide victims are killed by their husbands.
>
> The group of women most at risk for depression is married women who do not work outside the home and have three or more children under the age of twelve.[22]

Pastoral counselors are responsible to know these and other such realities in order to bring those kinds of lenses and resources to the stories that are told. This information does not make them experts on the counselee's life. She or he is the expert on that experience, and her or his narrative is the primary source of information for the counseling. But the lenses of power analysis are a primary part of the resources that the pastoral counselor brings to share with the counselee as appropriate for the sake of clarification.

This means that part of the pastoral counselor's task is to be able to look at and question the truthfulness of any and all assumptions that dominant systems of understanding have put out as truths. Much of that work is being done in the deconstructive projects of feminist, womanist, and other liberationist approaches to psychology, theology, and counseling practice. Pastoral counselors need to join that work by learning about the lies that have been taught to people about who they are and who they can be. These lies have been internalized and exist behind many of the problems that individuals and families bring to pastoral counseling.

Mary Daly offers some insight into that process in the radical theology/philosophy of *Gyn/Ecology*, where she talks about the primary rule of patriarchy as being that of deception. She suggests that in order for us to gain clarity, it is necessary for us to re-reverse the great

Reversals of patriarchy. Her assumption is that if most of the values that patriarchy holds dear and assumes as truths were reversed, those reversals would represent much greater truth for women's lives.[23] Mary Daly, in her thorough analysis of a sexist culture, also demonstrates the rather amazing power of language and the need for women (and for all whose language has been either eliminated or co-opted) to create language that more accurately and powerfully describes their authentic experience.

This is not unlike the process of the parables. This form of discourse, which appears to be authentic to Jesus in the scriptures, can be an important methodological resource as pastoral counselors attempt to help people and systems gain clarity about their lives and relationships. There are several dimensions to the parables that might be useful to consider for the work of clarification in feminist-based pastoral counseling.

First, many of the parables deal with the ordinary. There is a general respecting of the ordinary events in the lives of ordinary people of the time. These parables are often stories about marginalized folks going about their daily business. And yet, in the middle of those daily events, radical insight breaks in and nothing remains the same. God's spirit and wisdom are present in what might otherwise seem like a routine moment, and the characters in the parable are transformed—as is the culture that hears about this transformation. There are two points for us here. The parables are about people having their ordinary lives respected and valued as a way to experience God. Nicola Slee, when talking about the parables that are oriented toward the domestic life of women, says:

> The parables suggest that within the context of the domestic the unexpected, the wholly gratuitous and unlooked for, erupts—but in so doing, the very world of the everyday is irretrievably shattered, irreversibly transformed. This provides no easy solution to the conflicts women experience between the domestic and the professional, home and work, family and society, and others, but it does hint that to discover the presence of God within the confines of the mundane and domestic is radically and explosively to transform these realities—and this may be as uncomfortable as it is unexpected.[24]

Another aspect of this point is that the transformation experienced in the private, everyday sphere has radical implications for the listeners and for their world. Transformation is never merely a personal experience.

A second, important dimension to the parables that may be guiding for the pastoral counselor is the reframing or reversal (to use Daly's concept) that happens in the parables. The assumption of many of the parables is that the realities accepted by the dominant culture obscure truth. People have learned to believe lies and, thus, to put their own lives in danger or distress. This is also true for most of the people who come for pastoral counseling; they have lost themselves in attempting to live according to false definitions of who they are and what their world is really like. Thus the only way for the truth to be revealed is by turning everything upside down and, in the chaos of that, allowing new perspectives on truth to emerge. Counseling is a risky proposition. People come to counseling because their lives are not manageable any longer in the direction in which they are going. But many people come to the counselor without the ability to imagine life in another way. They often come asking to be helped to return to "normal," even though "normal" was the precursor to their experience of extreme distress. I worked with one very depressed and suicidal thirty-eight-year-old woman who wanted to be helped to get back to normal. When I explored with her what she was like before she was depressed, she was unable to locate any time in her adult life when she was not depressed. Is it ethical, much less feminist, for me to help her return to a state of functional depression? Counseling is risky because lives and relationships and contexts change because of it. Coming to and believing in a new kind of clarity may be very frightening.

A third dimension of the parables that serves as resource to pastoral counselors is one pointed out by Don Capps in his book *Reframing*.[25] Capps suggests that it is the storyteller—or, in this analogy, the pastoral counselor—who provides the story's frame. In other words, the content of the story belongs to the people who experience it, but the frame through which that story is seen is provided by Jesus in the parables and by the pastoral counselor in the counseling process. For example, in the counseling situation named above, Mary had spent several sessions describing a very oppressive household where she was not valued in any way except as the caregiver and housekeeper. She had managed to function for many years in this household, but finally her depression stopped her from being able to do even a load of wash or vacuum a floor. This threw her family into chaos and made them all angry with her, especially her husband. Mary was terribly upset by her inability to do her "job." I asked her what it would take to get her family to notice that she existed and had value? In light of that frame, we were able to see that she had chosen a rather powerful, and maybe the only, way to get them to pay attention. She had gone on strike in such a manner as to keep them from taking strong action against her. However, this choice was doing her harm. Once the frame had shifted from powerlessness to choice, Mary began to see new options for her to get her needs met. The change of frame shifted the truths about her life.[26]

It is important to note that the process of clarification moves alongside the process of gaining voice. It is not a distant, objective analytical experience to identify the counselee's problems so they can be solved. It is a coming to a new awareness—a transforming awareness—for the sake of empowering the self and enriching/reversing a culture that has been and continues to be toxic to many people.

Margaret, an African-American woman, is an example of a woman who was struggling for clarity when she came to pastoral counseling. Married to a police officer, Margaret had over one hundred unpaid parking tickets. She had attempted suicide three times and was considering another attempt. She worked for a collection agent in an unpleasant work environment, and she was in so much debt that most of her salary was garnished to pay her bills before she even saw it. She lived in an all-white neighborhood, and her children went to white schools where they felt uneasy and isolated. Her twelve-year-old daughter, especially, was engaging in risky behavior in order to find a way to belong. Margaret was worried, depressed, hopeless, and she saw herself as a failure.

What does it mean for Margaret to get clarity about her situation? Obviously, one of the most important dimensions of this pastoral counseling situation was to help Margaret find her own voice and language. Surrounded by an alien and hostile environment (both her all-white neighborhood and her angry, sometimes violent husband), Margaret framed her needs and possibilities in terms of the lives and language of others. As we worked to clarify the layers of her life situation, it became helpful to frame her depression as resistance to living in a toxic environment. The parking tickets and unpaid bills took very little reframing in order to see them as attempts to express what little power she experienced herself as having. When we began to understand her symptoms of depression and suicide through the lenses of racism, classism, and sexism, Margaret's options began to expand. She began to attend a Black church in another neighborhood and intentionally to develop a supportive group of friends there. She also got her children involved in the youth choirs, where they had the experience of being with other kids who shared some dimensions of their experience that the children in their schools did not. Margaret began to see her current experiences in light of her history of abuse (incest and racial threats) and to understand the nature of her healthy resistance to systems of oppression. Her need then became to find ways to resist that did not do harm to her. She created a budget that got the police department and the bill collectors to stop harassing her. Her husband (with the embarrassment of the parking tickets gone) was willing to join Margaret in counseling. He became aware of how he did not experience the same kind of isolation that Margaret did because he worked with a diverse group of colleagues. He also was able to talk about his childhood images of success, which included living in a white, middle-class neighborhood. Together they were able to find ways to build community and to strengthen their relationship. Margaret changed jobs and began working at a neighborhood after-school program where her six-year-old son could both spend more time with her and be exposed to a diverse group of playmates. Margaret's supportive friendships continued to flourish and expand. She also joined an incest survivor's group, which helped her continue to gain language and voice about her history of abuse and the way it impacted her life.

Gaining clarity around the complex interrelationships of power and powerlessness in one's life is an important dimension of the pastoral counseling process. Looking for resources, including resources masked as symptoms (for example, resistance, survival skills, and so on) is also an important dimension of the work. Whereas pastoral counseling has tended to look for "pathology" in the individual, a feminist-oriented approach looks for strengths, possibilities, and potential transformations at all levels.

## Making Choices

The above counseling situation certainly demonstrates the importance of making choices in pastoral counseling. One of the key features of pastoral counseling, especially in the parish context, is that it is time limited. The purpose of engaging in a process of pastoral counseling is to address specific life problems with the goal of setting in motion the process of their resolution. A feminist-based pastoral counselor seeks to empower the telling of the story in which the problem is rooted, to assist in the process of clarifying the issues by seeing them through a variety of cultural lenses and employing appropriate frames to better illuminate the real problems, and to empower the counselee to make choices that work to resist and transform the oppressive forces in her or his life and world.

People who come for pastoral counseling are usually experiencing considerable distress in their lives and are eager for help in relieving that distress. Usually they have tried all of the logical or reasonable solutions that any counselor could suggest. As brief-therapy theory has demonstrated, it is not only that people have generally attempted all of the reasonable solutions to their problems, but it is often the repeated efforts to solve the problem (the solutions themselves) that have become the problem motivating the counseling. For example, with Rebecca and Hyun Son's experience, Rebecca had become worried over time that she was achieving too much success compared to her husband's lack of success (as she and the Western culture defined it). Rebecca, in her anxiety and self-denigration, began to urge Hyun Son to change jobs and work harder. In response, he began to feel inadequate as perceived in her eyes, and he began to cling more to his Korean friends and his store in the Korean neighborhood for comfort. Rebecca became more anxious and began to try new ways to encourage him to succeed: leaving graduate-school catalogues around, cutting out want ads from the newspaper, making potential contacts and introducing him to them, and so on. This made Hyun Son more insecure, and he distanced even further—sometimes not even coming home. Rebecca felt that she was no longer attractive to her husband because of her greater success and that she was a failure as a wife. As a result she worked longer hours in order to stay out of the home, and Hyun Son felt that his wife no longer needed him or found him attractive in any way.

The original situation for this couple was nowhere near as big of a problem as the "solution" became. Because people who come for counseling have tried most or all of the reasonable solutions to their problems, prescribing or advising more reasonable solutions is a poor approach to the counseling. It is ineffective, and it reinforces the dynamics that created the problem in the first place. The feminist-grounded pastoral counselor is not about the process of advice giving but rather is oriented to helping the counselee see the root of the situation that is causing pain and opening up the avenues to understanding it so that the problem reframed becomes the generative source for the solution. In other words, it is important in the pastoral counseling process that the symptoms of the problem are understood to be potential resources and even strengths in the person or relationship rather than "pathology."

The phase of making choices, thus, needs to come after coming to voice and gaining clarity for two reasons. First, in coming to voice and finding language, the counselee is able not only to name the story accurately at its roots but also to feel entitled to having this story with all of its implications. This sense of entitlement is usually a key component to the counseling process. Second, in gaining clarity the counselee has learned how to frame the issues through a variety of helpful and even revolutionary lenses that orient the original problem in a new direction. These two approaches do not necessarily eliminate the pain or even make the tensions easier to live with. Sometimes a feminist-based pastoral counseling with all of its multivalent perspectives may create more chaos temporarily.

However, the process does give a sense of both hope and possibility to the counselee.

The dimension of making choices comes in this context of new language, new frames, and new sense of hope. Choices can be made out of a real ownership of the person's or relationship's whole narrative. New and transformative choices where there can be real accountability are possible only when liberation has already begun. An illustration of this, which I have found helpful, is in the chronology of the Exodus, where the people, who had been under oppression for a long time, needed to gain language and voice about their experience. In this they called to God for deliverance and, through the leadership of Moses, Aaron, and Miriam, came out of their slavery into the wilderness. Over the forty years of wandering in the wilderness, the people began to clarify and understand what it meant to live free of slavery. Once they had experienced this community of empowerment, never perfectly of course, they were called by God to a new kind of accountability—illustrated in the Ten Commandments. Choice and accountability came when oppression (internal and external) was being dismantled, and the dismantling of oppression was furthered by the choices made.

Choice is an important part of the counseling. Sometimes choices emerge as a natural consequence of clarification. However, in many cases, especially when the counseling has not been understood to be time limited, the counselor and counselee do not move to making choices but rather get stuck in the clarification phase. There is always more to know and to be clear about, so it is easy to be seduced by ongoing clarification. However, moving to choice acknowledges that the counseling has a purpose. The purpose is to address the questions, now relevantly framed and voiced, that brought the person into the counseling in the first place. One of the most important questions to keep in the foreground during counseling is that of how the counselee and the counselor will know when they are finished. Having this question before them serves three purposes. First, it clarifies the nature of the counseling. Counseling is to address issues and problems that are causing distress. In this, the evaluative question of knowing when the counseling is finished helps put boundaries around the counseling "contract," which is especially important when counseling is done in the parish context. Because parish ministry involves multiple roles, including the ongoing role of pastoral care, it is important that the beginning and end of this unique and time-limited relationship are clear. A second benefit is that this question helps to generate images of what it would be like to complete the counseling "successfully"—what it would look like to resolve the distress. Having an image like this begins to break what is often a stranglehold of despair and helps to generate an attitude of hope. Hope can facilitate a move toward empowerment. If one can imagine new possibilities, one can begin to move toward them. The third benefit is that it puts the evaluative task mostly in the hands of the counselee. It is the counselee who is mainly responsible for setting the goals of the counseling when she or he attempts to answer this question of the ending point.

Choices, of course, can take on endless shapes and directions. Consequently, it is helpful to have some sort of criteria by which to judge the helpfulness of choices made in the counseling process. The criteria that go into assessing the helpfulness of choices made might vary considerably based on the pastoral counselor's theology, on her or his vision of a just world, on his or her priorities for health, and on the particular contexts of the counselees. For the purposes of this chapter, I would suggest the following eight evaluative questions as useful criteria for assessing the helpfulness of choices made during the counseling.

> Does this choice address the real issues involved as revealed in the coming to voice and gaining clarity dimensions of the counseling?
>
> Does this choice empower the counselee in a nondestructive way?
>
> Does this choice reverse damaging patriarchal values?
>
> Does this choice enhance healthy relationships?
>
> Does this choice further the liberation of self, family, and/or society from oppressive and damaging forces without doing harm?
>
> Does this choice fit with the counselee's (and counselor's) understanding of God's ongoing lures for love and justice?
>
> Is there adequate support for the ongoing implications of this choice?
>
> Is there a method and a plan for evaluating the consequences of this choice/these choices at some point?

These criteria may not all be able to be answered positively, but when any are answered negatively, those negative consequences need to be carefully considered. The purpose of these criteria is for the counselor and the counselee to keep in mind what work they are really about.

When talking about making choices in pastoral counseling, the prophetic traditions of the scriptures may be helpful as resources. The foundational goal in pastoral counseling (for counselor and counselee) is the identification, resistance, and transformation of the ravages of patriarchal oppressions from sexism, racism, classism, heterosexism, ageism, and ableism intrapsychically, interpersonally, and institutionally. There is an obvious prophetic dimension to that process. Rosemary Radford Ruether suggests that the prophetic traditions can be helpful to a feminist analysis if they are first used internally to critique their own use in the scriptures. Without critique, the prophetic literature of the Bible can be used to support the patriarchal norms of which they were a part. As Ruether says, "Feminist theology that draws on Biblical principles is possible only if the prophetic principles, more fully understood, imply a rejection of every elevation of one social group against others as image and agent of God, every use of God to justify social domination and subjugation."[27] But used critically and thematically, they can be helpful and guiding for an analysis of today's patriarchal world.

Ruether suggests that there are four themes that are central to the liberating prophetic traditions. They are (1) God's defense and vindication of the oppressed; (2) a critique of the dominant systems of power; (3) the vision of a new age to come; and (4) a critique of the ideology that sustains the unjust order.[28] How counselors carry through these prophetic principles changes depending on the context, but the themes of this prophetic tradition rightly belong at the center of a feminist-based pastoral counseling theory.

One of the ways that this prophetic tradition is used is by the careful listening to those who have not been heard. These are the voices that are privileged in a feminist counseling process. This especially includes the voice of the one who has come to counseling, but it also includes an intentional focus on other left-out voices. As David Tracy says, "The prophetic voices of our present may be found best, as they were for the ancient prophets and for Jesus of Nazareth, in those peoples, those individuals, and those new centers most privileged to God and still the least heard in the contemporary Western conflict of interpretation on naming the present: the suffering and the oppressed."[29] As Tracy points out, it is these voices that must be brought into dialogue, with each other and with the dominant culture. It is these voices that need to regain their "mother tongue" and their entitlement to speak it. It is these voices who must be helped to gain clarity about the forces that work systematically against them in this culture. It is these voices, who sometimes come to their pastor in isolated, self-blaming despair, that need to be empowered to speak so that personal and cultural transformation may occur. And it is these voices that need to inform the theories and theologies of pastoral counseling.

This is an important reminder that, in helping counselees to come to voice, gain clarity, and make choices, pastoral counselors are not to operate as if one marginalized voice is either representative of a whole group or of all marginalized groups. They need to be very clear that the one voice of the counselee is expert on the narrative she or he is learning to speak *and* that the counselee's narrative needs to be set in the context of the diverse voices that have not been heard in building normative theories and theologies of pastoral counseling.

In helping counselees to make choices in pastoral counseling, counselors need to pay attention to these prophetic issues if the counseling is to be truly transformative to both people and cultures in distress. It is important to acknowledge in both the theories and the practices that making choices of this nature is not an easy process. Making choices against a system, even a destructive one, that has been deeply internalized as truth and that is persistently presented in culture as part of the natural order, is a frightening thing. These choices cannot be made without a great deal of personal and relational deconstructive work. "Corrective action" requires the undoing and challenging of "harmful adaptation."[30] When one begins to claim one's own voice and starts to break the "rules," punishment (either intrapsychic or in the immediate world of the counselee) is to be expected. As Ballou and Gabalac suggest, the counselee has become a healthy person in an unhealthy world, trying to make choices for ongoing health in both self and world. This is not an easy task.

Nathan found himself feeling insecure and worried in his relationship with his wife, Kay. Kay was an assertive, self-aware, and self-reliant woman, and Nathan had appreciated the mutuality of their relationship. After about a year of marriage, however, he began to worry that Kay would leave him; he was not sure what he had to offer her. He was also aware of, and somewhat committed to, issues that had arisen in the women's movement. He alternated between a vague guilt at his connection to the "race of male oppressors" and rage because of his own authentic feelings of helplessness and powerlessness.

As Nathan worked in the counseling to address his ambivalent feelings of worth and purpose, he was able to get in touch with the nature of his own models for maleness. He had learned that to be male was to be strong, stoic, a provider, a protector, and financially successful in a traditional male profession. Nathan was a graduate student in theology and preferred intimate conversations, nurturing his children, and spending time in contemplation and writing. Although Nathan was quite sure about his preferences, he did experience anxiety that seemed to reflect the anxiety about going against his male script so thoroughly.

In a combination of individual counseling, marital counseling, an increased network of friends, and some reading in gender studies, Nathan gained a greater comfort and confidence in his choices and in his primary relationships. As his counseling was ending, he made three intentional choices. The first was to reconnect with his father in order for them to try to know each other as persons instead of as stereotypes of what they each did not want to be. The second was to negotiate with his spouse, who loved the high pressure, intense job she was in, that he would take on more of the home and child care. The third choice was to write his doctoral dissertation (although discouraged by his advisers) on a creative and nontraditional topic that was deeply informed by feminist thought and that made a significant contribution to the field of gender studies. He built an adequate support network to help him through the institutional resistances to this work. These choices both came out of and contributed to his own healthy liberation and empowerment and his commitment to health in and for an unhealthy world.

## Staying Healthy

Staying healthy in an unhealthy and damaging world is a difficult challenge. It requires a persistent analytical lens of suspicion that is tiring and risky. It puts one at risk for punishment by the dominant system's representatives and by those who are just trying to get by on what little borrowed power they can get. It puts one at risk for feeling crazy and isolated or as being seen as a "one-issue person," or an angry man- (or fill in the appropriate object) hater. It puts one at risk for feeling hopeless in light of the persistent toxicity of the dominant culture. Staying healthy requires an active and intentional strategy that might well include some of the following options.

1. There is a need to continue assessing choices that have been made in counseling against criteria that one has decided measures personal and systemic health. This allows one not to get complacent, but to make changes as contexts and needs change. Choices are always just starting places and need to avoid reification.

2. One of the most important resources that people from nondominant groups can use for their envisioning and empowerment is personal and communal imagination. Because there are few patterns in the culture that identify healthy and energetic directions for nondominant group members, sometimes pastoral counselors have to find new directions from within their own

creative processes. Michael Cordner has suggested that the imagination is "the playground on which we meet God."[31] If pastoral counselors allow themselves to enter their imaginations and let new possibilities emerge from their own depths, then they are often able to bring together their knowledge, their personal narratives, their value systems, and a creative spiritual energy that can create remarkable possibilities. And in sharing these imaginative visions within safe and interested groups, they are able to test out those possibilities and find ways to live into them. Imagination is a powerful tool for transformation.[32]

3. Another important resource for staying healthy is to develop intentional and disciplined self-care. Without self-care, all people lose their ability to be in honest relationships with others. Too often, when pastors experience deprivation, they use other relationships, directly or indirectly, to meet needs they do not want to acknowledge. They also lose their capacity to be creative, to care deeply for others, and to be spiritually centered. As Laura Brown puts it, when talking to feminist therapists, "For women to give themselves focused attention, nurturance, good food, space, and time are all profoundly revolutionary actions."[33] Helping people to stay healthy means encouraging them to see themselves through their own needs rather than through the needs and definitions of others. Claiming one's "self" against the norms of the power system mandates good self-care. This is the only way to be able to care for the well-being of all creation.

4. Staying healthy also requires the development of a network of supportive people who can reality-test ideas and perceptions without judging them by the norms of the dominant culture. This is a network of mutuality where people who are engaged in a common struggle for personal and communal transformation and liberation can encourage, support, and challenge one another appropriately. The seductive and coercive strategies of the dominant culture are too strong for any one person to resist. George Orwell once wrote that insanity was a minority of one. Solidarity and support are the sine qua non of staying healthy from a countercultural perspective.

5. Another resource for health is a support network intentionally made up of people from diverse backgrounds and perspectives. It is necessary to intentionally seek out this kind of broad-based community, for cultural separatism is a norm for Western culture and is often even a norm for homogenous liberation-seeking groups (like white feminists). As David Tracy has indicated, voices from these groups must be in dialogue with each

other if the world is going to be adequately transformed.[34] Without this kind of commitment to communities of diversity, even liberation-based groups are in grave danger of repeating the exclusivist patterns of currently dominant groups, and there is no health for anyone in that.

6. Another resource for health, one named by Ballou and Gabalac in their health maintenance paradigm, is the intentional researching of one's particular gender, ethnic, and racial roots and the stories that may have been lost or, at least, not heard.[35] Claiming one's legacies of strength, of suffering, and of vision is a part of claiming one's place in the culture. It also helps generate resources and possibilities for current life situations.

7. Reaching out with one's new sense of voice and clarity to other people and groups in the culture can provide valuable resources for others while at the same time helping to keep the one reaching out healthy. This may take the shape of mentoring others (see Chapter 7). It may involve caring for others in need out of commitment to mutuality and shared humanity. It may mean taking political action in one's community to further the process of justice. It could involve helping others to see through the cultural lies and the need for reversals. Whatever shape it takes, it facilitates health to maintain an ongoing consciousness about the realities of an oppressive culture and the needs that arise as a consequence of that oppression. It is often easier to see those consequences in the lives of others than in one's own life.

When Terry came in for pastoral counseling, she was experiencing considerable isolation in her life. She was not in a context where she could be "out" very easily, and she had learned to keep her thoughts and feelings to herself. Over time in counseling, she learned to claim her own story and the worth of that story. Through individual counseling, a structured support group, and a training group in her profession, she also learned that other people were interested in her and her thoughts and feelings and ideas. She gained confidence and strength as she broke through the walls that had kept her from herself and from meaningful relationships. She made choices to come out where it was safe to do so and to develop a support network of lesbians who helped her to test her perceptions and her possibilities. She changed jobs to a less toxic environment, and she rebuilt some of her early relationships, such as one with her sister. She also began to work on projects in her profession in behalf of women, which specifically included lesbians. For example, she became part of a task force to support civil rights for all people who were at risk of being denied those.

Her efforts to stay healthy included these various ongoing support and outreach networks. In addition, she joined a woman's center that was committed to diversity and that intentionally recruited a diverse membership. She entered into a time-limited training process to help her learn to use her imagination to stay in touch with her feelings, with new possibilities, and with God. She worked to develop new and richly meaningful images for God—a God whom she could meet in the playground of the imagination and who could inspire her with empowerment and with hope. It is this hope that continues to keep Terry healthy and pulls her into a future that can be transformed. It is this hope—the belief in a promise larger than the lies of patriarchy and larger than the possibilities of any individual or any institution—that pulls all of us into a future that can and must be transformed. It is this hope, the hope that is a gift from God to the community of believers, that will empower all who receive it to participate in bringing in the just and liberative kin-dom of God.

## NOTES

1. John Patton, "Pastoral Counseling," in *Dictionary of Pastoral Care and Counseling,* ed. Rod Hunter (Nashville: Abingdon Press, 1990), 850.
2. There are many works in feminist psychology and psychotherapy that discuss the closed nature of traditional psychotherapeutic systems. For example, see Miriam Greenspan, *A New Approach to Women and Therapy* (New York: McGraw-Hill, 1983); Mary Ballou and Nancy Gabalac, *A Feminist Position on Mental Health* (Springfield, Ill.: Charles C. Thomas, 1985); Laura S. Brown and Mary Ballou, *Personality and Psychopathology: Feminist Reappraisals* (New York: Guilford, 1992); and Laura S. Brown, *Subversive Dialogues: Theory in Feminist Therapy* (New York: Basic Books, 1994).
3. See, for example, Howard Stone, *Brief Pastoral Counseling* (Minneapolis: Fortress Press, 1994); Charles Taylor, *The Skilled Pastor* (Minneapolis: Fortress Press, 1992); and the vast amount of secular literature in Brief Therapy, such as Jeffrey Zeig and Stephen Gilligan, eds., *Brief Therapy: Myths, Methods, and Metaphors* (New York: Brunner/Mazel, 1990).
4. Feminist pastoral counseling always has an element of education in it. This is necessary for the purpose of learning to make visible the often invisible lies of the culture. This education can happen in a variety of settings and is often more effective outside of the counseling office. In addition, no one counselor can adequately validate a person's story against the tidal wave of denial that comes from the power systems in the counselee's context. Thus, a group where women validate one another and a group reality begins to emerge is much more effective for

some of the counseling work than a traditional one-to-one relationship.

5. Gerda Lerner, *The Creation of Patriarchy* (Oxford: Oxford University Press, 1986), 239.

6. Rebecca S. Chopp, *Saving Work: Feminist Practices of Theological Education* (Louisville, Ky.: Westminster John Knox Press, 1995), 56.

7. The foundational motto for this wave of the feminist movement has been "The Personal is Political." This essential concept means that all of women's experience must be understood in terms of its political formation and that what happens in the culture ultimately affects the well-being of all women.

8. Brown, *Subversive Dialogues*, 23.

9. Dale Spender, *Man Made Language*, 2d ed. (London: Routledge & Kegan Paul, 1980), xiii.

10. Jean Baker Miller, *Toward a New Psychology of Women*, 2d ed. (Boston: Beacon Press, 1986), 47.

11. There is considerable literature on this topic in both culture and church. For example: Casey Miller and Kate Swift, *Words and Women*, updated version (New York: HarperCollins, 1991); Spender, *Man Made Language;* Mary Vetterling-Braggin, *Sexist Language* (Philadelphia: Littlefield, Adams, and Co., 1981); Keith Watkins, *Faithful and Fair* (Nashville: Abingdon Press, 1981); Brian Wren, *What Language Shall I Borrow? God Talk in Worship: A Male Response to Feminist Theology* (New York: Crossroad, 1989).

12. Nelle Morton, *The Journey Is Home* (Boston: Beacon Press, 1985), 127. This phrase has been important to many inside and outside the church. The sense of collaboration—of giving birth to one another's ability to speak truth—is at the essence of empowerment.

13. Greenspan, *A New Approach to Women and Therapy*, 233.

14. Lyn Mikel Brown and Carol Gilligan, *Meeting at the Crossroads: Women's Psychology and Girls' Development* (Cambridge: Harvard University Press, 1992), 216.

15. Ballou and Gabalac, *A Feminist Position on Mental Health*, chap. 4.

16. Miller, *Toward a New Psychology of Women*, 11.

17. Brown, *Subversive Dialogues*, 155.

18. The Mud Flower Collective, *God's Fierce Whimsy* (New York: Pilgrim Press, 1985), 134.

19. This is a well-known quote by Nelle Morton, *The Journey Is Home*, 52.

20. Mary Daly, "Why Speak About God?" in *WomanSpirit Rising: A Feminist Reader in Religion*, ed. Carol Christ and Judith Plaskow (San Francisco: Harper & Row, 1979), 212.

21. Julia A. Boyd, "Ethnic and Cultural Diversity: Keys to Power," in *Diversity and Complexity in Feminist Therapy*, eds. Laura S. Brown and Maria P. P. Root (New York: Harrington Park Press, 1990), 164–65.

22. See Christie Cozad Neuger, "Feminist Pastoral Counseling and Pastoral Theology: A Work in Progress," *Journal of Pastoral Theology* 2 (Summer 1992): 39–43.

23. Mary Daly, *Gyn/Ecology: The Metaethics of Radical Feminism* (Boston: Beacon Press, 1978).

24. Nicola Slee, "Parables and Women's Experience," in *Feminist Theology: A Reader*, ed. Ann Loades (Louisville, Ky.: Westminster/John Knox Press, 1990), 42.

25. Donald Capps, Reframing: *A New Method in Pastoral Care* (Minneapolis: Augsburg Fortress Press, 1990).

26. For more about this counseling situation, see Neuger, "Feminist Pastoral Counseling and Pastoral Theology.

27. Rosemary Radford Ruether, *Sexism and God Talk* (Boston: Beacon Press, 1983), 23.

28. Ibid., 24.

29. David Tracy, *On Naming the Present* (Maryknoll, N.Y.: Orbis Books, 1994), 21–22.

30. Ballou and Gabalac, *A Feminist Position on Mental Health.* These are Ballou and Gabalac's paradigms for the harm done to people in non-dominant power positions and for the therapeutic work of building a healthy self.

31. G. Michael Cordner, "The Spiritual Vision Within," *Journal of Pastoral Care* 35, no. 1 (March 1981): 42.

32. For more information on the use of imagination in pastoral counseling, see Christie Cozad Neuger, "Imagination and Pastoral Counseling," in *Handbook to Basic Types of Pastoral Care and Counseling* (Nashville: Abingdon Press, 1992).

33. Brown, *Subversive Dialogues*, 222.

34. Tracy, *On Naming the Present*, 22.

35. Ballou and Gabalac, *A Feminist Position on Mental Health*, chap. 5.

# 5

## ADMINISTRATION AS AN ART OF SHARED VISION

### Judith Orr

*Asking how I do church administration is kind
of like asking how I clean house. I just do it. I
don't think about how.*
— *46-year-old woman who grew up poor
and has been in ministry 22 years*

In spite of resistance by some women to doing so, the time has
come to talk about how women understand their work in the
church as managers, administrators, and leaders.

It has been said that many pastors find administration to be the
most time-consuming and least satisfying aspect of ministry.[1] And
even those who claim to do a satisfactory job at administration often do not find it satisfying. It is fair to say that much administration and leadership in the church leaves a lot to be desired, perhaps
because the paradigm out of which much current practice is shaped
is no longer viable. But there are also some—and a number of them
are women—who see administration and leadership at the heart of
what they do and have a deep joy about it.

Just exactly what is administration and leadership in the church?
Do women understand it in the same way as do men? What is the
influence of feminist theory on the ministry of leadership and administration? What are the actual practices of women doing church
leadership and administration? Are they the same as for men? Are
they the same as for women in nonchurch organizations? What
would the future of the church be if more administration and leadership were done by women? What if more were done from a feminist perspective?

### Listening to the Voices of Women in Ministry

Growing up in a white working-class family, I have never felt particularly prepared for or competent at administration or leadership.
I have assumed leadership roles on occasion because organizations
that I was a member of needed someone to do so, and in that process
I have, in fact, become better prepared and more competent. I have

assumed those roles believing that these organizations were accountable to the church, to society, and to God for seeking a different world, a world of justice and peace.

This chapter will present the results of listening to the voices of
women with varying levels of experience in ministerial administration and leadership as they begin to respond to the above questions.
It is done with the painful knowledge that it is not acceptable in some
religious groups for women to be in leadership positions at all.[2]

I am making several assumptions. First, the theological perspective of the study comes out of the traditions that emphasize Christ
transforming culture.[3] Change is to be expected and sought. Second,
scripture and tradition are resources for understanding this ministry, but the social sciences are also resources to help understand
and name women's experience. Third, it is assumed that church administration and leadership are shaped in the dialectic of theory and
practice. Fourth, a feminist critical perspective is brought to this
study, including a hermeneutics of suspicion regarding interpretation of patriarchal texts and practices.[4] This perspective also includes an advocacy of justice for women of all races, classes, and
cultures.[5]

Several methodological points need to be made.[6] First, only
women were interviewed for this study, because feminist approaches to administration and leadership in the church must start
with listening to the experiences of women. Distinctions between
administrative or leadership styles of men and women will be a re-
port either of the perceptions of the women interviewed or of sec-
ondary sources, for no men were interviewed.

Second, each woman was allowed to provide her own definition
of the term *feminist* so that they could claim or reject any existing
cultural definition and thereby define themselves.

Third, the sample is not intended to be random, but rather diverse
and suggestive of directions for further study. All the women are in
ministry in one of several mainline Protestant denominations in one
of several midwestern states, with the exception of one who lives in
a western state.[7] Women who claim to be feminist and women who
do not describe themselves in this way are in the sample.

Fourth, the study is focused on a self-report questionnaire of ten
questions regarding women's practices of and perspectives on administration and leadership. Nineteen of thirty-six women responded for a 53 percent response rate.[8]

Fifth, in most cases the women reported that they were helped by
being asked to engage in these questions and by volunteering to
wrestle with answering them. I am grateful that the process was of
benefit to them as well as to me.

The method used here, therefore, reflects a feminist perspective in two ways. First, the stories of women are being reclaimed. Little of the research in church administration and leadership is by or about women. This chapter seeks to change that fact. Second, a feminist, justice-seeking perspective is brought to bear to critique theories of administration and leadership as well as practices embedded in the stories told. For example, a fifty-year-old white woman says that feminists believe in shared leadership, but her style is to take the lead and delegate. This is confirmed when she talks about a vision for the church. It is *her* vision, not a shared vision. The feminist perspective thus elicits the telling of women's stories and provides a critical perspective through which to hear and understand all stories.

## Defining Terms

A review of the literature indicates that the terms *management, administration,* and *leadership* are sometimes distinguished in meaning and sometimes used interchangeably. They always refer, however, to sets of practices in relationship to a group. From the insights of Robert Greenleaf[9] and others, the following definitions are proposed. They are in line with the comment of a forty-four-year-old woman in full-time ministry for seven years who said, "There's not a great deal in the church that's not about working with paper, people, and what's possible." One might say this is management, administration, and leadership captured succinctly.

*Management* is the functional, technical dimension of a group working toward its goals.[10] It includes such activities as long-range planning, goal setting, budget setting and monitoring, and time management. Management serves a conserving and maintenance function for any organization through maintaining a balance of operations. Good managers have a sense of self in harmony with tradition—of doing one's duty and meeting one's responsibility with integrity. Managers solve problems and act so as to limit choices.[11] The word *management* comes from the Latin root *manus*, meaning "hand," and carries the meaning of "handle, direct, control." Its focus is on precise processes.[12]

*Administration* is the enabling and empowering dimension of a group coming to discern its needs, hopes, and goals, and then coming to believe in and care for itself in such a way that it is motivated to care for and serve something beyond itself. In the church, according to Campbell and Reierson, it is the centripetal force of building up the body of Christ.[13] Administration is nurturing and motivating the group to move toward ministry, toward service (Latin: *ad* = toward; *ministrare* = serve). Its focus is on empowering people.

*Leadership* is the centering and visionary dimension of a group coming to discern its purpose and working together to live it out.[14] Goals are shaped from ideas, desires, and expectations rather than from necessity. From these the leader helps the group to imagine and vision what it is called to be and to do so that people catch the spirit. Through opening up new options and developing choices, the leader shows the group the way to move toward their shared vision.[15] Leadership represents the centrifugal force of a group, according to Campbell and Reierson, equipping the saints for ministry, thrusting the group beyond itself into the world to its higher/ wider calling than maintaining the status quo. According to the *Oxford English Dictionary,* "to lead" (Old English) means to accompany, to show the way, to guide by going in advance. Its focus is on the passionate pursuit of purpose.

Nine of the women interviewed for this study did not distinguish between management, administration, and leadership, and most understood these three dimensions to be indispensably interrelated to one another.[16] They believe, for example, that one can lead with lasting effects only if people are served and empowered and if careful processes are managed within which they can do their work. Otherwise, leadership is "a lot of hot air." And if people manage the work of committees and attend programs without a sense of purpose inspired by visionary leadership, they eventually "burn out." Amid the fragmentation the body dies, and often the leader leaves.

The nineteen women interviewed understand themselves to be doing management, administration, *and* leadership as they engage in ministry. The administrative dimension was mentioned most frequently in response to the question "When you are doing church management, administration, and leadership, what are you doing?" Fifteen women mentioned the importance of connecting with people and helping them be connected to one another and to a larger purpose or mission. One woman noted the importance of "being friends with everybody," by which she meant to indicate the importance of staying connected to folks and not excluding anyone from the community. Fourteen women noted the importance of enabling or empowering people, including helping them to identify their gifts and discover their own authority, inviting them into ministry, fostering their involvement in the life of the community, training people for different roles in the church, mobilizing leadership resources, coaching people in their work, recognizing their ministry as valid, and appreciating it as valuable.

Three women understood administration as "oversight," by which they meant some form of relational attentiveness ("making sure people don't get lost in the system" or "overseeing programs in a way that shows people we care about them" or "overseeing things so I know where I can be of help and resolve conflicts, so the church can come alive"). Two of these women are judicatory administrators, and one is the organizing pastor of a new church.

It is clear that these women have much clarity of identity around the administrative functions of connecting with and empowering people. The middle-class women tended to connect with people one-to-one to discern their needs and dreams. The women from poor and working-class backgrounds were more likely to talk about being with people to "work together" or "build together" and noted the kind of solid community that happens from doing so.

The second most frequently mentioned set of responses to the question "When you are doing church management, administration, and leadership, what are you doing?" is related to leadership. Eight women affirmed the importance of visioning and accomplishing/achieving the purpose or mission of the church. A forty-five-year-old woman who is new to ministry said:

> It's a flow of paperwork. But it is also visioning. Getting people together and focused. It involves group dynamics, identifying lay leaders, getting their dreaming going, linking them to training resources, and scheduling time together to plan, to work, and to be the church.

Additionally, three women mentioned the importance of modeling to describe their task as leaders. By this they meant modeling "what it means to be the church" or "wearing the vision." In one case it meant being an example by being willing to take the initiative, doing things first, as a way to promote initiative in others toward the vision.

Four women were particularly clear that their leadership is contextual. A twenty-nine-year-old woman in full-time consecrated ministry said:

> My practice is actually different with different groups. I may use shared leadership and share ideas with the Committee on Children's Ministries, but on the [regional] Board of Ministry all the disciplinary requirements and needed accountability require moving into a more hierarchical form of leadership. I'm trying to sort it all out.

A forty-eight-year-old woman in ministry for fifteen years, who recently entered intentional interim ministry, understands leadership to be "how I can use my gifts in this setting to accomplish its mission." The life situation of both women contributed to their keen awareness of the importance of context for the shaping of leadership. The same is often true when women serve multiple churches.

Finally, these women were not oblivious to the importance of management for ministry. They recognized the necessary tasks of planning (7 responses), paperwork (7 responses), solving problems or resolving conflicts (5 responses), organizing (4 responses), and financial management (2 responses). A forty-eight-year-old woman in ministry for four years is in her office doing a number of these tasks each week, but she often does so with her "door open with people in and out. To me those aren't interruptions. They are what I do— catching up with people, connecting with people." Management and administration come together easily for her.

The women were also asked what they liked best or found easiest about management, administration, and leadership, as well as what they disliked or found most difficult about these dimensions of ministry. What these women liked best is leadership. They liked accomplishing the goals of the church and making a difference (8 responses: 5 from women with poor or working-class backgrounds and 3 from middle-class backgrounds). They liked visioning (4 responses). And they also liked leading through preaching and teaching, for these are ways to clarify the church's mission as well as building up the body of Christ. As a fifty-year-old woman in ministry for eight years said, "I have the ability to see the vision or goal, and I have the faith it can be attained. I believe people want to find a place of ministry to be a part of something greater than themselves."

Some women mentioned liking the administrative work with people (7 responses) and seeing people change and grow (3 responses). A forty-five-year-old woman said, "I like the people part of it. I like the one-to-one, but I find the group work especially energizing. For example, the worship breakfasts we have to plan worship services are bread and drink for me!" Here real communion takes place for her through administration.

And others genuinely liked or found easiest the management aspects of ministry—helping to set up goals, tasks, and procedures (4 responses) and organizing ministry with others (3 responses). Again management, administration, and leadership all come together in the comment of a forty-four-year-old woman in ministry for seven years who said, "Pushing paper is easy for me, for I was in the business world. But I really love the creative stuff we do. I settle for low pay, because I get my jollies setting up systems and getting people together to make a difference."

There were also some aspects of management, administration, and leadership that women disliked and/or found difficult. At the top of the list was paperwork (10 responses). But the response of a thirty-seven-year-old woman in ministry for seven years is revealing of its importance in ministry: "I dislike the paperwork, the endless nature of it. But I once had to deal with a case of harassment and misconduct by a retired minister. Protesting such injustices can be a kick, but I found out you have to do the paperwork well for justice to be served."

It is interesting to note that five women (over 25 percent of those interviewed) mentioned not having a clerical staff or having difficulty with an ill-trained, undependable clerical staff. Women in ministry as a second career were especially frustrated that either the low pay or no money in the budget usually caused this dilemma. Although several women mentioned their willingness to pitch in and do tedious work in the church, others are clear that they can't do everything and need good help to pull it off healthfully for all.

Women also found difficult or disliked conflict (4 responses), people resistant to change (3 responses), ecclesiastical politics (2 responses), and not being heard (1 response). Only one—a forty-three-year-old woman with a middle-class background in ministry for thirteen years—mentioned her dislike for using her authority.

> [I resist acting] as a compelling agent, as opposed to collaboration, in conflict situations. I can only do it with a lot of prayer. Then I try to get as much information as possible about the persons involved, and try to differentiate between my feelings and what the situation needs. For me to say, "I'm in charge here and this is how it will be" is a last resort.

Five of six women who mentioned not minding the occasional need to assert their authority in a compelling way grew up poor or working class or were racial/ethnic women.

Women are obviously quite engaged in management, administration, and leadership in the church and have their likes and dislikes about them. In what ways do these perspectives and experiences provide a challenge to traditional practices and to the construction of new practices of leadership in the church?

### Three Theoretical Perspectives Related to Management, Administration, and Leadership

The literature suggests that there are several theoretical perspectives that have informed management, administration, and leadership in the church up to the present. Clarifying these will provide a starting point for understanding the feminist challenge to these theories as well as the ways in which feminist thought contributes to construction of new theory. Most of the literature suggests three such theories, generally called "management theories."[17]

First, in *classical management theory*, power is understood as a commodity, as a zero-sum game regulated by marketplace rules of competition and supply and demand. The more you have, the less I have; may the best individual win. The institution is a bureaucracy, an efficient machine arranged as a pyramid or hierarchy with clear lines of authority. People relate through their roles rather than as persons. The leader, who is in control, is the formal authority and expert who establishes systems of management, collects information, makes rational decisions based on empirical evidence, and gets results. Certainty is important; mistakes, doubts, and ambiguity are rarely acknowledged publicly. Morality is centered on abstract principles that confirm the values of duty, obedience, and conformity.

Classical management theory is rooted in a positivist epistemology that separates means and ends as well as facts and values. Because of the pyramid structure, the leader can appear remote, impersonal, inaccessible, insensitive. Because information is carefully controlled and decision making so centralized, an institutional atmosphere of secrecy, suspicion, distrust, and defensiveness is not uncommon. In this theoretical perspective, power is covert and context is ignored.

A subset of classical management theory that also views power as a commodity, although it is organized in shifting power blocs, is *organizational management theory*.[18] The institution is a composite of formal and informal groups vying for control of institutional processes and outcomes. The leader is mediator and negotiator between the shifting power blocs. The latent political nature of classical management theory here becomes overt.[19]

Second, in *human relations management theory,* power is understood as capacity. One with power is able to do or create something. The institution is a collegium, a community of equals. The leader, first among equals, seeks participation and democratic decision making. Behavior is open, vulnerable, and trusting, with the need to take risks recognized. Ambiguity, contradiction, and conflict are tolerated. Morality is more person centered, and emotion and experience are valued. Some hierarchy remains in differential power. It is marked by gradualness of decision making. This perspective is rooted in theories of humanistic psychology.

Third, in *systems management theory,* power is understood as energy circulating throughout a system as in a helix, such that both people and institution simultaneously exercise and are influenced by it.[20] The institution is a cultural system of shared meanings and beliefs in which organizational structures and processes are invented. The leader is a facilitator and catalyst whose task is to communicate guiding principles such as guiding visions, strong values, and organizational beliefs so as to maintain focus rather than control around organizational meaning. A leader's context and embodiment of leadership is more important than the leader's distinctiveness and particular actions. Whoever communicates those principles and maintains the focus is leader. Collegiality is understood as differentiation within the holism of the relational system. Diverse viewpoints are sought, information is shared, disequilibrium and conflict are brought to the surface to provide new information, responsibility for creating something that can be systemically supported is expected, and trust is fostered. All participants convey power, for each is both teacher and learner. Change happens not incrementally but in small starts and quantum leaps. Laughter at the surprises of creation is a mark of systemic health. This perspective is rooted in the systems theory of biology and quantum physics.

As noted by Martha Stortz, there is a place for each of these perspectives in wholistic ministry.[21] Because varying forms of leadership may be required in various contexts, knowledge of all three is important. Likewise, leaders should have at their disposal various forms of conflict management for differing contexts.[22] Several women interviewed for this study confirmed the importance of that kind of eclecticism in the interest of a wholistic and integrated ministry.

### Women's Affinity to Systems Management Theory

Because both culture and church manifest the effects of the sin of dualism, it may not be surprising that some studies find that the practices of men are often congruent with classical management theory and organizational management theory, and that the practices of women are often congruent with systems management theory. Both men and women have occasion to use practices congruent with human relations management theory. Judith Rosener's study of "transactional" male leadership and of "transformational" and "interactive" female leadership is instructive in this regard.[23] Likewise, the perception of the nineteen women interviewed here is that there is a difference in the administration and leadership of men and women, although quite a number were admittedly hesitant to engage in gender stereotypes.

When asked, "How is what you do different from the practices of men engaging in management, administration, and leadership?" the most frequent response was that women used shared leadership and team decision making more frequently than did men (6 responses). A thirty-two-year-old in part-time ministry for four years said:

> Men are more hierarchical—they make decisions and expect them to be carried out, or they just decide and go do it. They

become the answer person, the little dictator. For example, a senior pastor I once worked with went out and bought a van for the church. He said, "I'm the leader. They pay me to make decisions and I did. So what are they so upset about?" Well, I try to get close to consensus. If everybody's not on board, I don't do it.

Or a thirty-eight-year-old in full-time ministry for thirteen years said:

> Men may do shared leadership, but not to the extent I do. I have a very deep value for and structure about team decision making. We have a *lot* of team meetings. I probably don't make any decisions alone. No men in our group tested as high in "collaborator" [in Speed Leas' five conflict management styles] as I did.

A number of women perceived that men tend to focus more on numbers and women focus more on feelings or on people (5 responses). Typical is this response of a forty-five-year-old in ministry for two years:

> Men's concerns seem to relate to numbers and building projects, status, and tasks to do. There is less talk about the affective components, such as "What does it mean to have five funerals in six weeks?" or "How much of what I'm going through do I let show to others?" They seem more concerned about presentation. Women seem more concerned about connection.

Several women also mentioned the distinction between assuming a role and being real (4 responses). For example, a thirty-eight-year-old woman in ministry for eight years said, "I have an openness about who I am that works for me. Men tend to walk into a role. Women are more who they are than the role. They are more real, intimate—willing to talk about dogs and kids that don't behave." A thirty-two-year-old woman in ministry for eight years said:

> I think I'm clearer than men that people are individuals—they're not my mother, etc. I try to keep others in perspective with multiple claims on their lives. I also think I give someone the authority to do something when I turn it over to them. I try to take responsibility for my mistakes and not blame my subordinates. I try to deal with everyone as a peer with different tasks to do. And I have decided to be a healthy person so I'm not unjust with others.

Some women perceived that men do more talking and women do more listening (3 responses); that men break things up into pieces, whereas women see the connections between things and how each thing affects everything else (3 responses); that women don't mind admitting they are vulnerable or weak or mistaken (3 responses)[24]; that men more than women engage in win-lose dynamics (2 responses); and that women are often more attentive to details and to cleanup (2 responses). The perceived differences are perhaps most powerfully captured by a forty-three-year-old woman in ministry for thirteen years:

> I probably let my feelings get involved more. And I don't break up what I do into little pieces. They like to play with numbers more than I. Often I feel we're speaking the same language, but it's my second language. When it comes to power, I don't want to overstep my bounds. Their power seems more indigenous. I am intentional about using mine. It's as if this is their native land, and I'm an immigrant.

Women have various ways to characterize their own style of administration and leadership. Nine of the nineteen women used such terms as *collaborative, collegial, shared,* and *team* leadership. One judicatory administrator said, "My style is collaborative. I don't use a compelling style very often, and there's usually not enough time for consensus. I hope for a level playing field and try to create it." The importance of not getting lost in all the shared leadership, however, was noted by a woman serving as co-pastor in ministry with her husband who said, "It's a team effort. There's mutual exchange while recognizing and owning my own expertise."

Women also understand themselves as enabler, coach, midwife, facilitator, or catalyst. As a forty-seven-year-old woman in ministry for twenty-two years said, "My style is a catalyst who turns up the heat and gets people together so they can do what they can't do alone. Before a proposal is offered, I've already talked to five people about it. I'm people oriented as a part of being task oriented so we can reach consensus."

Three women described their style as eclectic or contextual. A forty-four-year-old in ministry for seven years said, "My choice is to be collegial, but in the current transition [of a small urban congregation trying to reach out to its neighborhood] some direction is needed. Some groups can brainstorm freely while others need the structure of selecting among options presented to them. So I can be directive, but mostly I need to be flexible." Another poignant example of the significance of an eclectic, contextual style is from a forty-five-year-old woman new to ministry:

> My style is eclectic and pretty contextual. One congregation I serve is depressed and has no energy. The skills I use here are more directive. There's not even any leadership in the

town, because there's been a lot of loss. I do a lot of one-on-one talking and listening there. At another church I can float an idea and it takes off. I play with them. They have strong lay leaders. So I need a whole rainbow to draw on. The danger of eclecticism is that it can fragment me, and it's wearing to shift gears all the time. But the theological foundation stays the same—being an imaginative community discovering what grasps us that opens us up into a community of faith. The particular vision is different with each church, but there *is* a vision in each case.

Finally, the remaining women described their style variously as visioning/creating (2 responses), consensus (2 responses), modeling (1 response), and self-differentiation (1 response).

When the nineteen women were asked if their style was feminist, three said no, ten said yes, and six indicated either that they weren't sure or that the answer was both no and yes. Whereas eight of the youngest ten women in the sample (ages 29–45) claimed to have a feminist leadership style, only two of the oldest nine women (ages 46–64) claimed to have a feminist style. No racial/ethnic woman said yes. A Native-American woman who was asked if her style was feminist distinguished between tactics and commitments when she said, "Yes and no. Two pastors have said, 'I don't want her in my pulpit.' Well, I don't take that authority just to demand my rights. I don't argue in public, I don't demean someone in public. I cut it off. This is my calling by God. Yet I do stand up for women's rights." When asked if her style was feminist, an Asian-American woman said, "Not particularly. But it is strong, feminine, powerful. I see it in men and women. 'Feminist' means white people. 'Womanist' fits a little more closely—maybe 'womanly.'" An African-American woman said, "No, my style is liberationist. People are helped to become their own person, to be set free from oppressive things. As Martin Luther King Jr. said, 'I can't be all that I can be until you can be all that you can be.'"

Most striking among the racial/ethnic women in this sample was the sense of leadership involving a commitment to lead one's people as a people. It meant a passionate commitment to reordering relationships *within* the community—that "demeaning women" and "sexual misconduct" were not acceptable, for example, within a community. But it also meant that one worked with some clear understandings about the important ways racial/ethnic communities take shape over against the dominant culture, and one knew when and how particular actions would lead to justice and when they would mean only further oppression for the community. All three of the racial/ethnic women were among the five women who saw their leadership happening through preaching and teaching. They know how to use those very public moments to take the lead in articulating the values of the community that get lived out in various smaller group or relational situations at other times. Women in this study were asked to characterize what was feminist about their styles. Some of the characteristics they listed appear in Table 1. This cluster of characteristics is fairly descriptive of the systems management theoretical perspective on leadership that informs the orientation of many women. These characteristics also describe values of liberal feminism in response to sexist culture. The six women (nearly one-third) who responded with uncertainty or with "yes and no" to the question asking if their style was feminist named a number of these characteristics as they went on to describe someone else they considered to be feminist. This cluster of characteristics reflects a period in the development of feminist theory and practice that affirmed the values of egalitarianism and inclusiveness of women and men in the human community. These values are limited, however, in confronting the ideology, structures, and practices of power in gender relations.

Other responses of the nineteen women interviewed form a second cluster of characteristics reflective of radical feminism. This cluster reflects theory and practices that focus on the distinctiveness of women's experience within a power structure of dominance–submission and on the need for justice. For example, these women believed feminism promotes women's authority over their own

### Table 1. Self-Identified Feminist Characteristics

| Characteristic | Number of Responses |
| --- | --- |
| Nurturing/caring/attentive to feelings of self and others | 7 |
| Value every voice | 5 |
| Express own beliefs and values | 5 |
| Use shared leadership with various persons at center | 4 |
| Make connections to build trust | 4 |
| Flexible and contextual | 3 |
| Rely on shared information | 2 |
| Let go of tradition as needed | 2 |
| Explore future possibilities | 2 |
| Discover common goals | 2 |
| Move toward conflict | 2 |
| Affirm and embody community | 2 |
| Whole is greater than sum of parts | 2 |
| Integrative, keep the big picture | 1 |
| Trust an inner authority | 1 |

N = 19

bodies, the power of naming and using women's language to tell the particularities of women's experience through story, seeking and welcoming diverse perspectives of race–sex–class in order to come closer to truth, opposing structures of dominance–submission and abuses of power, repentance that reminds women that they are human, and (especially among women of color) strengthening just connections among one's own people.[25]

## A Feminist Critique of
## the Three Management Theories

Using these two clusters of characteristics, a feminist critique of the three management theories becomes possible. In classical management theory, hierarchy can promote a structure of dominance-submission through which established lines of authority can become authoritarian and those nearer the bottom of the hierarchy are disempowered. People who are less important than their role become anonymous, and those deprived of information and decision-making power are sacrificed for the sake of efficiency. Someone always loses, and the nonconformist is punished. Intolerance for mistakes promotes a rigid perfectionism, and an atmosphere of suspicion prevails that is damaging to everyone's health.

A feminist critique of human relations management theory reveals its limitations. The leader holds control over the structure of the group and the allocation of positions. The hierarchy remains intact as the leader remains first among equals. The implications of difference in gender–class–race may be masked because all participants are presumed equal. Participation is encouraged, but power is not shared (minimal delegation of power). And the potential for abuse increases, because a human relations management structure encourages open and trusting behavior at the same time that it discourages rules and legal procedures.

A feminist critique of systems management theory is also important. An emphasis on process may hamper accomplishment of goals, and the chaos of structurelessness may prevail. Because a theory of power relations is masked, inequalities of power cannot be redressed. In such cases, to seek mutuality through dialogue may exacerbate the injustice. Additionally, there is no built-in structure of accountability, and painful restructuring often becomes necessary.

The critique of traditional management theories that feminism offers is deconstructive work of the most significant sort. Transformative leadership practice, however, also requires the constructive accrual of structure and meaning for ministry in the church today. Informed by my own Wesleyan and Reformed traditions,[26] as well as a liberation hermeneutic, management, administration, and leadership in the church come together for me in the metaphor of covenant making—in the task of a particular people of God giving shape to their covenant for the journey into the world.[27] It is a task requiring the participation of all of the church known as the people of God (*laos theou*) coming together in their "peoplehood." It is a task of discerning the mission and character of discipleship of this people of God. It is a task of fashioning an agreement about the mutual promises and obligations between a people and God that takes a unique shape in this time and place. It is a journey with its own wilderness moments of conflict and fear, but also a journey of hope that in encountering the world, both the world and the people of God might be transformed from death to life. It is a profoundly biblical metaphor for liberative leadership in the church.

### Biblical Metaphors for Leadership

The Exodus covenant, in memory of God's covenant with Abraham-Isaac-Jacob, was born out of the deliverance of the Israelite people through the God-inspired leadership of Moses, Miriam, and Aaron.[28] Miriam claims her own prophetic role and thus exemplifies a more inclusive, team model of leadership.[29] As a good leader, she has stirred the devotion of her people. It is her song—her words—that Moses uses to begin his song to the Lord (Ex. 15:21). The power of her language has brought the people together in community. She models the joy and passion of leadership in singing, dancing, and gratitude for what God has done. It is also she who is punished by God with leprosy when she and Aaron criticize Moses (Num. 12:1, 9–16). And she dies while the Israelite people are still fighting for survival in the wilderness, hoping for deliverance (Num. 20:1). Her story is replicated in the lives of many women in leadership in ministry—women whose ministry ends while they are still hoping for change.

Just as "by strength of hand the Lord brought [the Hebrew people] out of Egypt [w]hen Pharaoh let the people go" (Ex. 13:16b—17a), so today deliverance of the people of God from bondage (of pride, aimlessness, oppression, death) occurs with the leadership of one who knows the people, dwells among them, and by Christian baptism *is* one of the people willing to take their hand for the journey.[30] Just as the Hebrew people "went up out of the land of Egypt prepared for battle" (Ex. 13:18b), so today a faithful leader helps a people to discern when and how resistance against evil is an expression of faithfulness on the journey. Just as "the Lord went in front of them in a pillar of cloud by day, to lead them along the way, and in a pillar of fire by night, to give them light, so that they might travel by day and by night" (Ex. 13:21), so today the people of God are best led by one who knows to call on the God of spirit and truth, the God of wisdom and life as the source of power and guidance that does not depart from them.

Just as the Hebrew people cried to Moses, "What have you done to us, bringing us out of Egypt? . . . For it would have been better for us to serve the Egyptians than to die in the wilderness," and just as Moses said to the people, "Do not be afraid, stand firm, and see the deliverance that the LORD will accomplish for you today" (Ex. 14:11b–13a), so today a leader must encourage the people when fear and doubt loom large. And just as "Moses and the Israelites sang this song [of Miriam] to the LORD" (Ex. 15:1a) after deliverance from Pharaoh's army, so today leaders bring the people together in praise and thanksgiving to celebrate what God has done in their midst. And then as now, keeping the Sabbath is our "perpetual covenant" (Ex. 31:15–16).

In the New Testament a variety of gifts evoke various forms of leadership (1 Cor. 12:28). But in each case power and authority are based on a social reality enlivened through the creative power of the Holy Spirit for a life of discipleship by participation in a community of grace. One woman interviewed for this study suggested that the vital and participative leadership she tried to embody was "not too different from the New Testament church."

In time, of course, such charismatic power becomes organized into offices that are ordered hierarchically. Throughout the history of the church, these offices have often excluded women. But women also have found ways to practice leadership roles in marginal religious groups that deemphasized the masculine character of God, tempered or denied the doctrine of the Fall, denied the need for ordination to lead a congregation, and viewed marriage as one (but not the only) faithful way of living.[31]

This perspective on scripture, tradition, and leadership emerges from a particular view of the church. According to Peter Hodgson, numerous crises of postmodern times are prompting the emergence of a new ecclesiological paradigm that challenges the monolithic hegemony of the Western patriarchal church.[32] This is an emerging church that is nonhierarchical, nonprovincial, lives in the dialectic of the historical and the spiritual, engages in liberative praxis, and lives out an ecumenical mission. It is a new/old church led by the paradigm of Jesus, whose ministry was collegial, inclusive, liberating, suffering, and impelled by the Spirit of life. It is an ecclesial paradigm that is influenced, Hodgson admits, by feminism.[33]

Feminist theologian Letty Russell, as well as Hodgson, understands the church still to be one, holy, catholic, and apostolic in its character and values.[34] For her this means that the church finds its unity in one baptism, in all who call on Christ's name finding Christ in their midst, and in crossing barriers of diversity. The church is holy in fulfilling its covenant relationship with God by living out justice, mercy, and faith so as to put the world right. It is catholic in the universality of Christ's presence in the world, its invitation to all nations as connected, and in its orthopraxy of the church's witness. It is apostolic in its true witness to Jesus' own story, its faithful preaching with a mission of justice and peace, its commissioning of leadership sent out to tell its story, and its quality of life as participating in God's liberating action.

The gifts of the Spirit making the true community of the church are revealed in values of justice, vitality, love, and wisdom, according to Rebecca Chopp.[35] Justice is present in the equal access to speak and in standing in solidarity with others toward liberation. Vitality is present in the ability to risk and to sing a new song. Love is present in listening, in celebrating difference, and in the willingness to be changed. And wisdom is present in guiding the community in the best use of its resources and in the most insightful decisions, in knowing the community's tales of the past, and in discerning its vision of the future. Out of these shared values of true community, a people will grant a leader authority to lead them.

A leader can lead only when freely granted the authority to do so by the people.[36] In the church there is a sharing in the same Spirit that authors the lives of the people of God, including the leader, and a sharing in the values that the Spirit lifts up. Leader and people come to articulate those values and discover their common identity through their encounter with the stories of the biblical people and the stories of those in the church across the generations similarly stirred by the Spirit.[37] As noted by four of the nineteen women interviewed in response to the question "How is administration by women in the church different from administration by women in other organizations?" the empowerment of ministry by God and the shared values of the community rooted in a shared story are the primary differences.

Hence, in this new/old ecclesial paradigm, authority is dialogical, shared, and cooperative rather than hierarchical. True authority is life-giving and critiques abuses of power that are death-dealing. True authority is embodied, recognizing our fragile and vulnerable condition, aiming at restoring the balance of mind and body, and aiming to discover a variety of gifts. True authority tells the "truth of the whole" by listening to the marginalized as well as those with power and by speaking up. True authority seeks to restore justice in the world and says so. True authority creates the possibility of life for the present and future.[38]

## Issues Raised from a Feminist Perspective

There are a number of issues to be raised in connection with management, administration, and leadership in the church from a feminist perspective. First, women in leadership will cause conflict. It is the kind of conflict that comes with the shaking of hierarchical foundations or the birth pangs of a paradigm shift. It is to be expected and anticipated. Good leadership knows to head into conflict rather than avoiding it. But the road will not be easy.

Second, the shifting of the paradigm will mean that women must find ways (most especially through support systems) to maintain the dialectic of envisioning, risk-taking, and confronting inequities and injustices, while also being able to be nurturing and compromising when needed. To "speak the truth in love" remains a difficult task.

Third, feminist leadership in the church must maintain a solid theological and spiritual foundation. Henri Nouwen has suggested that Christian leaders must avoid the temptations to be relevant, to be spectacular, and to be powerful by learning the disciplines of contemplative prayer (to connect us to our First Love), confession and forgiveness (to keep ministry communal and mutual), and theological reflection (reflecting on life's realities with the mind of Jesus to discern where we are being led).[39] Our feminist leadership will be strengthened on such a foundation.

Fourth, claiming one's authority and developing the skills of leadership does not come overnight and needs to be learned. Women in this study learned leadership and administration in a variety of ways, including role models, formal instruction, in-service training, reading, learning by doing, listening, watching, and being with other women. A forty-seven-year-old woman in ministry for twenty-two years indicated that in addition to her mother, it was the church that taught her some of the basics of management and administration: "The organization of Youth Ministry taught me about scheduling meetings, rotating leadership, mailing lists and notices, how to communicate with pastors in writing, learning to do minutes, financial reports, budget projections—all before graduating from high school."

But a number of women also indicated that women need to know more. Several women mentioned needing not only role models but mentors for learning leadership (see chapter 7). They also need more texts written by women, especially in the church. Most frequently mentioned was needing opportunities—where risk taking and imagination were encouraged. Some thought women could be helped by intentional self-reflection, but more commonly peer review or conversations with other women about leadership were seen to be important. As a forty-eight-year-old woman in ministry for fifteen years said, "Women really need to talk about it together before talking to men."

## Envisioning Future Leadership from a Feminist Perspective

The women in this study were invited finally to envision leadership in the future of the church if more of it were done by women and if more were done from a feminist perspective. Many women were very clear that more women in leadership would not necessarily solve the problem. They said: "it would not necessarily be kinder and gentler"; "it may not be different—the same people may rise to the top"; "sometimes women get co-opted into men's way of doing things"; "it won't be different if women use the same old model—in fact, it could be worse, since women wouldn't be playing with their own rules"; "it requires a different view of life—a view more alive and vibrant"; and finally, "gender is probably not as important as values."

Given all this, the interviewees did believe that if there were more women in leadership in the church, there could be more inclusive ownership of ministry, more gifts shared, more voices heard and valued, more new ideas, more styles tried, more decision making shared. A forty-three-year-old woman in ministry for thirteen years believed that "ministry would be less fragmented because women can do more than one thing at a time, and laity would be listened to more because women have a tendency to listen more." And a fifty-year-old woman in ministry for eight years said, "I've heard pastors say that laity don't want to do anything, but I think they do. They have a calling. Our task is to help them come alive, so they can be in ministry and build up the body of Christ."

They also believed that if more women were in leadership in the church there would be "less one-up and one-down, which keeps us from using our gifts and keeps us adolescent" (forty-two-year-old woman in ministry for eight years). In addition, one believed, "We wouldn't use numbers to evaluate ministry, but would celebrate programming, commitment, growth in faith. Like Stan Hauerwas says, 'we're supposed to be living the gospel, not just being effective'" (thirty-two-year-old woman in ministry for four years).

The women were also invited to indicate how they thought the church would be different if more management, administration, and leadership were done from a feminist perspective. Many women believed that the actual structure of churches as organizations would need to change, that the hierarchical structure would be broken down, that power would not be so centralized like a commodity to be fought over and won. The watchword might be "know your authority—meaning everyone has some." This would have the effect of being more empowering, just, and equal to all so that "there would be more actual ministry happening."

But it would also mean "taking more risks against the status quo." It would mean promoting, not simply accepting, diversity. It would mean creating "a place for people who don't fit the mold, walk the walk, and talk the talk," and it would mean "the voices of women and children and the oppressed would be heard and their experiences valued, more women and people of color in leadership." It would mean "getting more people from different perspectives together and having a better overview of God's will coming." It would mean that leaders would need to "wear their authority lightly" and that "our attitudes, including our need to impress everyone, might change." It would mean that "women might no longer be demeaned" and that "there would be less guilt and self-sacrifice needed, so that we could carry on what's life-giving." It also would mean that "men would be better leaders" and that "we'd be free to be the church of God."

These are difficult times for leadership in the church. The perspectives and practices of women give us both pause and hope for the future. We are still in the wilderness trying to survive, but the vision of a new day is becoming clearer. Not all of the leaders seeking justice will arrive in the promised land, but they have helped plant seeds that our faith tells us will bear fruit. We get tired and weary fighting the battles, but hope of a new day and a new home inspires us still. Feminist leadership is prophetic leadership that creates the possibility of a renewed covenant community of justice and peace where all women and men are gathered as God's kin-dom to share in the commonwealth of new life.

## NOTES

1. David Luecke and Samuel Southard, *Pastoral Administration: Integrating Ministry and Management in the Church* (Waco: Word, 1986), 11.
2. For a comprehensive history of women in leadership in the early church (including the prohibition of their being bishops or elders), see Carl A. Volz, *Pastoral Life and Practice in the Early Church* (Minneapolis: Augsburg Publishing House, 1990), 180f. Nadine Pence Frantz and Deborah Silver, "Women in Leadership: A Theological Perspective," *Brethren Life and Thought* 30 (Winter 1985): 37–40, note the Church of the Brethren position that women in leadership violate the God-given order of family life and church life, and that women are actually seeking self-exaltation when seeking church leadership.

3. H. Richard Niebuhr, *Christ and Culture* (New York: Harper, 1951). Thomas C. Campbell and Gary B. Reierson note similar assumptions (except the fourth) in *The Gift of Administration* (Philadelphia: Westminster Press, 1981), 18. They note that the theological perspective adopted can be found in Calvin, Knox, the Puritans, the Separatists, the Wesleyan tradition, H. Richard Niebuhr, and Paul Tillich.

4. According to Elisabeth Schüssler Fiorenza, this critical perspective means that conscious partiality rather than objectivity is sought, that the view from below (the perspective of women) has scientific as well as ethical and political dimensions, that spectator knowledge must be replaced by participation, that the starting point is to change the status quo, that research is a process of consciousness-raising that assists women. Cited in Jeanette Sherrill, *Power and Authority: Issues for Women Clergy as Leaders*, dissertation at Hartford Seminary, 1991, 8.

5. I have been influenced greatly by womanist authors who generally speak more cogently to the connections between race, gender, and class than do feminist authors. My being white determines my perspective as feminist, however, with strong prowomanist commitments.

6. See Jill Blackmore, "Changing from Within: Feminist Educators and Administrative Leadership," *Peabody Journal of Education* 66, no. 3 (Spring 1989): 21, for foci of most literature on feminist leadership: (1) individual female administrators who have been successful in male terms, (2) life histories and life cycles of men vs. women, (3) woman's work culture created by their subordinate position, (4) feminist epistemological concerns, for example, why a study excludes female experience, (5) woman's ways of knowing, thinking, making moral judgments. See also Virginia Schein, "Would Women Lead Differently?" in *Contemporary Issues in Leadership*, eds. William Rosenbach and Robert Taylor (Boulder: West View Press, 1989), 156, who suggests that trait theory of leadership is limited.

7. The women range in age from twenty-nine to sixty-four. Nine are married and ten are single by choice, death of spouse, or divorce. Thirteen have children, one has stepchildren only, five have no children. They represent lay ministry (N=1), consecrated ministry (N=2), and ordained ministry (N=16) in local church (N=14), parachurch (N=1), and judicatory (N=4) settings. Their experience in ministry ranges from twenty months of part-time ministry to twenty-four years of full-time ministry. Sixteen of the women are Caucasian, one is African American, one is Asian American, and one is Native American. Although nearly two-thirds of the women understand their families of origin to have been middle class, seven grew up working class or poor.

8. A letter of introduction inviting participation, a questionnaire, a return card requesting phone numbers, and a self-addressed/stamped envelope were mailed to thirty-six women. With the exception of two face-to-face interviews, all interviews were completed by telephone. With a few exceptions, the conversations lasted between thirty and forty minutes.

9. Robert K. Greenleaf, *Seminary as Servant* (Peterborough, N.H.: Windy Row Press, 1983).

10. Kathleen S. Hurty, "Ecumenical Leadership: Power and Women's Voices," in *Women and Church: The Challenge of Ecumenical Solidarity in an Age of Alienation,* ed. Melanie May (Grand Rapids: W. B. Eerdmans, 1991), 91.

11. Abraham Zaleznik, "Managers and Leaders: Are They Different?" *Harvard Business Review* 55, no. 5 (1977): 67.

12. Thirty years ago Alvin Lindgren suggested that there are two basic approaches to church administration: programs and principles. The view espoused here is more complex. See Alvin Lindgren, *Foundations for Purposeful Church Administration* (Nashville: Abingdon Press, 1965), 19.

13. Campbell and Reierson, *The Gift of Administration,* 38.

14. Campbell and Reierson point out that Paul Tillich talks about leadership as the social analogy to centeredness, that leadership is to the corporate body what centeredness is to the individual body, in *Systematic Theology,* vol. 3 (Chicago: University of Chicago Press, 1963), 82.

15. See Lovett H. Weems, Jr., *Church Leadership: Vision, Team, Context, Integrity* (Nashville: Abingdon Press, 1993), 34.

16. See James D. Anderson and Ezra Earl Jones, *The Management of Ministry* (New York: Harper & Row, 1978), 78. The authors use the terms *management, administration,* and *leadership* interchangeably at times, but they cluster various tasks of ministry similarly to the three emphases here: (1) Efficient Organizational Management (managing task groups, buildings, communications, fund-raising, budget); (2) Effective Associational Leadership [read: Administration] (conflict management, visitation, governance, social witness, community outreach); and (3) Authentic Spiritual Direction [read: Leadership] (preaching, teaching, prophetic leadership, prayer, sacraments, crisis support, counseling).

17. See Daniel A. Wren, *The Evolution of Management Thought* (New York: Ronald Press Co., 1972). See also Martha Ellen Stortz, *Pastor Power* (Nashville: Abingdon Press, 1993), 17–18; and Ben Kimmerling, "Women and the Church," *SEDOS Bulletin* 10 (November 15, 1988): 344–51. Jill Blackmore also makes some helpful remarks on theory in "Changing from Within." Brian P. Hall and Helen Thompson refer to these as "leadership theories" in *Leadership through Values* (New York: Paulist Press, 1980).

18. Estela Mara Bensimon, "A Feminist Reinterpretation of Presidents' Definitions of Leadership," *Peabody Journal of Education* 66, no. 3, (Spring 1989): 143–56, understands organizational management theory as a fourth theory rooted in sociological organization theory. Although its theory base differs from that of classical management theory, the understanding of power as commodity and the importance of control in power's use and expression are thematic connections that both classical and organizational management theories share.

19. According to James McGregor Burns, *Leadership* (New York: Harper

& Row, 1978), it is a male bias that sees leadership as mere command or control, as in classical and organizational management theories. The male managerial stereotype was not confirmed, however, but a managerial stereotype reflective of both men and women was confirmed (including high dominance, high achievement, and low nurturance) in Otto C. Brenner and Jeffrey H. Greenhaus, "Managerial Status, Sex, and Selected Personality Characteristics," *Journal of Management* 5, no. 1, (1979): 107–13.

20. Michel Foucault understands power as something that circulates. See "Two Lectures," in Colin Gordon, ed., *Power/Knowledge: Selected Interviews and Other Writings, 1972–1977* (New York: Pantheon Books, 1980). One who uses the image of power as helix is Margaret J. Wheatley, *Leadership and the New Science: Learning About Organization from an Orderly Universe* (San Francisco: Berrett-Koehler Publishers, 1992).

21. For Stortz power is *power over, power in,* and *power with.* Power as authority (power over) is appropriately used to protect the helpless, guarantee survival against threatened siege, and hold persons accountable. A leader has appropriate and legitimate authority to set boundaries, delineate roles, and foster individuation. Power as charisma (power within) is appropriately used to attract and empower others, discern the spirits, challenge idolatrous expressions, create new life and new forms. The leader appropriately encourages self-knowledge, assessing one's assets and limitations. Power as friendship (power with) is coactive power that cannot happen without the other and is appropriately used to foster mutuality, the common good, equality of power and status, reciprocity, benevolence, knowledge. See Stortz, *Pastor Power,* 43–122.

22. See Speed Leas, *Discover Your Conflict Management Style* (New York: Alban Institute, 1984). It is interesting to entertain the possibility that the styles Leas describes may be appropriate to each of the management theories described here: Compelling or Forcing Style (classical management theory?), Bargaining or Negotiation Style (organizational management theory?), Persuasion Style (human relations management theory?), Collaboration Style (systems management theory?).

23. Judith Rosener, "Ways Women Lead," *Harvard Business Review* (November–December 1990). Rosener found that men depended on the power of position and described their leadership as "transactional" (exchanging rewards for services or punishment for inadequate performance). Women depended on the power of personal charisma, interpersonal skills, personal contacts, and hard work, and described their leadership as "transformational" or "interactive" (getting subordinates to transform their own self-interest into shared interests by focusing upon a broader goal). It goes beyond increased participation (a characteristic of human relations management theory) to shared power and information, enhanced self-worth of others, energizing and inspiring people.

24. This confirms the observation of Anne Marie Neuchterlein and Celia A. Hahn, *The Male-Female Church Staff: Celebrating the Gifts, Confronting*

*the Challenges* (New York: Alban Institute, 1990), 25. See also Donna Schaper, *Common Sense About Men and Women in the Ministry* (New York: Alban Institute, 1990), 74.

25. An important methodological point is being made in suggesting that all nineteen women, including women who claim not to be feminist, can contribute to shaping principles called "feminist." Two who claimed not to be feminist are racial/ethnic women who made the claim because of the perceived exclusiveness of feminism as an ideology and practice of white middle-class women. Another was a fifty-eight-year-old white woman who perceived feminists to be excluding men. This was also a point mentioned by several women who said they were not sure if they were feminist. Feminism as an ideology took shape and continues to change shape as a result of practices that make and deny its claims in its many forms.

26. Born into the Methodist Church (later to become United Methodist), I transferred thirteen years ago to the United Church of Christ. See note 3 above for theological and denominational assumptions.

27. Luecke and Southard, *Pastoral Administration*, 31, suggest that it is "to give shape to the covenant for the journey."

28. The authority of scripture is dependent on the authority of the persons with whom it is associated (the Torah is associated with Moses, and the Psalms are associated with David), as noted by Claudia Camp, "Female Voice, Written Word: Women and Authority in Hebrew Scripture," *Embodied Love: Sensuality and Relationship as Feminist Values*, eds. Paula M. Cooey, Sharon A. Farmer, and Mary Ellen Ross (New York: Harper & Row, 1987), 99.

29. Schaper, *Common Sense*, 61. See also Ruth Daughterty, "Issues of Leadership into the 21st Century," *Viewpoint 13* (Summer 1991) for a reminder that Jesus Christ had a regenerative rather than a merely reflective relationship with society because he dwelt in the midst of the people.

30. See Letty Russell, "Feminism and the Church: A Quest for New Styles of Ministry," *Ministerial Formation* 55 (October 1991): 28–37, for seeing in the Miriam story clues to feminist/womanist leadership.

31. See Mary Farrell Bednarowski, "Outside the Mainstream: Women's Religion and Women Religious Leaders in 19th Century America," *Journal of the American Academy of Religion* 48, no. 2 (June 1980): 207.

32. Peter C. Hodgson, *Revisioning the Church: Ecclesial Freedom in the New Paradigm* (Philadelphia: Fortress Press, 1988), 13, 18. The five crises he lists are cognitive, historical, political, socioeconomic, and religious.

33. Ibid., 81, 98. Barbara Brown Zikmund, "The Contributions of women to North American Church Life," *Midstream* 22 (July–October 1983): 373, further notes that feminism has influenced theology through a strong ecclesiology grounded in a sense of mission, skepticism about the authority of scripture and tradition, affirmation of women's experience, and an incarnational theology (confronting "body" issues such as prostitution, slavery, mental illness, lynching, prison reform, child

labor, temperance, birth control, rape, capital punishment, abortion, and homosexuality).

34. Letty Russell, *Church in the Round: Feminist Interpretation of the Church* (Louisville, Ky.: Westminster/John Knox, 1993), 131–34. Jürgen Moltmann also explains the church as one (uniting in freedom), holy (sanctifying in poverty), catholic (comprehensive in partisanship for the oppressed), and apostolic (commissioning the lordship of Christ in the cross), in *Church in the Power of the Spirit: A Contribution to Messianic Ecclesiolgy* (New York: Harper & Row, 1977), 341.

35. Rebecca S. Chopp, *The Power to Speak* (New York: Crossroad, 1989), 97.

36. For more on the dynamics of people looking to those in authority to evoke their consent to experience security and direction in their lives, see Letty Russell, *Household of Freedom: Authority in Feminist Theology* (Philadelphia: Westminster Press, 1987), 21–23. See also Richard Sennett, *Authority* (New York: Vintage, 1981), 16–21.

37. Claudia Camp, "Female Voice, Written Word," 109, 111.

38. Susan Ross, "He Has Pulled the Mighty . . .": A Feminist Reflection," in *That They Might Live: Power, Empowerment, and Leadership in the Church*, ed. Michael Downey (New York: Crossroad, 1991), 145–59. See also Letty Russell, Feminism and the Church," 28–37.

39. Henri Nouwen, *In the Name of Jesus: Reflections on Christian Leadership* (New York: Crossroad, 1989).

# 6

## ETHICS AS AN ART
## OF DOING THE WORK OUR SOULS MUST HAVE

*Emilie M. Townes*

On Doing the Work Our Souls Must Have

o sing to me a song of hope
a song of tomorrows
a song of todays

o sing to me a song of hope
a song of days gone by
and moments unborn

o sing to me a song of hope
that gives me ways
to walk the path

o sing to me a song of hope
that leads me home
that leads me home
—Emilie M. Townes

Many African-American women in the theological disciplines
have gravitated to the use of Alice Walker's term *womanist* as
both challenge to and a confessional statement for their own work.
Walker's four-part definition that contains the elements of tradition,
community, self, and critique of white feminist thought provides a
fertile ground for religious reflection and practical application. The
challenge, which is an interstructured analysis[1] that begins with
race, gender, and class, provides for a dynamic tension in womanist thought for all of the theological disciplines. Such an analysis is
not only descriptive, but prescriptive as well. Womanist religious reflections provide descriptive foundations that lead to analytical constructs for the eradication of oppression in the lives of African Americans and, by extension, the rest of humanity and creation.

The confessional element of *womanist* means that it is a term that
cannot be imposed, but must be claimed by the Black woman who
is engaged, from her own faith perspective and academic discipline,
in the eradication of oppression. Therefore, the use of the term
*womanist* to describe a theorist's or a practitioner's work is one of

avowal rather than denotation. This confessional stance is crucial, for the womanist engaged in theological reflection is also holding in tension her own identity as a Black woman with the vicissitudes of the theological discipline or ministry in which she is engaged. This provides an organic undertaking of constant self-reflection in the context of the "doing" of one's vocation and avocation. Also, the womanist is not free to name others as womanist if this is not a term they claim for themselves. For example, describing Black women from the nineteenth century as womanists is inaccurate. Although many like Ida B. Wells-Barnett, Sojourner Truth, and Anna Julia Cooper employed an interstructured social analysis in their activism, none of these women claimed the term *womanist* for herself. At best, and most faithfully, these women embody nascent womanism that provides a rich framework for womanists of this era to flesh out.

There is no one voice in womanist religious thought, but a symphony that at times may move to a cacophony. There is still much debate about the need to hold all of Walker's definitions within the womanist frame versus picking and choosing the elements one finds helpful in her work. There are some womanists who challenge, in the second definition, Walker's inclusion of homosexuality as a desirable norm in the African-American community. Others resonate with the themes of the mother-daughter dialogue in the first definition and see this as pivotal for their work. Still others are drawn to explore the dimensions of self-care and self-love and affirmation in Walker's third definition. Some womanists focus on the need for a piercing critique of white feminism (academic and practical) implied in her fourth definition. Finally, there are those who believe all four parts of Walker's definition must determine one's theoretical and analytical framework.

This debate has just begun and is far from settled. However, the commitment to work through these issues is strong. Therefore, there are many times in which the passion of the ideas turns into a marvelous and creative cacophony that refuses to settle for uneasy truces and obsequious compromises to appear united and of one mind in and to the theological academy or in the halls of the Black Church.

This has been, in the language of the Black Church, a homecoming for womanist ethicists. The dynamics of womanist thought immediately challenges the normative discourse and theoretical constructs of traditional ethical reflection. Rather than argue for universals, womanist ethics begins with particularity. It does so with the knowledge that claims about universalities often evolve out of particular communities and ideologies that have been dominant, yet unacknowledged for being so. What is dominant is seen as the norm and therefore neutral.

Womanist ethics questions this hegemonic notion. Rather, a womanist perspective argues that because all discourse is rooted in the social location of those who speak (or are silent or silenced), such discourse is particular and ultimately biased. The task of womanist ethics is to recognize the biases within particularity and work with them to explore the rootedness of social location and the demands for faithful reflection and witness in light of the gospel demands for justice and wholeness.

As a womanist ethicist, I begin with the realization of the traditional role and place to which African-American women have been assigned and relegated. Katie Geneva Cannon points out that the assumption of dominant ethical systems implies that the doing of ethics in the Black community is either immoral or amoral.[2] This traditional reflection is predicated on the existence of freedom and a wide range of choices. As Cannon notes, this "proved to be null and void in situations of oppression."[3] This freedom is not available to white women and women and men of color, as well as to poor people and representatives of marginal groups in United States society.

Cannon goes on to note that dominant ethics makes a virtue of qualities that lead to economic success: self-reliance, frugality, industry. It assumes that the moral agent is free and self-directing and can make suffering a desirable norm. In Cannon's view, this understanding of moral agency is not true, however, for African Americans. The reality of white supremacy and male superiority forces Blacks and whites, women and men, to live in different ranges of freedom. In situations of oppression, freedom is not a choice, nor is self-reliance. Frugality is enforced and suffering is present, but neither is chosen. Cannon believes that Black ethical values cannot be identical with the obligations and duties that white society requires of its members.

## Descriptive Notes

An African-American woman as a moral agent must contend with race, sex, class, and other sources of fragmentation. The challenge for a womanist ethicist is to create and then articulate a positive moral standard that critiques the elitism of dominant ethics at its oppressive core and is relevant for the African-American community and the larger society.

Black women continue to play a highly functional and autonomous role within the family and Black society because of economic and social conditions that have devalued and ill-defined the Black woman historically and forced African-American men and women into ill-fitting negative stereotypes. Black women are forced, as are other women of color and white women, into images of womanhood imposed by a larger society. African-American women also know that they will never reach this model because of the constraints of race and class. One aspect of racism is that it has structured dominant and subordinate roles and relationships between Black and whites and placed African Americans within a relatively closed system while blaming deviant behavior on them.

Black women have been called matriarchs, Sapphires, and castrators. This is in large measure because of the active role many Black women have had to play in the support of children, husbands, and Black society. All have usually assumed the Black woman's capabilities. Black women who have the legacy of clearing the fields, caring for the children of others as well as their own, and functioning in marginalized roles—while being called on to provide the backbone of African-American values—are considered a deviation from the norm and an anomaly in United States society.

Key for me as a womanist ethicist is the notion of justice. Justice involves the radical act of truth telling—of reality testing and reality challenging. As both a people and as genders, African-American women and men have been stereotyped, categorized, scrutinized, and dichotomized into a people straining against the bonds of double-consciousness and triple-consciousness. As a womanist ethic of justice emerges, it must be radically rooted in the truth tradition and history of African-American life and witness. It cannot succumb to a praxeological framework in which all the women are white and all the Blacks are men.

The task of the womanist ethic of justice is to move within the tradition descriptively yet jump for the sun to climb beyond the tradition prescriptively. An ethic of justice must be based on the community from which it emerges, for it can degenerate into flaccid ideology if it does not espouse a future vision that calls the community beyond itself into a wider and more inclusive circle. This circle is neither tight nor fixed.

## Descriptive Leanings

Contemporary womanist ethicists can take important cues from slave women who practiced forms of resistance to the onslaught on the humanity of Black people. These women practiced abstinence in refusing or attempting to avoid intercourse with white masters. In this vein, they also delayed marriage to a slave male with the hope that childbirth would happen in freedom.[4] Abortion and infanticide were also methods of resistance, but were less common than abstinence. Black women's resistance to sexual exploitation had political as well as economic implications. By using resistance, women negated, through individual or group action, their role in the maintenance of the slave pool.

A womanist ethic of justice responds from its own well of history and sociopolitical methodology: we cannot bring together that which we do not know. A unity forged on imperfection, romance, poor vision, limited knowledge, and fissured reconciliation will always benefit those who have the power and leisure to enforce and ignore differences. Unity as a teleological goal can be dangerous and life defeating, for it can overwhelm and neglect equality. Unity is only vigorous in an atmosphere that is unafraid of difference and diversity—an atmosphere that does not view difference as a barrier, but rather as the proverbial stew whose aroma is richer and whose substance provides greater sustenance for the work of justice.

The collective experience of Black women, like the experience of any group, can inform and challenge the dominant worldview. African-American women must seriously consider a womanist analysis of society, culture, and history. Such an analysis calls for an integrated and multitextured survey of church and society. It also helps ground Black women within our community as we seek to applaud and admonish our communities for the work they do and leave undone. For a Black woman to forget her blackness is to deny a rich heritage that crosses the continent of Africa, moves in the waters of the Caribbean, touches the shores of South America, and is vibrant in the rhythms of Alice Coltrane and Sweet Honey in the Rock. She loses part of her very soul if she turns away from Zora Neale Hurston or Phyllis Wheatley. African-American women must continue to draw from the deep well of the lives of Fannie Lou Hamer and Septima Clark.

However, care must be taken neither to idealize nor to romanticize African-American women. An even greater danger is to confuse collective with monolithic. Strength, determination, and steel will are part and parcel of the Black woman's heritage. Yet this does not mean that this heritage is always healthy. She has been the breeder and the unwilling mistress. She has been the big mama and the prostitute. She has suffered in kitchens and borne child after child. She needs not only to celebrate her heritage, but to take a long, hard look at it.

With such a rich history—one of tragedy and triumph—what cues are there for us in ethics? It is my deep belief, from the particular perspective of the Black woman in the United States, that an ethic of justice is rooted in two concepts: liberation and reconciliation. These concepts are the components of transformation for the individual and society. Liberation and reconciliation respond to the experience of African-American women in this country and in churches. However, liberation and reconciliation move beyond the particularity of African-American women's lives to touch the Black community at large and to call to the whole church and the whole society.

Liberation has spiritual and social dimensions. The aim of liberation is to restore a sense of self as a free person and as a spiritual being. The spiritual dimension of liberation concentrates on the acquisition of power that enables each person to be who she or he is. This power is not one that dominates and subordinates. Rather, it fosters the security to give that self to others in a love that requires no response in kind. This does not mean that a person participates in self-abnegation. Giving of oneself does not mean the automatic forfeiture of dignity and worth. One gives through love, but not at the expense of self. A delicate balancing act achieves spiritual liberation, for one must give through the God-presence in each of us and not solely through the fully human parts of oneself. The challenge of spiritual liberation is choosing between wholeness and destruction.

Social liberation is participation in the world. It is a concern for others as we bring ourselves together to witness our faith. Liberation requires that each person acquire an attitudinal mind-set that refuses to accept any external restraint that would deny her or him the right of being. Implicit in this is a strong self-affirmation that cannot be challenged successfully by any external force.

This is not a carte blanche opportunity to justify unjust or inappropriate behavior because we "feel" or "sense" that persons or structures are trying to "control" us. There are contexts, such as in guidelines and rules regarding clergy sexual misconduct and clergy professional ethics, where such structures of accountability are apt and proper external restraints on our behavior. Unfortunately, in our humanness, we can stray off the pathways of righteousness, and we need help in holding ourselves and each other accountable to proper conduct.

Similarly, there are times when our colleagues, our families, and our friends can rightly intervene in stopping us from doing destructive behavior such as self-abnegation. There are times when the demands of ministry are great and there are a multitude of tasks at hand. It is important that if we are unable to set limits bounded by our humanity, that others help us set them. A key thing to remember is that the gift and the tragedy of the atonement are our legacies, but it is not our mandate to relive them in our ministries. Like the women who stood at the foot of the cross and the women who were at the tomb, we are called to be witnesses and heralds of the good news. We are not called either to knock Jesus off the cross or to spend a lifetime in ministry rolling the stone back into place.

Social liberation and spiritual liberation are tremendous challenges and awesome gifts for us, for liberation combats the double-consciousness all of us live under in this society. This double-consciousness is seeing ourselves through the revelation of others. This tragic twist of self-perception was explained by W.E.B. Du Bois in his discussion of double-consciousness:

> After the Egyptian and the Indian, the Greek and Roman, the Teuton and Mongolian, the Negro is a sort of seventh son, born with a veil, and gifted with second-sight in this American world—a world which yields him no true self-consciousness, but only lets him see himself through the revelation of the other world. It is a peculiar sensation, this double-consciousness, this sense of always looking at one's self through the eyes of others, of measuring one's soul by the tape of a world that looks on in amused contempt and pity.[5]

Double-consciousness wreaks a particular kind of disfigurement for women in leadership positions in the church. It is more than external conditions that impinge on our living; it is also the terror from within that is the mutilation of the spirit and the body. The challenge is to refuse dehumanization and affirm and value the gifts women bring to society and to the church.

An important distinction must be made; liberation and freedom are not the same. Liberation is a process. Freedom is a temporary state of being. It is more of an event we point toward, work for, and hope for. Freedom is that moment of release in worship where we know that God loves us and holds us tenderly. Freedom is that moment of triumph as we watched Nelson Mandela walk into freedom for the first time in twenty-seven years. It is the hope of freedom that drives liberation.

Liberation is the product of freedom. Liberation is God's work of salvation in Jesus. Because Jesus died for us and lives yet again in us, we have the promise of wholeness through our brokenness. Liberation is the process of struggle with ourselves and with each other that begets the transformation of all of us to our full humanity. Liberation establishes freedom, yet it must go on to explore greater dimensions of personhood. Liberation cannot be content with the situation, despite the health it may produce for people. There is always the possibility of being transformed anew. Through liberation, freedom may be made manifest, but that freedom is not a permanent state of being. When we are made whole, we are asked to give of that wholeness. Our act of giving fragments us. This fragmentation opens us to the possibility of new and greater transformation. Liberation is dynamic. It never ends.

Reconciliation has both an objective realm and a subjective realm. The objective realm is God's activity in our lives in which God creates a new relationship with us. This new relationship is the gift of freedom. This freedom is the new being whom God creates in us through our faith. There is the freedom honed through liberation that is our activity. The objective realm also holds the freedom that is God's activity of love and grace in our lives.

The subjective realm of reconciliation is what we do among ourselves. This realm is the restoration of harmony with groups and with individuals. In this realm, we acknowledge a respect for the world we share and our need for others and their experience. The subjective realm of reconciliation is what we do to remain faithful to God's gift of freedom in our lives.

Through the objective realm, God liberates us for freedom; through the subjective realm, we acknowledge and then accept God's gift to us through faithful and loving relationships with others and the whole of creation.

Liberation and reconciliation must occur in order for whole women and men to emerge. There is no proper ordering of liberation and reconciliation when the goal is transformation of the person and also the society and church in which she or he lives.

A nonreconciled people cannot be a liberating people if the goal is transformation. Similarly, a nonliberated people cannot be a reconciling people. When the goal is transformation, the oppressive structures of this society and our churches must be challenged if the event of freedom found in the midst of transformation is to lead us beyond the wounds of injustice. Working together, liberation and reconciliation, pointing toward the freedoms found in transformation, name the oppression of our lives and our institutions for what they are—sinful—and demand that we work with God for a new thing—the reign of God in all of life.

## Prescriptive Leanings

The prescriptive elements of a womanist ethic of justice must be as relentless in its analysis as it is inclusive in its recovery of history and sociopolitical analysis. A womanist ethic cannot be content with a justice that addresses only a particular person or group's wholeness. A womanist social ethic must embrace all segments of society if it is to be thorough and rigorous. We must continue to push ourselves into a critical dialogue that presses the boundaries of our humanness. Race, sex, and class analyses are crucial. Still, we need to challenge ageism (of both the young and the seasoned),

homophobia and heterosexism, the myriad of issues around acces-
sibility, our own color caste system, and the "Pandora's box" around
issues of beauty. The work we are about is not only eradicating an
unjust white social order that names us as less than; it is also about
the ways that we help that system find new ways to deem us children of a lesser God.[6]

Two voices emerge from womanist ethics: the pastoral and the
prophetic. Both are necessary and are complementary forces that
coalesce into a day-by-day ethic that serves both the mundane and
the extraordinary in our lives and in the witness and work of the
church.

## The Pastoral Voice

The pastoral voice[7] entails the ability to be self-critical, to provide
comfort, to accept others, and to encourage growth and change. The
pastoral voice, the voice of leadership in community, must always
be prepared to consider all of the information, the varying social
contexts that groups and individuals bring to bear, the various
means of social analysis. No one element in the world or in the society contains all of the truth—all of what faith-filled Christians
need in discerning God's will. Leadership in community will be ineffective if we do not accept the humanness of being human. We can
understand structures, but if the pastoral voice is poorly developed
or undeveloped, then we do not fully consider the need to care for
the people behind the institutions. We are not able to accept and recognize the diversity that can occur around any ministry of the
church.

Combining the prophetic with the pastoral is crucial, in my view.
Passion for a faithful witness must be deep and abiding. However,
it can be difficult to make our passion flesh if we are unable to accept the reality of human failing, human wavering, human ambiguity. It is imperative that a leader struggling for a faithful witness and
an ethic of justice hold in tension personal and social transformation. If we address only one form of transformation, the person seeking an ethical witness cannot be a full participant in community or
mobilize that community for ministry.

Developing a go-it-alone mentality in ministry and failing to work
effectively with other church leaders or church groups is all too
easy. We can be tempted to put forth our agenda and take unilateral
actions that destroy any notion of community and dialogue. Unilateral actions can hurt or anger others to the point that we become
marginalized and sometimes completely cut off from the decision-
making process. Perhaps a first reaction to this will be embitterment
rather than self-examination. However, self-examination is crucial

if one begins to suspect or recognize that one is caught in a pattern rather than an occasional misunderstanding.

There are times in ministry when we must be innovative-creative because that is the only way to express our concern for justice. As innovative-creative persons, we can perform the invaluable service of debunking myths and stereotypes about peoples and groups. We can be strong and passionate voices for justice, but we must temper this with life in community. If our moral standards are so rigid that we have no room for grace, then we fail to allow for human failings and weaknesses—even our own. Clinging to a fiercely high moral code of conduct for others and for ourselves can alienate people because of our attitudes of disdain and disapproval, rather than empowering people through our attitudes of justice and hope.

We must strive to understand that the personal side of transformation in which people are being changed and renewed requires an entirely different set of critical and analytical skills to effect a faithful witness. As agents for agitation seeking to bring in the new heaven and new earth, we can help others find their witness, their voice. Still, we must hold as precious the humanity of all people and the blessedness of creation. We must reach out to others with tenderness, concern, and grace, and never forget that the pastoral voice must also blend with the prophetic voice in a womanist ethic of justice and hope.

## The Prophetic Voice

Being innovative-creative also suggests the notion of a prophetic voice. Christian womanist ethics must take the Bible and the life and ministry of Jesus seriously. Passion for justice and ethical witness has within it a concern for right relationships among peoples. We must have a strong and willful prophetic voice in response to the injustices we see heaped on people and on the rest of creation. We must grow and cultivate a social analysis embedded deeply in our faith.

The Black Church (and much of Black theo-ethical thought) has its own peculiar form of patriarchal oppression. It reflects the same patriarchy as the society, but it is also imbued with the dynamics of racism of the dominant white society. Therefore, Black women must deal not only with the negative effects of racism, but with Black men's own virulent form of sexism as well.

There are no lasting shortcuts to curing the complexity of problems a womanist ethic of justice faces. It is better to take the long, hard, steady route in which a womanist ethic explores both the individual and the African-American community. The route is forged from the knowledge that womanist ethics not only seeks to understand white folk; it also needs to be in a dialogue for understanding and solidarity with the various tribes of Native Americans, the Hispanic cultures, and the Asian-American cultures. It must also carry on a search for understanding globally. As Marian Wright Edelman says so well, justice is neither cheap nor quick; it is a hard, ongoing process.[8]

A prophetic voice contains six key threads.[9] *The first is the desire and the ability to discern the will of God.* God is on the side of oppressed peoples. Therefore, the primary task of the Christian ethicist is to transform the present unjust structures into just ones. The measure of a just structure is found within these six key threads.

The search for justice must have both manifest and latent functions.[10] The manifest function, our conscious motivation, will vary according to contexts and conditions. There may be common ministry issues that we face—spiritual malaise, violence in the community, disagreements among those with whom we are in ministry, poor educational structures, and so on. However, how those issues take on a peculiar cast when placed within the varying contexts in which we do ministry is an important question. The structures and individuals behind the issues we face in ministry reveal the latent function of our work. A simple solution to violence and crime is to build more prisons and draft tougher laws. However, crime and violence are often the result of the impact of drugs in our communities—be they rural, suburban, or urban. We cannot settle for simplistic analyses.

The church, and we as its representatives, must work hard and long to discern God's will in the midst of injustice and hopelessness. The issues we face in ministry go much deeper than the surface and require us to develop the ability to move beneath the surface to the heart of the issues that people face today.

Transforming unjust structures into just ones is a colossal task. However, we can take comfort in scripture and be challenged by it. Many more of us live our lives as Esther than as Ruth. Yet both women are there for us in the biblical record to draw from for our own witnesses and ethical reflection. The tragedy of Sarah and Hagar leaps out to us as a call to examine the story-behind-the story in our social relationships and how we are to act in faithfulness.

Transforming unjust structures into just ones will not happen quickly, and this transformation may never happen within our lifetimes or within our ability to see into the future. However, each act we take to move ourselves away from the mayhem of evil is a step closer to transformation. I suggest that no act for justice is too small or too insignificant. It is tempting to conclude that we are acting faithfully only when we can see the tangible results from the work we do. Ethics is not so neat a discipline, and it is often far from the tangible. Ethical reflection and action are found in the mundane and the everyday. It is found as much, if not more, in the small acts we do each day in response to God's voice of love, compassion, and judgment in our lives. In the words of Shug to Celie in Alice Walker's novel *The Color Purple*, "it ain't a picture show."[11]

Second, in discerning the will of God, *the prophetic voice also exposes the oppressive nature of society*. The committed Christian must stand for justice and transformation. There are times when the only recourse open to us is resistance. Oppression uses many tools to repress our attempts to live faithfully in a world that often denies humanity. Obvious tools such as racism, sexism, classism, ageism, and ableism have caused many of the roads of oppression when such evil structures are named as greater goods. We live in a time when the small gains of affirmative action are increasingly disdained as repressive forces for those who no longer benefit from the overt tools of oppression and destruction. We live in a time when we are hearing much of the public discourse argue for a mythical "even playing field" where, if one works hard and long enough, her or his natural talents will bring them to the level of living and wholeness to which they aspire.

Myths are precious when they represent that which truly lives beyond our grasp and are a call for us to live into the new heaven and earth. Myths are deadly when they are grand narratives of progress that fail to mention the very unequal places we all begin from in life. As some of us inherit privilege, some of us inherit despair. Our tasks are to acknowledge where we begin and work to craft a church and a world that are not bending on faithful knees to economic gain and social status—even when these come in the forms of the ministry we do.

Third, *the prophetic voice must be an agent of admonition*—pointing out the wrongdoing in society and stressing the need to have human action (and inaction) conform to God's will. In dealing with the myths of injustices in our society, we must acknowledge that our drive toward unchecked progress and upward mobility is killing many of us and threatens the very fabric of creation. To sanction any form of oppression in the name of a false god such as progress is to turn away from the realities of the histories of how we have destroyed others so that a few might prosper.

Fourth, *a womanist ethic is unapologetically confrontive*. The root meaning of confront is "to face together." Implicit in this is a relationship between equals. There must be mutual respect for the dignity of others, a willingness to engage in dialogue, and an awareness and acceptance of diversity. If one thrives in a power dynamic that places one over and against rather than with, all prophetic voice is lost. We must learn to trust and respect the gifts God has given us to speak the truth and act through our faith. Black women need not apologize for naming injustice for what it is or for challenging the Black Church and the church universal to live into more of what it is called to be.

Fifth, *the prophetic voice seeks to create a community of faith, partnership, justice, and unity.* This speaks of the need to engage in a pastoral relationship as well as a prophetic one. To omit the very human need for affirmation, respect, and acknowledgment makes empty and incomplete any move to be prophetic. We must take seriously the promise of a just world and devote our lives to attaining that for all peoples.

This is why coalition building is crucial. Our partners are those folk committed to the struggle against oppression—those who understand the need to act and reflect and analyze. Few social problems, and certainly not the multitude of social problems that face the contemporary church and society, can be solved with a single strategy. Therefore, womanists, like the church and folk we love and critique, must move beyond ideological boxes and obtuse language.

Justice is beyond history. It is not limited to the realities and limitations of this world. The divine future breaks into the present with each thorny act of justice. The womanist agenda for justice recognizes and relies on the gospel message of justice, and not one crafted solely from human desires and idiosyncrasies.

Within the church and without, women and men are competing for life. This competition is a cruel wager on scarce resources in a hegemonic culture and social structure. Playing out this wager means settling for an imposed hierarchy in which only one gender's concern is addressed at a time. The result is a praxeological disaster and an endangered community. A community affirms the worth of the people who are in it and invites others to join it because it offers life and health. To set up a hierarchy of needs based on femaleness and maleness is shortsighted and discriminatory. This lives out the model of the white power structure and any version of Christianity that condones oppression.

If we are to model justice together, as female and male, then the descriptive and prescriptive elements of such a justice must be scrutinized with the utmost care. As womanists we must listen to our stories, our experience, before we try to shape the new creation. Such care-filled listening, construction, and reconstruction are mandatory in a rigorous praxis. A rigorous praxis is at the heart of a womanist ethic of justice. However, the tunes are not only sung by African-American women. Peoples of all colors have a word to say to us. Rather than commit the modernist sin of universal presumptions of knowledge and reason, womanist descriptive evaluation seeks to listen to the plethora of voices as we discover our own voice in the ring shout.[12]

This means that class analysis must be a part of our tool kit for justice. Such analysis cannot remain descriptive. It must critique and offer a new vision for African-American society and the Black Church. Until recently, with the work of Marcia Y. Riggs, the impact of the rise of the United States Black middle class in the 1870s has not been studied with precision by African-American people of faith.[13] Race analysis has so dominated inquiry and rhetoric that class and gender issues are assumed as mere appendages to justice. The incomplete praxis and inadequate reflection that have marked feminist theory and ethics is evident in Black theory and ethics as well.

Failure to analyze and strategize with class consciousness will doom all our efforts to mediocrity if not defeat. It is imperative that we begin to address the peculiar dynamics of a class within a class. African-American society has its distinctive features that cannot be explained by using the descriptions of hegemonic culture. Collapsing all African-American experience as the "Black experience" is the worst kind of modernist turn.

Finally, *self-critical inclusivity is mandatory*. The challenge of womanist ethical discourse and action is to guard against using the masters' tools to dismantle a supremacist house:[14] arrogance, universalism, progress, grand cultural narratives, renovation, domination, subordination. This challenge is done with the acute awareness that the cultural narratives and cues we learn from birth may tempt us to create new systems of domination and subordination. The task constantly remains for us to evaluate goals and standards in light of the gospel understanding of justice. This justice is dynamically revelatory—always within our grasp and just beyond it.

## Living Out the Call

As parish pastors approach the task of a womanist understanding of being an ethicist and a pastoral/prophetic voice in the congregation and the culture, we must work to understand where our gifts and liabilities are in our ministries. This is crucial, for the work of ethics and the demands of both the pastoral and the prophetic voices are significant, if not daunting. Harkening back to spiritual and social liberation can help us realize our limits. In doing so, we may well discover that we have moved beyond our limits, but we also see that we have not yet lived into our limits. The task of living out our call can help us uncover the realities and possibilities in our ministries.

Part of being an ethicist in pastoral ministry is opening the doors in the rooms of our lives and being willing to walk into them to discover the grace and hope and judgment that may be in each. This, at first glance, may be the last thing in the world we want to do in the midst of births and deaths and board meetings. However, if we develop the ability to assess and reassess our ministry, the direction in which it is going, and ask ourselves if this is the path of God or the path of ecclesiastical reward or human folly, we will find more energy and commitment to do the work that God would have us do. Key to the task of the ethicist is the ever-developing ability to analyze and critique the world we find ourselves in (and the worlds of which we are not a part).

Tools such as discovering how we understand and use liberation and reconciliation can move us into such an analysis. Perhaps one of the greatest gifts women in pastoral ministry can offer themselves and the church is the ability to ask the tough, yet faith-filled, questions about justice and righteousness and the church's response to the challenges of our time. For example, an easy solution is sought to the complexities of suicide or deaths by accidents. The ethicist in us can help people find a God who is large enough to take our rage, our confusion, our questions, and perhaps our unbelief, and continue to love us and hold us close in times of trial and confusion. The ethicist can work with youth groups when a friend or peer takes her or his life or if someone is killed in an automobile accident. So many of the youth I talk with in my own church resent an answer like "This was just the will of God" when they are faced with their own mortality and the loss of a friend in the same breath. What they yearn for, and what we can provide, is a person from a community of faith who hears their fears, their anger, and their confusion, and helps them walk through this time and, in the process, find a deeper, and often a richer, understanding of God working in their lives.

The pastor as ethicist can help these moves happen as we lean on both the pastoral and the prophetic voices in our ministry. For the pastor as ethicist in parish ministry needs to be both a comforter and an agent of hope. When a church is faced with the hard task of discerning the direction of its ministry, the parish ethicist can help set in motion a process (liberation) that leads the church through asking questions and seeking answers to those questions about its own gifts and abilities. This becomes crucial in our chaotic times. So often churches respond in an either/or manner to chaos—becoming insular and concerned only with the membership of the church or seeking to answer all the problems and providing all the solutions to those problems through its programming and worship services. The problem arises when neither response calls out the gifts and abilities of that church—or its pastor. Using the tools of a womanist ethicist, people in pastoral ministry (of all races and ethnic or class backgrounds or sexual orientation) can begin to set in place a structure for dialogue and discernment in the life of the church. This structure is important, because as a church seeks to discover and/or affirm its ministry, the members of the church may well feel vulnerable, uncertain, excited, and anxious. Often these emotions can come all at once from various individuals or within each individual. A clear structure that all can see and be confidently guided by can help the church and its pastor continue on the path of discernment and faithfulness.

There are also times in the church when there is a serious rending of the community's fabric. Such times come when there is a legacy of clergy sexual misconduct that the pastor inherits from a predecessor. They come when a husband who has a history of physical abuse with his wife and children kills or is killed by a member of his family. They come when a member of the congregation who is trusted and respected is discovered misappropriating funds either in the church or in her or his workplace. They come when a child reveals the sexual, emotional, and physical abuse he or she has endured. These times signal a soul-deep shredding of the "life" of a congregation and can become like deaths in the community. Such times call for the pastor as ethicist to call on our pastoral and prophetic voices as well. There is a human need present in which healing is crucial. There is also the opportunity to name social and individual sins in our midst, discover how they are interconnected, and invite a time of naming those sins out loud. We can discover how, as a community, we can walk through these times of death and mourn them in healthy and creative ways and vow to work faithfully to refuse to allow such injustices to go unnamed or unaddressed.

Key in all of this is that the parish pastor as ethicist learns that we cannot do this alone. It takes nurturing and prodding a community to take on its call. It also means that we must learn to lean on and truly trust God who is the Spirit and Hope in our lives. This is not always easy. Waiting on a community (which is not a passive activity) takes patience. In the waiting, the pastor must be working to cultivate and grow the community into a more faithful witness. No opportunity is too small—incidental conversations, counseling sessions, working with committees, celebrating the ordinances of the church, experiencing our leisure time.

However, the greatest work is what we must do within ourselves and in our relationships with God. The gifts of reconciliation are truly in evidence here. God's covenant with us is an ever-present and sustaining one. There are times when we will "know" this in ways that are too profound for words or human reason. It is in these times that our partnership with God will be unquestionable and our journey on the path God sets before us clear. These may be fleeting times, but as we allow God to work in us, they do come as blessing and as gift. There will also be times when God seems far off and the pathway unclear. These are times when spiritual disciplines such as prayer and fasting are imperative. Each of us must find her or his own spiritual pathway to God, but find it we must. It is in these times that God's covenant and our search for faithfulness will carry us home. It is from this objective realm that we can move into the subjective realm of reconciliation—and vice versa. For as we seek the restoration of harmony with others that is the work of the subjective realm, God's covenant with us may be seen anew.

This is the song of hope for which we must find the words, the meter, the key, and the notes. It is tempered with the high cost of living and also the knowledge of how precious is this journey.

## Conclusion

In her 1974 essay, Theressa Hoover states: "To be a woman, black and active in religious institutions in the American scene is to labor under triple jeopardy."[15] This state of affairs has not changed. In United States society, African-American women are at or near the bottom of the economic ladder. Women compose nearly 75 percent of the traditional Black Church, yet the higher levels of decision making do not reflect this statistic in proportionate numbers.

There are increasing numbers of African-American women in seminaries, the ordained ministry, and in the ranks of lay professionals. A growing body of literature and reflection is emerging from African-American women in academic theological circles on the nature of the Black Church and the church universal; the mission, identity, and scope of ministry; social and theological ethics; and biblical hermeneutics. Lay professionals and laywomen join in the chorus of resonant voices in articulating the experience and also the gifts of African-American women in the church.

A womanist ethic of justice provides rich resources for a church and a people seeking faithfulness. It models a witness that can be adapted for various racial ethnic contexts, genders, ages, and denominational identities. The voices of this ethic, pastoral and prophetic, are attempts to live life fully and faithfully in an age where we often struggle to see the next dawn. We must be about the business of promoting the full partnership of children, men, and women in creation with God. We search for the possibilities; we pray for the will to grasp them. In the process, we may well be outrageous, audacious, courageous, or willful in our behavior. We do yearn to know more and in greater depth than was considered good for us. We may actually be responsible, in charge, and serious. Nevertheless, we must always seek first God's vision and live our lives into that good tomorrow. This is our song of hope that leads us home, leads us home.

## NOTES

1. For a further discussion, see Marcia Y. Riggs, "The Logic of Interstructured Oppression: A Black Womanist Perspective," in *Redefining Sexual Ethics: A Sourcebook of Essays, Stories, and Poems*, eds. Susan E. Davies and Eleanor H. Haney (Cleveland: Pilgrim Press, 1991), 97–102; and her book *Awake, Arise, and Act: A Womanist Call for Black Liberation* (Cleveland: Pilgrim Press, 1994).

2. Katie Geneva Cannon, "Moral Wisdom in the Black Women's Literary Tradition," *Annual of the Society of Christian Ethics* (1984): 172.

3. Katie Geneva Cannon, *Black Womanist Ethics* (Atlanta: Scholars Press, 1988), 2.

4. Darlene Hine and Kate Wittenstin, "Female Slave Resistance: The Economics of Sex," in Filomena Chioma Steady, ed., *The Black Woman Cross-Culturally* (Cambridge, Mass.: Schenkman Publishing Co., Inc., 1981), 291.

5. W.E.B. Du Bois, *The Souls of Black Folk* (Greenwich, Conn.: Fawcett Books, 1961), 16–17.

6. Mark Medoff, *Children of a Lesser God* (New York: Dramatist Play Service, 1980).

7. This category of voice is an attempt to appeal to the African-American religious experience of the role of the pastor as comforter. Max Weber's classic essay "Politics as a Vocation" offers the categories of an ethic of ultimate ends and an ethic of responsibility. These are helpful categories in reframing the question of leadership. See Weber, "Politics as a Vocation," in *From Max Weber: Essays in Sociology*, ed. and trans. H. H. Gerth and C. Wright Mills (New York: Oxford University Press, 1946), 120–28.

8. Marian Wright Edelman, *Families in Peril: An Agenda for Social Change* (Cambridge: Harvard University Press, 1987), 106.

9. Jacquelyn Grant, "Tasks of a Prophetic Church," in *Detroit II Conference Papers*, eds. Cornel West, Caridad Guidote, and Margaret Coakley (Maryknoll, N.Y.: Orbis Books, Probe Edition, 1982), 137–38. Grant's essay points to a broader understanding of the prophetic church. I expand her original five categories to discuss the nature of a prophetic voice in ministry.

10. Robert K. Merton, *Social Theory and Social Structure* (New York: Free

Press, 1968), 105, 114–18. Merton defines manifest functions as "those objective consequences contributing to the adjustment or adaptation of the system which are intended and recognized by participants of the system." Latent functions are "those which are neither intended nor recognized."

11. Alice Walker, *The Color Purple* (New York: Washington Square Press, 1982), 176–77. This conversation is about the nature of God. Much of what the character Shug argues for about the way one brings God with them rather than waiting for him [sic] to show can also be said about the nature of faith-filled ethical reflection.

12. See my discussion of the ring shout in Emilie M. Townes, *Womanist Justice, Womanist Hope* (Atlanta: Scholars Press, 1993), 72. Also helpful are Albert Raboteau, *Slave Religion: The "Invisible Institution" in the Antebellum South* (New York: Oxford University Press, 1978), 62–71; and Sterling Stuckey, *Slave Culture: Nationalist Theory and the Foundations of Black America* (New York: Oxford University Press, 1987), 62–63.

13. Riggs, *Awake, Arise, and Act,* see esp. chaps. 1–3.

14. Audre Lorde, "The Masters' Tools Will Never Dismantle the Masters' House," in *Sister Outsider* (Trumansburg, N.Y.: Crossing Press, 1984), 110–13.

15. Theressa Hoover, "Black Women and the Churches: Triple Jeopardy," in *Black Theology: A Documentary History, 1966–1979,* eds. Gayraud S. Wilmore and James H. Cone (Maryknoll, N.Y.: Orbis Books, 1979), 377.

# 7

## MENTORING AS AN ART
## OF INTENTIONAL THRIVING TOGETHER

*Pamela Holliman*

> *My first step from the old white man was trees.*
> *Then air. Then birds. Then other people. But one*
> *day when I was sitting quiet and feeling like a*
> *motherless child, which I was, it come to me:*
> *that feeling of being part of everything, not sepa-*
> *rate at all. I knew if I cut a tree, my arm would*
> *bleed. And I laughed and I cried and I run all*
> *around the house. I knew just what it was. In*
> *fact, when it happen, you can't miss it.*

—*Alice Walker,* The Color Purple

Women have always mentored other women. Grandmothers, mothers, and aunts have mentored daughters in the ways of surviving as females. The most powerful ways were manifested in their day-to-day lives, modeling how to carry themselves, how to relate to men, and how to think and feel about themselves as women. Throughout much of history and in most cultures a woman's well-being depended on how well she learned those lessons. At the same time, women have paid a high price in depression, lower income, and as victims of violence. Survival for many women has not meant thriving.

Alice Walker, in her novel *The Color Purple*, created a powerful mentor in Shug Avery. Celie had learned difficult lessons in living; Shug Avery had learned to thrive. Shug invites Celie into a greater reality that encompasses hardship, but also celebrates the freedom and transcendence that is revealed and experienced in the ordinary. Shug mentors Celie in ways that begin to transform Celie's life. Shug's mentoring includes calling into question socially accepted ways of thinking about God. Once Shug is free from that "old white man," she begins to thrive. Shug understands Celie's despair; she also recognizes her struggle. Shug embraces both within the hope she lives and dares to share with Celie.

To mentor other women is to become increasingly conscious of cultural expectations and the limits placed on us, to hold with and for each other the pain and fear of risk, to create possibilities for growth and change, to celebrate the giftedness of each woman. Women in ministry today have many opportunities to mentor.

Women in significant numbers have entered ordained ministry in the last fifteen to twenty years. Many women who entered the profession did so in a climate of suspicion, if not outright hostility. Finding one's way in fulfilling one's call, exploring and claiming gifts and graces, could be both exhilarating and daunting. Learning to be a "minister" as a woman meant a new task with guidelines developed and demonstrated mainly by men. Women have, of necessity, been creating out of their experience guidelines and models of what it might mean to be a "woman in ordained ministry." Beyond survival issues that occupied much of a woman's time and energy in the early years of women's ordination, there is now a significant range of experience that women have to share—experience gained through increasing responsibility and accountability in positions of leadership in parishes, judicatories, related organizations, and differing ministries.

Taking an interest in the professional development of both women and men is crucial. The increased complexity of the tasks of ministry, the challenges of balancing roles and one's personal life, and the continually changing demands of the church community can be daunting to all who seek to serve in ministry. Although this chapter will focus on women and mentoring, the need for mentoring of men is increasingly apparent as we seek to build new models of community within the church.

This chapter discusses the role of mentoring as an *intentional* part of ministry. Opportunities are available in whatever setting a woman ministers. Claiming one's authority by valuing one's experience, knowledge, and skills is crucial to beginning to mentor. As this chapter will demonstrate, mentoring occurs in many ways. Often it is only on reflection that one realizes one has been mentored or has mentored someone else. Intentional mentoring means being alert to possibilities for mentoring. Intentional mentoring means affirming one's life in community. Intentional mentoring means taking responsibility for what God has revealed in one's life. Intentional mentoring means being accountable both to one's teachers and mentors as well as to those with different gifts and vision who follow. Intentional mentoring means caring deeply about ministry. Intentional mentoring means investing carefully in the well-being of women who minister.

## Definition of Mentoring

Mentoring is sharing one's wisdom with another. Wisdom is born of experience, knowledge, and skills combined uniquely in each person. It is self-conscious wisdom. That is, a mentor recognizes that wisdom becomes only wisdom as each person is able to appropriate it in ways that enhance her integrity. Mentoring involves the whole person, because mentoring at its core is a relationship between two persons. Although many other relationships may involve sharing one's wisdom, mentoring is usually a chosen, as opposed to an assigned, relationship.[1]

The focus of the relationship is on the development of an individual often in the context of other more formalized roles, such as student–advisor/teacher; parishioner–minister; supervisee–supervisor; group participant–group leader; younger friend–older friend. In addition to whatever formalized roles exist, the relationship may develop into a mentoring one. A person may perceive in a potential mentor admired characteristics, similar history, a particular vision, shared lifestyle, or specific abilities. A potential mentor may identify gifts, potential, and problems, or recognize familiar struggles in a student, colleague, friend, or parishioner. Intentional mentoring evolves as one person chooses to share her insights about her process of decision making; the why of her choices; the lessons from her mistakes; her "insider's" view of the profession; how she navigates the politics of congregation, faith group, or faculty; how she balances self, family, and job; and how she maintains her integrity and vision. The mentor also is intentional in providing opportunities for networking, opening doors and making introductions to key persons and committees, encouraging the development of the other's abilities through inclusion in programs, committees, and publications. The mentor's wisdom is apparent in both what she offers and how she offers herself. The mentor's wisdom is apparent in her primary emphasis on the development of the individual amid careful listening to the issues important to the other.

### Women and the Value of Mentoring

A search of the literature yields more on supervision and ministry than on mentoring per se. Supervision of women in ministry is a growing literature.[2] Mentoring of women in ministry is mentioned only in passing and then only in a few references.[3] The literature about women in business yields more emphasis on the importance of mentors for a woman's full participation in her career. Sally Helgesen's book *The Female Advantage: Women's Ways of Leadership,* for example, is a resource for mentoring women. She emphasizes the differences in women's and men's leadership/management styles.[4] Women stress relationships, process, networking, sharing information. Men tend to stress achievement, identify with their jobs, have difficulty sharing information, and focus on completion of tasks. Men emphasize vision. Women emphasize voice, finding their own and helping others express their voice.[5] Although both styles are successful ones, it is important for women to affirm their style. Helgesen's book does so by telling the stories of several successful women in corporations. Their day-to-day routine expresses their values and methods of leadership.

Belenky and her associates discuss the development of women as learners toward the goal of helping women become active participants in the world. They stress the importance of women trusting their gifts and abilities before they are willing to take on more complicated risks and challenges.[6] Jean Baker Miller and her colleagues at the Stone Center have stressed the greater capacity of women for relatedness, emotional closeness, and boundary flexibility.[7] Although these characteristics increase a woman's capacity for empathy, for caring for others, they can also make it difficult for a woman to attend to her own needs, to separate from destructive relationships, and to deal with transitions in life.[8]

Lynn Rhodes, writing about supervision in parish settings, outlines certain feminist implications for women in ministry. These provide guidelines not only for supervising women in ministry, but also for mentoring:

> Women need to learn to reflect theologically upon their own experience. They cannot rely upon the accepted theologies of the patriarchy.
>
> Women need to learn how to empower the least powerful people, so that mutuality may be practiced more fully. They need to learn how to be in solidarity with those who are different and whose voices are not being heard.
>
> Women need to learn how to co-create rituals that embody the visions of inclusion and women's experiences of the Holy.
>
> Women need to learn social analysis skills so that they can think strategically and contextually.
>
> Women need to learn how to make connections between personal experience and social realities so that the personal-as-political makes sense to people and so that our spirituality is not split into body-spirit, personal-political, or contemplative-active dichotomies.
>
> Women need to learn the economic realities of work in the United States and learn some skills in organizing the community around work issues. Sexism will not end until women have equality in the economic life of this society.

Women need to learn the art of working experimentally and experientially in community. Thus they need to learn not to avoid conflict, but know that it is part of the process that occurs in transformative communities. They will need the skills of working collaboratively through conflict.[9]

Mentoring provides a relationship in which a woman can experience support, affirmation, and challenge about her uniqueness and gifts. Mentoring is a relational space where a woman can critically examine her assumptions and those of the culture, and evaluate her choices, opportunities, and realistic limits.

### Talking to Women About Mentoring

Because the literature about mentoring women in ministry is quite limited, research for this chapter involved gathering seven women, including the author, for a three-hour recorded discussion of their experiences of being mentored and mentoring. The participants followed a list of prepared questions that form the substance of this chapter.

Each of the seven women represents a different faith group: Episcopal, Presbyterian (PCUSA, Presbyterian Church [USA]), Lutheran (ELCA, Evangelical Lutheran Church in America), Mennonite, Baptist (ABC, American Baptist Church), Roman Catholic, and United Methodist. The range in age is thirty-three to forty-eight. The experience in *ordained* ministry is from one to twenty-one years. The Roman Catholic woman had been in a religious order for twenty years until 1986 and is now in ministry as a pastoral counselor. The experience in ministry, nonordained or consecrated or ordained, ranges from nine to twenty-nine years, for an average of seventeen years each.

Participants had served in a wide variety of roles in ministry, including solo pastor, associate pastor, interim pastor, chaplain, missionary, campus minister, and Christian education director; three had been social workers before entering the ministry. At present, participants are active in ministry as pastoral counselors, solo pastor, associate pastor, and director of a religious nonprofit organization. In addition, all participants are serving in various capacities as leaders in their faith groups and professional associations.

All seven participants indicated they had been mentored by both women and men throughout their careers. Male mentors tended to be persons with whom participants had "formal," more traditionally hierarchical relationships: home church pastors, seminary professors, clinical pastoral education (CPE) supervisors, therapists. In addition, two women named their husbands, who had preceded them into ministry as mentors. Although female mentors included seminary professors, therapists, and pastoral counseling supervisors, they also included women whom they knew in less formalized relationships. Three women had been mentored by laywomen who had been active in their particular faith group. Women pastors were mentors to two women. Neither were parishioners of these women. All seven women had at one time or another participated in a women's group: a seminary, faith group, or professional caucus, a religious community, a support group, a study group, and/or a theological reflection group. Most identified this group as a central mentoring experience in their development in ministry. Participants talked about their women mentors by name more often than they did their male mentors.

## Types of Mentors

Given the diversity of settings in which mentoring occurred, it is important to make some distinctions about those settings and their relationship to mentoring. Participants agreed that some of the persons they named as mentors would probably be unaware of the influence each had. We might think of these mentors as *models*. Mentoring models included female women professors. The professors' interests and attitudes both inspired and helped participants articulate their experiences. Models also included women pastors who were influential in the early stages of a participant's entry into ministry by helping them to understand parish life. They were generally women who shared a similar life experience, such as attending seminary after having several children or ministering in a primarily male setting. There were also female and male supervisors who not only helped a participant develop gifts and skills, but also modeled how to be in the professional relationships of ministry. The influence of these models as mentors was apparent to participants mainly in retrospect when reflecting about their movement into ministry.

Persons became models as women identified with certain characteristics of teachers, supervisors, or pastors. Models provided ways for women to imagine themselves in particular roles, to claim authority, to negotiate demands, to manage responsibilities, and to be in ministry. They were proof that women could reach their goals, could contribute, and could survive. These models were also inspiring. They were mentors in their behavior, choices, and status. They shared their wisdom through the ways they lived their professional lives.

A second dimension of mentoring described by these participants involved a relationship with an individual around a specific event or experience that proved to be at a decisive point in the participant's life. We might call these experiences *mentoring moments*. One participant remembered an active laywoman who "opened doors for me" in the political structure of the diocese and attempted to bring lay and clergy women together for dialogue in the early days of women's ordination. Learning about the diocesan structure and being introduced to key persons and committees added immeasurably to this participant's visibility and to her opportunities for leadership. During a struggle for ordination in her faith group, one participant was affirmed by her male CPE supervisor: "You have the gifts for ministry and are called by those gifts." Another recalls her home pastor as being "forward thinking, supportive, and advocating" for me in ministry. One participant, taking a course on "Women's Ways of Preaching," felt her call to ministry confirmed further when narrative and story were emphasized as a typical style of preaching for women.

Common to these mentoring moments was an experienced person recognizing the possibilities by identifying gifts and providing opportunities for using those gifts. These can be significant points in empowering a woman to claim her abilities more fully. Each participant could identify moments when a timely and thoughtful intervention of support was formative for her development in ministry. These moments often occurred within the context of an ongoing relationship where a woman was exploring her interests and skills for ministry. The intervention combined the leader's sensitivity to the personal plus her or his experienced perspective of the profession. Wisdom in these instances was the leader's capacity to imagine the uniqueness of another within the requirements and needs of the profession at a particularly vulnerable or significant time.

Several participants described an ongoing relationship with another person that, among other foci, also served a mentoring purpose. These relationships are more clearly *mentoring relationships*. In two instances women had been mentored by their husbands who were already in ministry. Both husbands were in ministry in settings that paralleled the work or interests of their wives. Mentoring occurred as consultation, support, and information from the perspective of experience. Two women indicated they had experienced mentoring within the context of a therapeutic or counseling relationship with another woman. Both of these women sought counseling at a crucial turning point in their lives: one, after a divorce, and the other, while working as a lone woman in a male academic setting. Both were evaluating their futures in relation to beginning or continuing ministry. Mentoring in the therapeutic setting was a combination of support to claim self more fully and to risk change to follow a perceived call to ministry.

One participant described a mentoring relationship with a graduate school male professor, who in addition to being a teacher and adviser spent time discussing options, opportunities, and pitfalls inherent in her chosen field of ministry. Mentoring involved the emphasis on the life of the professional as well as the skills and knowledge required. Another participant told an unusual story about finding a mentor. Needing housing for a summer CPE unit, a friend gave her the name of a woman pastor in the town where she was going for the summer. She ended up staying with this clergywoman that summer and the next. Over the two years a mentoring relationship developed as the clergywoman introduced her to other women pastors in the area, got her involved in programming and in synod activities, and was a model in parish ministry. Her mentor took a personal interest in someone she did not know, opened her home and her professional life, and enabled another woman to learn and grow in her knowledge, skills, and personal experience of ministry.

These relationships with mentors were complex and evoked more from each person in the relationship. There was intentionality over time, focus on goals, a willingness by both persons to reveal their lives in some depth and breadth, and a primacy on the developing person in ministry. Each of the above relationships existed at least two years, and most continue in the present. The therapeutic relationships were time limited but were of sufficient length to include an awareness by the clients of the therapist's investment of self in the process. In the relationships with their husbands, the women trusted their spouses' capacity to focus on them as they explored issues and concerns. There was an investment by each mentor in the other person's growth and development apart from the many other concerns each mentor might bring to the relationship. As one woman said, "She spoke the truth, and she let me speak the truth."

All seven women had participated in a group composed of women committed to ministry. The timing of each woman's participation in a women's group was decisive as to how strongly each felt about the group's mentoring her development in ministry. For those women entering seminary in the 1970s a seminary women's caucus or similar group was a formative and validating experience. The groups served various functions for women: support, political advocacy, study, theological reflection, social connections, and most important, a safe space to explore and reflect about being a woman in ministry. These groups were often creative places for strategizing for more women faculty; developing liturgies with inclusive images; consulting about being the "first" woman in a field education placement, the "first" woman ordained in a particular faith group, the "first" woman clergy in a town, the "first" woman to apply for a graduate program, the "first" woman to . . . Women quickly established patterns with and for each other, based initially on negotiating the various obstacles each faced, the strong call to be in ministry, and the experience of each other's gifts and limits. Women mentored each other as they gained wisdom. Women experienced an exhilarating confidence in their quest, while at the same time looking to each other for a developing shared wisdom about being women in ministry.

By the 1980s, networks had developed with women faculty, for women who had graduated and were serving in ministry, and for women in faith groups at regional and national levels. Despite the growth in the numbers of women clergy, and depending on the particular faith group, women entering seminary in the 1980s had varying levels of success in finding other women to share experiences. Two women initially attended seminaries where there were fewer than five women students and no women faculty. Both eventually finished at seminaries where there were both women faculty and more women students. The results of this change included increased connection with women and opportunity for group mentoring. Most important, however, was a reduction in the time and energy they gave to defending their call and at times their personhood. They no longer had continually to translate issues from a male perspective to a more female perspective.

Another woman entered a seminary in the 80s that had both women faculty and a large group of women students. It was only after she entered her first parish that she really understood at an emotional level her difference as a woman in ministry. Serving in an area where she was the only clergywoman, she quickly realized how she had taken the support and mentoring of women at the seminary for granted. She states, "I didn't realize how different I was until [I found] the parish norm wasn't to be connected with other women." She began to seek ways to meet with other women clergy. The woman who left a Roman Catholic order was alone for the first time in her professional life in ministry in a setting populated predominantly by men. She lost the group that had embraced a strong mentoring milieu. Her connections with women became more one-to-one as opposed to being in a group setting.

Each of the participants had sought to join a group of women whenever she moved into a new setting in ministry. It was usually

easier to make connection with another group if she entered a training or study setting to develop her skills or increase her education.
These groups usually included mentoring related particularly to
how to enter the larger arena of a training program, school, or specific area of ministry. Groups outside these educational settings provided support and consultation, but participants experienced mentoring less in these groups. Mentoring, most participants agreed,
was much more difficult to find if one was not a student.

Participants agreed that finding an individual mentor was particularly difficult after school or training. This conclusion identifies a
continuing desire and felt need to be with and learn from others
with more and different experience. Regardless of their years in
ministry, participants agreed that they continued to struggle with
direction, choices, and vision for their ministry. Each recognized
that she would value the opportunity to meet regularly with another
woman who might provide mentoring at this stage in her career in
ministry. Many women continue to serve in isolation, to have moments of great uncertainty about themselves in ministry, to be un-
sure of their options, and to lack the support of other women. The
relationship of mentoring is one possibility for reaching out to one
another in ministry.

## Characteristics of Mentors

Whether via models, moments, relationships, or groups, a mentor possesses these characteristics: she is more seasoned, relates
collegially, helps the other to name and claim her gifts, recognizes
the potential of the other within her uniqueness, is competent, is
actively supportive, cares about the individual and the future of the
profession, and is connected with others professionally. Participants agreed that a woman chooses a mentor based on particular
needs at particular times in her life. A woman identifies in the
other a similar interest, a particular attitude or belief, a specific
style of relating, a common lifestyle, or sees a woman doing what
she hopes to do. By identifying with the other, a woman expects
that her model will understand in some ways the issues she is
struggling with in her life. As one participant noted, "I was looking
for women who were both feminine and competent . . . not being
a female in male garb." Another said, "I could begin to imagine doing ministry in the parish the way she was ministering." One participant said, "I valued the ways he related to others and main-
tained his integrity." Group experiences provided opportunities
for women to struggle together with similar concerns, as well as to
practice with each other, risking themselves in new settings and

experiences. A summary of many participants' feelings might be: "The women's group meant I wasn't alone. We were together in a shared commitment."

As the participants discussed what they had received from the mentoring process, they realized several common results. These results were based in the important capacities that mentors brought to the relationship by way of shared characteristics. Mentors were able to create a secure space for the mentoring relationship to develop. They consistently named and affirmed specific gifts of participants in ways that enabled them to claim their talents more fully. Mentors were strong advocates as they guided participants in the practical and political realities of ministry.

Participants spoke of their experiences of being mentored as "supportive," "a refuge," "protection to experiment with images and ideas." Feeling secure with others to risk, to practice, to "try on" new ways of using one's abilities, to raise uncomfortable or "dumb" questions, confirmed the presence of a possible mentoring situation. As a relationship developed with a mentor, a woman found she could increasingly count on the other to understand, to bring insight, to be fully present to her concerns. There was opportunity to explore her growth in ministry in a safe place.

Mentors affirmed the gifts a woman has in ways that encouraged her to use those gifts and to begin to trust herself in different ways. One participant noted, "She [a seminary professor] was the first person to point out to me how 'alive' I became when I presented in class." Mentors often confirmed intuitive insights that women had been unable to articulate. One woman said, "He integrated theology and psychology in ways that made sense to me and fit my experience." Another said, "My mentor called me beyond myself to see possibilities I didn't know existed." One woman, having lost her base in ministry and questioning her direction, used her work with a mentor to reclaim her gifts in liturgy and retreat work.

Mentors were advocates. They "opened doors" to denominational involvement, to opportunities to develop and present programs in different settings, and to networks. They took women to professional gatherings, made key introductions, explained formal and informal political processes, encouraged participation in activities where participants would meet others who shared their interests, concerns, or lifestyle, and consistently related in ways that demonstrated to others that the mentors saw them as colleagues. One participant coauthored a book with her mentor. Early in her career another became very active in regional denominational activities because of the advocacy of her mentor.

## Process of Mentoring

As a result of our discussion, we began to articulate a process of mentoring as experienced by the person mentored. Our tentative schema included four stages. The initial stage is one of *idealization*. Each woman could recognize that she had chosen a mentor at a time when she was feeling particularly vulnerable. This vulnerability was precipitated by being a student or trainee, after a loss, during a transition, in a new setting, or in exploring options. She was excited and anxious about her present and future, as well as feeling more dependent. She was also encountering tremendous obstacles toward her new goals. She was beginning to take increased initiative to deal with these challenges. Identifying a mentor involved finding someone who had "done it," or in the case of a group, were working together to "do it." This person or group became a secure anchor, a sounding board, and was seen with an idealized hope that she/he/they would know "what to do" regardless of the circumstances, or at least in most circumstances.

This idealization has at least two important functions. The first is to allow the woman the opportunity to see the mentor in ways that she needs to see him or her. In other words, through idealization a person sees only what she wants to see, and in the case of a mentor what is seen is very positive. To be able to imagine identifying with another's words, actions, or choices enables the person to compare her life and to affirm her similarities. Idealization leads to identification with the other. Idealization also creates the expectation of being safe, of being known in ways that are protective—the expectation that the other will relate in ways that one needs and wants and in ways that respect who one is. Idealization establishes the possibility that one will be safe to be oneself with this person.

Idealization leads eventually to some experience of *disillusionment*. As one woman expressed it, "One day you find out your mentor has clay feet." Disillusionment is inevitable. How the disillusionment is experienced and dealt with in the relationship determines the eventual outcome of this stage. Disillusionment is also necessary if the one mentored is to integrate the wisdom experienced with the mentor. Disillusionment is always painful and can be quite confusing and disappointing. Mentors do not always have the answers, they are not always patient, they make mistakes, and they disappoint. The experience of disillusionment can begin with rather innocuous events. One woman recalled excitedly telling her mentor about reading most of the works of a particular and, to her, very important theologian over the summer. She was eager to hear her mentor's thoughts about this theologian's work. Her mentor had never read him. Another remembered her disappointment when observing her mentor in a setting where she was flustered and not particularly articulate. Disillusionment also occurs as the one mentored begins to develop areas of expertise or interest that the mentor cannot or does not share. The disillusionment coalesces as the one mentored realizes that she is different in some particularly stark ways from her mentor. She may then make choices that the mentor may not understand or affirm. Even with the blessing of the mentor, she realizes she has moved into new territory that is uniquely hers. She may experience a mentor increasingly seeking her view on a project, idea, or problem.

Successfully resolving disillusionment issues results in increased differentiation. This stage of *differentiation* is a period of integration, growth, and mourning. Moving away from the mentor is most significant emotionally. The individual relates to the mentor in a different way, with more distance. The individual has taken what the mentor offered and integrated the experience. The mentor's wisdom has been formative in the individual's development of a new sense of self, that is, a professional identity. For both persons there is a sense of loss within the change. The mentoring relationship is forever changed. The individual may realize she knows more in certain areas, or has developed a skill beyond her mentor's ability, or has taken a different stance toward issues once shared in common. The mentor experiences a loss of direct influence and affirms the changes and accomplishments of the one mentored. In some cases the distance becomes a permanent one, with continued contact greatly limited or nonexistent.

Most women in our group continue to have contact with past mentors. They experience their relationship now as peers. Moving to *peership* is a gradual process usually marked by a period of transition. The person mentored graduates, or assumes a different role in ministry, or moves out of the area. For the one mentored it is a time of integration, practice, and continued growth professionally and personally. Continued contact with a mentor is most often initiated by the one who was mentored. To move to peership requires the mentor now to be able to value the uniqueness of the other as resource. It is important that the one mentored be able both to appreciate what she has learned as well as be able to claim realistically her development as an individual. Although a mentor may continue to have more knowledge or skill and experience in certain areas, the person who was mentored now experiences herself in a mutually collegial relationship. Both persons may consult each other. Continued contact seems to be determined by whether both continue to share a professional setting or similar professional responsibilities. Persons who are married to their mentors find their unique gifts valued by their partners. Several women reported that they consider their former mentors as mutual "allies."

Mentoring to peership can be an immensely satisfying experience for both persons. Participating in the development of another's professional growth is a contribution to the future; it is also a source of joy in the richness of the gifts of a colleague. Being mentored is to be privileged to receive the investment and interest of another person, to experience the trust and confidence of one who has struggled with similar issues and concerns, and to not feel so alone in becoming a woman in ministry.

## Mentoring, Supervision, and Therapy

It is important at this point to make some comparisons between mentoring and supervision and between mentoring and therapy. Most women in ministry have been in supervised ministry settings: field education, clinical pastoral education, a probationary period during the ordination process, clinical supervision, as well as supervision from academic advisers, senior pastors, or faith group administrators. Many women have also entered a therapeutic relationship. The process of idealization, disillusionment, differentiation, and possible peership evident in mentoring can also be similar in the process of supervision and in therapy. And, as is obvious from this small group of women, supervisors and therapists can also be experienced as mentors. Supervision in ministry settings also combines an emphasis on the development of professional identity and usually includes focus on knowledge, skills, and the person of the supervisee. Therapy attends primarily to personal growth and resolution of recurring patterns in one's life. All of these aspects are interrelated; problems or changes in one area affect all the others to some degree.

Supervisors and therapists generally possess more experience, a broader knowledge base, and a wider perspective on ministry or psychological development than does the supervisee or therapy client. As with mentoring, these attributes indicate an initial "temporary inequality" or initial hierarchical relationship. Jean Baker Miller defines this temporary inequality as necessary in some relationships where the purpose is to impart particular qualities, knowledge, or perspective to another, but the relationship of inequality is to be temporary. The goal is full parity where the relationship may continue.[10] It is particularly the goal of mentoring that a relationship of collegial mutuality develops. Mentoring, supervision, and therapy can be crucial in a woman's professional and personal development and functioning in ministry.

There are several characteristics of mentoring that distinguish it from supervision. Almost all supervision involves the exchange of money or the earning of grades and an assessment and evaluation. The supervisee must usually apply for a position in which supervision occurs. Interviews, written applications, formal contracts are expected. Supervision is usually time limited based on the structure of an institution, such as an academic period or training year. Supervisors are usually accountable to a system or institution, such as a school or professional association, as well as to peers within the system. The supervision relationship exists within a specified larger context to which both supervisor and supervisee are responsible and accountable. Certain parameters of the relationship are dictated by the requirements of the system. Both persons are evaluated on their performance within those parameters. These characteristics of supervision generally are not part of a mentor relationship.

There are other more subtle distinctions between mentoring and supervision. Although both are hierarchical relationships, the nature of the hierarchical relationship differs. The hierarchy in the supervisor-supervisee relationship is based in the institutional system in which it functions. The hierarchical relationship of mentoring is based in the experience of the mentor, acknowledged by both persons as the basis of the relationship. Further, although a person may have some choice in a supervisor in some settings, a person almost always chooses a mentor and in some cases initiates formally contracting for that purpose. A mentoring relationship begins, even within the hierarchy of differing experience, with an emphasis on collegiality by virtue of its independence from systemic requirements.

There are, of course, differences between therapy and mentoring. Therapy, like supervision, includes payment for services, usually an evaluation or assessment period, and a larger system to which the therapist is responsible, such as state licensing or a certifying body. A primary distinction is the therapeutic goal of the psychological or emotional growth or change of the client. This priority determines the nature of the relationship based on the therapist's theory of development and change. Feminist therapy particularly stresses social and cultural context and its effect on a woman's identity, growth, and development.[11] As a therapist validates the reality of a woman and helps her to claim more of her abilities through trust in herself, there may be a mentoring aspect, though this is not the primary focus. Likewise, both supervisors and therapists as models of competent women serve a mentoring function for many women.

The focus of supervision is on task primarily. Depending on the setting of supervised ministry, more or less emphasis is given to the person of the supervisee as central to how the task is understood, learned, and conducted. The focus of mentoring is primarily the person who is mentored. Tasks, skills, and knowledge are concerns within the context of the functioning of the whole person in ministry. Who a person is and how she functions is as important or more so than what she does. The mentor can be more self-revealing about more aspects of her or his experience, for the emphasis is on how the mentor came to be who she or he is in ministry. Although both supervision and mentoring help a person enter a profession, a supervisor does so primarily through education and skill development; the mentor, primarily through hospitality.

## Mentoring Other Women

Participants discussed not only their experiences of being mentored, but also their experiences of mentoring. All but one person in the group indicated that they had mentored others. Their experiences varied, with most recognizing occasions when they had served as models for other women or had experienced a mentoring moment with a woman. Two women in the group realized on reflection that they each had been important mentors for another woman. One woman had recently established an intentional contract for mentoring another.

Most who had served in the parish realized that there were women who looked to them as models in ministry, as well as models about what it means to be a woman who has authority and leadership responsibilities. They felt they were a part of the process of helping other women "get their voice." They were aware of their influence on other women by virtue of the role in ministry they held. Yet they could still be surprised to hear from a parishioner how their word or an action or decision was a defining moment for another woman. All also related how important women in their parishes were to their development as pastors.

One woman realized that she had been serving as a mentor to students she had taught in junior high school. Several students continue to call or write to her at transition times in their lives. She remains a source of wisdom for these students.

Two women had been significant mentors in different settings of ministry. One woman did not realize how significant her relationship was to another woman until several years later. She had been a parishioner in the local church where this woman was a parishioner. She encouraged the woman's gifts and introduced her to regional denominational activities. Later, the woman who had served as mentor was invited to preach at her former parishioner's ordination.

A second woman was asked to mentor a woman new to parish

ministry. They served in two different parishes. When the senior pastor at one parish resigned abruptly, the new associate was suddenly left with responsibility for the parish. The two women established a contract for meeting regularly, at which time the woman being mentored would bring a "critical incident" from her parish to discuss. The mentor felt much freedom in her role because the two women worked in different parishes. The mentor could focus on the other woman free from the constraints of balancing the competing roles as leader of a particular parish and mentor of a staff member. The woman being mentored was in fact older than her mentor. The two have developed a peer relationship over the years. This relationship mixed supervision and mentoring. The emphasis was on mentoring, and the mentor had no direct responsibility for how the other performed in ministry.

The third woman has a contract with a younger woman for mentoring as she enters the specialized ministry of pastoral counseling. The student approached the older woman to discuss her struggles as a woman in ministry. The student asked questions about the other's journey in ministry, how she negotiated her commitment to feminism and women with the demands and limits of the church. After two or three such discussions, the older woman suggested they clarify their relationship as a mentoring one. To do so meant contracting about the limits and boundaries of the relationship. For instance, given the emphasis on mentoring, they have agreed that they will not establish a supervisory relationship in order to avoid a formal evaluation focus. The content of their discussions centers mainly on sorting out the student's concerns related to the profession and clarifying opportunities for growth and involvement with other women in the field.

Although all of the women had been mentored by both women and men, they were more intentional about being mentors to other women. At least one in the group indicated she had made the decision several years ago to mentor only women. Mentoring men meant less time and energy to invest in women. United States society remains largely a sexist, racist, and patriarchal culture. The church continues to be dominated primarily by white males, particularly in terms of power and core values. Women in many arenas are still expected to adopt the patterns of the dominant gender, class, or race. Becoming aware of internalized sexism, racism, homophobia, and classism is a tedious, difficult task that one can rarely do without the assistance of others. Feminism's emphasis on the personal as political is a central tenet in the necessity for women to find competent, savvy mentors. Women's individual identities and futures are inextricably tied to the fate of others and of the physical earth. Understanding the interdependence of persons and social and governmental structures is crucial to empowering women and affirming the differences that women bring to the political and social arenas. Regardless of women's experience, competence, and expertise, they continue to need each other to remain clear in the midst of oppression and devaluation of the feminine and of women's journeys and gifts.

Particularly in the church, women bring insights and images of God's work in this world. As in the larger world, the church most often is entrenched in preserving the power and prestige of authority and tradition. To counter this, to even test out other possibilities, ideas, and theologies based on differing experiences is perceived as threatening the core of faith and the authority of the church.[12] Women's capacity to sustain and nurture different visions incarnate in the lives of women makes necessary our willingness to invest in each other's development, to call each other to accountability and responsibility, to challenge each other to hear and trust our own voices.

## Cautions and Concerns

Discussion of being mentors elicited cautions and concerns related to mentoring. Each person was aware of the seductive nature of someone choosing her as a mentor. It is tempting to focus more on attempting to help the other woman develop in ways the mentor thinks important and less on hearing the other's concerns and valuing her uniqueness. Thus it is primarily the mentor's responsibility to be alert to and to manage the idealization of the one mentored. Although one may be greatly admired by another, one does not have to participate either in accepting the admiration or going out of one's way to deflect the idealization. The goal is to establish parameters that encourage the person being mentored to test out her assumptions about the mentor as she questions and evaluates her concerns and issues. Thus, for example, it is important to be able to discuss one's limits, what one does not know, and one's mistakes. The emphasis is on the reality of one's humanness within the context of valuing one's limits and learning from one's mistakes. What one does not know can be an opportunity of empowerment for the woman mentored. There is an opportunity to learn together, or for the mentor to be taught by the other woman.

Each person was aware of mentors who developed followers instead of participating in the other's process of differentiation. When these mentors leave, their followers are often devastated and plunged into disillusionment. It is tempting for the mentor, from a position of more experience and advanced skills and knowledge, to believe she can direct a person's life better than the one mentored. It is always easier to imagine how to improve another's life. Tolerating, even encouraging, difference between the one who mentors and the one who is mentored is key to managing our tendencies to direct another. Those mentored can be reluctant to express difference and deal with the normal disillusionment with the other and the threatened loss of connection. For women this can be particularly difficult to resolve. Valuing difference within a close relationship such as mentoring can provide needed support for women both to affirm their uniqueness and to experience the other's continuing in relationship with them. Valuing difference in relationship also conveys to the other that the mentor has something to learn from the experiences of the other. The mentor, as well as the one mentored, can be changed in this relationship.

A third caution involves boundaries. The mentor is responsible for maintaining appropriate boundaries. Mentoring lacks the accountability structures inherent in supervision and therapy, making the mentoring relationship a particularly vulnerable one. Thus it is especially important that a mentor take responsibility for maintaining appropriate boundaries. The group tended to agree that one is likely to cross boundaries when one is feeling the most needy and/or vulnerable. Boundary violations include depending on the mentoring relationship to meet one's own support needs. Evidence of this is when the mentor is so caught up in her struggles with the institution or her personal problems that they dominate and color her discussions with the woman she is mentoring. A more subtle boundary crossing results from the mentor's needs to be admired and to be experienced as special by someone else. The mentor finds herself preoccupied with the other person or initiates more appointments than the other is requesting. A mentor from her own emotional needs can "get ahead" of the other person by pushing resources, activities, and other people before the one being mentored indicates interest or readiness. A mentor can take advantage of another's dependency needs by placing herself as the final arbiter of all decisions made by the other. Finally, sexual boundaries can be crossed when the mentor is not clear about the imbalance of power in this relationship. Clear boundaries provide safety and predictability and promote a developing mutuality.

A final concern involves the importance of mentors finding other women to consult with about their formal and informal mentoring. Several women spoke of getting into relationships that initially seemed to be straightforward requests from women for help in sorting out issues related to ministry, which over time became very complicated. Managing the expectations inherent in the idealization and dealing with the disappointment in disillusionment can be confusing and wearing. Sometimes individuals are unable to reflect on their effect on others, are unable to modify their expectations in the face of reality, or are unable to accept difference and find ways to stay connected with another. Other individuals may be using the relationship to work out patterns that are difficult in all their relationships. Moving to differentiation with any of these issues is extremely difficult and makes mentoring particularly stressful. Thus it is important for mentors to have other peers and colleagues to review their mentoring relationships in a confidential setting. Sometimes a mentoring relationship must be ended.

Despite these cautions, participants enthusiastically supported the need for mentoring of women in contemporary ministry. At the same time, they admitted to a reluctance to claim ourselves as mentors intentionally. They realized that each of them continues to struggle with how they are doing, putting together their lives in response to the demands of family, work, and professional obligations. Having a group structure to mentor each other was key to their willingness to consider raising their awareness of opportunities to mentor others. As they age personally and professionally in ministry, they realize again that they are entering territory where few women have explored. To survive with health and energy, they must find ways to again mentor each other.

## Theological Commitments and Implications

Our enthusiasm and motivation for mentoring was grounded in a deep commitment to women and to the church. The primary theme permeating both commitments is the necessity of community for the survival, growth, and well-being of individuals. Participants were aware that they are part of a larger community to which they have responsibility by virtue of their involvement in ministry. One part of that community is other women, lay and clergy. One participant noted that her interest in mentoring is based on "the high priority not to treat other women the way I was treated by some women when I was ordained." Reaching out to other women in ways that are supportive, rather than competitive or suspicious, builds communities that are nurturing for all of us. Building community also means being available to women entering ministry. One pastoral counselor said she made a decision to respond readily and with extra time if necessary to women inquiring about ministry in pastoral care and counseling. Another said she participates in her denomination's women's group, "not only for myself, but to be present with my sisters."

Mentoring women in the church is a means, a participant said, "to regenerate the spirit of the church . . . so ministry isn't embodied in one person or one kind of role." Mentoring can be "an invitation to community," where people "have permission to become more fully themselves in God" instead of "becoming like someone else." The community of the church can be a place where persons hold faith for each other, continue to believe for each other when some cannot believe. Mentoring plays a role in developing this type of community by acknowledging the interdependence of persons in working out salvation. All persons within that community are vital to the salvation of each person. Mentoring can provide a relationship with women that both *is church to them* and empowers them to *be church with others.*

A second theological theme that emerged was a prophetic one, both for women and for the church. Mentoring is prophetic for a woman when she is heard and seen by another in ways that call forth gifts, creativity, and potential that she has not known or valued. Working with each other to free ourselves from expectations about how one is supposed to be, how things have always been done, and what one is allowed to do is a prophetic work. Discerning with each other where God is in our questioning, our visions, our call, our doubts is a prophetic activity. Consistent in participants' stories of being mentored was the power of being freed from seeing ourselves in light of limiting and often oppressive expectations. Telling our stories to others is to bear witness to the presence of God who is continually holding the promise of transformation and renewal.

Mentoring is prophetic in relation to the church. Mentoring women in ministry is, according to one participant, "the breaking open of the word that brings a new day." The word is broken open "in action and word, in a prophetic voice." Diversity within the community of the church challenges people to experience traditional expectations in different ways. As one woman related, "Things in our clergy district changed significantly when there were five women in our group. We came to be who we were. We came and talked about who we were. We modeled something new." Another said, "We are yeast rising, overflowing, infiltrating the system." Mentoring emphasizes the uniqueness of the individual, that which only that person can live in a particular manner. Mentoring women in ministry is an opportunity for women to claim more of who God is calling them to be; it can also provide the support to understand the risk inherent in living that call.

## Developing Mentor Relationships

Mentoring opportunities are many. Most important is the welcoming of women. Simply noting the entry of new women into a judicatory, a professional meeting, the church down the block, and introducing oneself is a beginning. Helping new, or younger, or less experienced women meet other women by inviting several women to an informal lunch or dinner, just to get acquainted and talk about themselves is also a part of the hospitality of mentoring. Seeking out women to work with them to understand the particular politics or system of the region or committee or town can be a central aspect of mentoring as can being alert to women struggling to fit in, to figure out what is going on. Mentoring means finding ways to give visibility to a woman's interests, talents, and ideas: inviting her to a group, recommending her to others, asking her advice or counsel.

Finding a mentor means evaluating what one's needs are. What are the particular struggles, issues, growing edges at this time in one's life, at this point in one's career? Finding women who are doing similar work and may have expertise in a particular area can lead to a relationship for consultation and mentoring. Most women would probably find it helpful to have someone with whom they could regularly discuss issues related to their work and its impact on their lives. Most people respond to requests for help positively and appreciate being seen as someone who has something to offer another.

Mentoring is hospitality. Mentoring is welcoming. Mentoring is sharing one's experienced wisdom. Mentoring is investing in another's journey—journeying with another for a period of time. Mentoring is helping to "launch another woman beyond where I am. . . . Their launching carries a part of me into the future." Mentoring is the power of naming. One participant told of observing another woman during a committee meeting dominated by men in numbers and by talking. As the meeting progressed, she sank further and further in her chair, looking confused and lost. After the meeting they talked, "I told her what it was like for me the first few times I attended. I would make a suggestion that would be ignored. Later, a man would make the same suggestion and he would be heard. I began to share with her what I had learned about the "rules" of the group. She was relieved, and we agreed that our similar experiences had left us feeling dumb and crazy. Later we strategized ways to change those rules."

Women can have a vision of community that includes both support and risk, nurture and confrontation, tradition and prophecy, solidarity and diversity. The church remains an institution as well as a community. Women's wisdom *as women* is a crucial and needed resource to break open with each other. Mentoring is both a call and a challenge to establish relationships with other woman where that resource can be revealed.

## NOTES

1. A notable exception is in clinical training where mentors are often assigned to students and to candidates for clinical certification.

2. Lynn Rhodes, "Supervision of Women in Parish Contexts," *Journal of Supervision and Training in Ministry* 10 (1988): 198–207. Robert Cotton Fite, "Ethical Dimensions of Gender Issues in Supervision," *Journal of Supervision and Training in Ministry* 12 (1990): 145–52; also in the same volume, Karen Lebacqz and Ronald G. Barton, "Power, Intimacy, and Supervision," 162–69. Francis C. McWilliams, " 'I Found God in Myself and I Loved Her Fiercely': Women's Identity and CPE Supervision," *Journal of Supervision and Training in Ministry* 13 (1991): 99–112. Denise Haines, "The Power to Lead: Forming Women for Public Ministry," *Journal of Supervision and Training in Ministry* 15 (1994): 190–99. Eugene Robinson and Miriam Needham, "Racial and Gender Myths as Key Factors in Pastoral Supervision," *Journal of Pastoral Care* 45 (Winter 1991): 333–42.

3. See above, Lebacqz and Barton, "Power, Intimacy, and Supervision"; and Haines, "The Power to Lead."

4. Sally Helgesen, *The Female Advantage: Women's Ways of Leadership* (New York: Doubleday, 1990).

5. *Ibid.*, 5–40.

6. Mary Field Belenky, Blythe McVicker Clinchy, Nancy Rule Goldberger, and Jill Mattuck Tarule, *Women's Ways of Knowing: The Development of Self, Voice, and Mind* (New York: Basic Books, 1986).

7. Jean Baker Miller, *Toward a New Psychology of Women* (Boston: Beacon Press, 1986).

8. Janet L. Surrey, "The Relational Self: Clinical Implications," in *Work in Progress* (Wellesley College: Stone Center, 1983).

9. Lynn Rhodes, "Supervision of Women in Parish Contexts," *Journal of Supervision and Training in Ministry* 10 (1988): 198–207.

10. Miller, *Psychology of Women*, 4.

11. See especially Mary Ballou and Nancy Gabalac, *A Feminist Position on Mental Health* (Springfield, Ill.: Charles C. Thomas, 1985); Lynne Bravo Rosewater and Lenore E. A. Walker, eds., *Handbook of Feminist Therapy: Women's Issues in Psychotherapy* (New York: Springer, 1985).

12. Witness the response to the November 1993 Re-imagining Conference, Minneapolis, Minnesota.

# CONCLUSION: THEMES AND THOUGHTS ABOUT THE ARTS OF MINISTRY

This book has attempted to address several major issues in the life of the church. First, it has described ministry praxis in a variety of congregational arenas—Christian education, pastoral care, preaching, pastoral counseling, administration, ethics, and mentoring. In each of these topics, the author not only has talked about the ministry practice under consideration, but also has reflected upon such issues as method, mission, and ecclesiology, as well as the theological foundations for her theoretical construction.

Second, most of the chapters in this book have either implicitly or explicitly offered a method for practical theology done in the context of the discipline being discussed. These methodological insights are helpful as the nature of practical theology is considered from liberation perspectives.

Third, the authors of these chapters have attempted to demonstrate the radical reorientation to their disciplines that a feminist or womanist perspective makes possible. The revolution in epistemology and anthropology that feminist scholarship has brought to theology (and, indeed, to all of the academy) is visible in the assumptions and proposals for ministry discussed in these various chapters.

Consequently, these chapters help to reveal some important contributions to the nature of contemporary practical theology in terms of method, process, and goals. Because practical theology is in a great deal of transition right now, the insights from these chapters may helpfully contribute to the dialogue currently taking place.

Finally, the insights from these chapters offer important lenses into the work of ministry as a whole. When ministry is explored from the perspectives of those who have not generally influenced theory and practice in the church, then both the understanding of ministry and the activities of ministry are transformed. Insights about ministry as discussed in these chapters may very well represent crucial resources for the church's revitalization in our world today.

It is these topics that will be explored here in the conclusion, beginning with a look at some of the common concerns raised by the authors of these investigations into ministry.

## Exploring Common Concerns

Although there is a rich diversity in the images, themes, problems, and proposals named in these chapters, there are also a variety of shared concerns. For the purposes of this conclusion, I have identified three such themes that, despite the different ways of addressing them, show a particularity of focus in practical theology and ministry done from feminist and womanist perspectives.

### Particularity and Social Location

The first concern has to do with each writer's attention to the particularities and social locations of themselves, of the theorists they use, of the people they talk to and work with, and of the ministry contexts in which they are involved. This concern takes on different levels of intensity and reflection in the various chapters but is present in all of them to one degree or another.

Several writers identify themselves according to their own backgrounds, agendas, experiences, and biases. Billman and Hess spend a considerable amount of time in their chapters telling stories of their own experiences that have shaped the way they understand their ministry tasks. They find the immersion in their particular experiences to be an important vehicle of communication for understanding the theories and theologies they go on to develop. They have also used those personal experiences to generate their initial research questions.

Other writers go about this task differently. Smith, for example, is direct and explicit about her social location in terms of race, gender, education, sexual orientation, physical ableness, and class. Smith, although more explicit than some of the other writers, joins them in acknowledging the importance of these categories as they impact the perspectives and goals of theoretical construction. These categories, which determine arenas of privilege and disadvantage, provide necessary information for making decisions about what constructions one will authorize as having appropriate and relevant truth claims for one's life and work.

The two writers who focus primarily on empirical method and the descriptive task, Orr and Holliman, carefully describe the social locations of those who are providing information and experience. Again, there is a concern to make sure that the grounding for these descriptions is available. Neuger's chapter provides specific information about the recipients of pastoral counseling in terms of their social locations so that theoretical constructions and clinical strategies can be seen in their concrete and particular contexts. Townes identifies the importance of confessional claims as she talks about the nature of womanist thought and the need to make one's assumptions about womanist thought particularly clear.

All in all, the common concern raised here is about the particularity of experience and standpoint in the building of and learning from theoretical constructions. This takes shape in the identification of the theorist, in the delineation of the sources, and in the nature of the ministry contexts. There is a tendency to move away from universalizing of experience for the sake of making larger claims about truth and general applicability. There are certainly claims within these chapters, important claims about unjust structures, resistance to evil, and transformation in the lives of people and institutions. Yet the claims are generally made in the acknowledgment of the particularity of the author's standpoint. The claims may prove to be larger, but they have to be evaluated in light of their originating standpoints.

This focus on social location, standpoint, and the importance of particularity in exploring experience as normative for theory building means that these feminist and womanist authors work within acknowledged complexities that shape their work. For example, Billman puts forth four tensions or dialectics out of her own experiences within which the religious leader must live when doing ministry from a feminist perspective. Through these dialectics the pastor lives in the reality of complex power relationships that impact the way she or he understands and makes normative claims for ministry. For example, when religious leaders live in worlds in which they exist as both oppressor and oppressed, as Billman says, they learn to develop "a keen sense of how important it is to be aware of [their] "place" in relation to those for whom [they] care—the delicate dynamics of power" (see chapter 1). Several authors focus on the realities of coexisting as oppressed and oppressor as central to their constructive work. These tensions also reinforce the belief that there is the goal of shared power, partnership, and collaboration in their formulations of ministry. Power is identified so that it will not be as likely to be abused and so that mutuality can exist in the pastoral relationship and in the shared work of ministry. These chapters share, to a great extent, a commitment to collaboration and partnership in ministry as well as in theory building. The focus on particularity in many of the chapters also fits with the invitation to and appreciation of diversity across lines of power and experience. These are strong common themes throughout this text.

## The Nature of Experience

One of the issues in all research revolves around the question of whose experience is going to be privileged in the conversation and theory building. Although this question has always existed in scholarly research, it was not until the African-American liberation movement, the feminist movement, and the rise of other nondominant perspectives in research efforts that the question became explicit. The privileging of voice and experience is certainly at issue in the chapters of this book.

The various authors, as discussed above, describe their own social locations and the assumptions and implications that arise from those standpoints, in part to indicate those voices to whom they grant authority. It is to those voices that the authors listen carefully and deeply. One of the great benefits of feminist and womanist research has been a tearing down of universal experience where "the partial paraded as the whole" and offering instead access to voices that have been left out. Yet there is often a tendency to generalize the perspective of the new focus group as if there can be a new universalizing from hearing some of the previously marginalized perspectives. This tendency will probably always exist; it seems to be human nature to seek commonalities and connections. Yet the chapters in this book deliberately work against this universalizing of particularities by seeking out and naming diverse experiences.

What stands out in these chapters is the commitment to the power of naming when using experience as the starting point. For these writers, the naming of experience with authentic language that legitimately reflects the reality of the subject is, at the very least, the starting point in a liberative method for ministry. Thus the writers focus on listening deeply to the diverse voices of the people whose experience is at stake in these constructions of theories and practices of ministry, and helping people to find language for their experience that is meaningful *and* transforming. Whether it is the focus on naming as the starting place for a feminist-based pastoral counseling, or the dangerous consequences of being named by others as discussed in the chapter on Christian education, or the very method itself in Holliman's chapter of listening carefully to women trying to name their experiences of being mentored, the starting place for understanding experience is the exploration of how naming is occurring. When one is denied the right to participate in the naming of self and context, then truth and wholeness are also denied at all levels of the culture.

In each chapter, certain experiences are listened to as being more authoritative than other experiences. Privileging the hearing of women's voices and experiences is common to all of the chapters. However, there are differences from that point on in which women's voices are focused upon, on the sources of those voices, on which voices are allowed to join those privileged voices, and on whether or not those experiences and voices are used as a direct source of theory building or whether they are viewed and critiqued through other lenses as part of the hearing. These are important methodological considerations.

For example, in Neuger's chapter on pastoral counseling, women's experiences are heard as normative—women theorists, women who have been counselees, women who do ministry. But in addition, the experiences of men who have sought pastoral counseling are also heard carefully as a way to try to understand the contexts in which a feminist-based pastoral counseling might operate. Gender is a primary category, though, in giving authority to women's experiences and needs. For Townes's chapter on ethics, women's experience is seen as normative, but race and class are equally normative, categories. So the experience granted the most authority in the theory building is that of African-American women (whether historical or contemporary), and it is that experience which is used to build and test theory. For Hess, gender is again the primary category, but she listens carefully to the life-span experiences of women so that girls' voices are raised up alongside of women's. Orr is particularly interested in the dynamics of class as well as gender and race, so she makes sure that diversity around class and race is carefully heard and noted. She also makes a clear point that the voices of women over time as recorded in feminist theory and theology serve as critical lenses through which to hear the voices of the women she interviewed about leadership. Critical reflection is an ongoing process.

The point of looking at whose experience is recorded and how that experience is interpreted and used is to see how important it is to avoid universalizing experience without naming its particularity. There is a clear consciousness within each chapter that we live in a world of interlocking oppressions that must be seen clearly and whose dynamics must be carefully analyzed. There is no such thing as "essential human experiences" in these theoretical positions, and thus the particular human experiences and their contexts must be carefully named. It is only when those experiences are carefully named that we can look for places of convergence and divergence in them that help us to build more substantial theory across diverse lines.

## Questions, Interpretive Norms, and Theoretical and Theological Resources

As already noted, the writers in this text begin with experience, as do most writers using liberation methods. The nature and context of that experience varies from writer to writer in terms of whose voices take priority in setting the research questions and concerns to be addressed and in how much that experience is universalized. The scholars walk a fine line between recognizing the importance of a variety of diverse voices in setting research agendas and privileging a particular set of voices whose experiences have not been taken into consideration in the meaning-making tasks of our theories, theologies, and practices. It seems clear that, despite the research focus, the authors are aware that, as paradigms shift as a result of these new perspectives, all experiences, including those of the dominant groups, will have to be heard as part of the ongoing theory-building processes. We cannot just add left-out experiences to those already dominant and have a viable set of theories and practices. The process is much more radical than an additive one as indicated in many of these chapters.

In the methods used in these chapters, not only is marginalized experience attended to in the gathering of information and perspectives, but it is also granted a certain level of authority in determining the questions to be asked, the resources to be critiqued and utilized, and the interpretive principles or norms to be used in the research process.

### Questions

In general, research done from liberation perspectives starts with the questions brought by the researcher himself or herself. This inclusion of self in the research process is a hallmark of liberation methods and is evidenced by the initial emphasis on the writer's social location and experience related to this topic. Too often in feminist liberation work, the questions raised by the researcher's experience have narrowly determined both the experiences to be observed (they have to be similar to the author's) and the questions seen as valid for the research (they have to reinforce the questions of the author). Because liberation methods make the researcher's standpoint evident, this tendency can be observed and critiqued.

In each of these chapters the researchers have begun in their own experience in terms of raising the questions and have then moved to, at the least, an investigation of whether those questions are relevant and useful to a larger population. Many of the writers have then attempted to listen to a more diverse population in terms of whether the questions are useful and have attempted to hear what other questions might be helpfully addressed. They have made intentional and persistent efforts to seek out and hear voices that represent experiences beyond their own social locations. In a number of cases, that listening to diverse experiences has changed the nature of the questions in important ways. For several of the authors, this has resulted in the naming of dialectical tensions within which these investigations must be made. Billman, for example, raises four such tensions explicitly as the contexts for her research questions—tensions that name the realities of being oppressed and oppressor, of experiencing both anxiety and possibility, of exploring the questions through both empathy and critical analysis, and of knowing the destructive power of systemic sin as well as the radical power of hope. These tensions emerge out of her own experience, but even more profoundly they emerge out of her testing her experience in diverse communities. This method of exploring experience and the resulting tensions within which questions are raised is especially evident in the chapters by Billman, Hess, Smith, and Townes.

The questions that are raised within these liberation agendas demand response. They are not abstract questions. They are not merely questions of interest or curiosity. They are questions of survival, of resistance, of possibility, of faith, and of justice. They raise additional questions about what resources can provide adequate response and what interpretive lenses that reflect their particularities might be applied to investigating those resources.

### Interpretive Norms

The interpretive norms that emerge from these chapters reflect the life experiences—including experiences of oppression, injustice, marginalization, and suffering, as well as those of insight, resourcefulness, resistance, and vision—of a variety of individuals and communities. The interpretive norms that surface from the conversations within and between these individuals and groups bear the weight of both the needs and the strategies of their experiences. The authors have attempted to name the norms as they turn to traditional and contemporary resources for assistance in developing meaningful and relevant ministry practices.

These norms do two things. First, they help focus the author on which resources are useful given these life experiences, and second, they provide the critical principles through which those resources can be evaluated and utilized. The norms identify useful themes, voices, and visions in the resources chosen and focus the lenses through which those might be used. The interpretive norms are critical norms that link the researcher, the people and communities whose experience is being privileged in the research, and the various sources for analysis and strategy. The researcher or interpreter, to some degree, becomes responsible for conveying the experience of these diverse voices in developing the interpretive principles and applying those in the investigation of normative texts. When this happens, the interpretive principles are used, in part, to grant a renewed authority to those authoritative texts. This is a pragmatic authority in that the texts become useful when viewed through these interpretive lenses to guide and facilitate the liberation of those who have been oppressed and the transformation of unjust and evil structures that maintain oppressive power relationships. These interpretive principles create the possibility for building ministry practices that empower individuals, communities, and structures to flourish within the vision of God's salvific kin-dom. Ministry in these liberation perspectives has as much to do with social transformation as it has to do with individual flourishing.

The experiences of the people represented in the particular research arenas, with their hopes and needs, form the matrix through which the researcher/minister seeks tools of analysis and resources for strategies that will speak positively to these individuals and communities, and offers both visions and strategies for assistance. The matrix frame is made up of the interpretive/hermeneutical norms that seek points of relevant access to the necessary resources.

The interpretive principles that emerge from the various perspectives and disciplines in this text have much in common and yet reflect the diversity of their contexts. For example, most of the authors use an interpretive norm of liberation in their work. This is close to a universal norm as represented by this group of researchers. Liberation has both personal and structural dimensions in each chapter and serves as a guiding norm for evaluating the resources as well as the theories and practices that emerge in the construction.

A second almost universal norm in these chapters is that of suspicion, framed in a variety of ways. The implication of this norm is the necessity of adequate deconstruction of patriarchal and oppressive texts using these principles of suspicion and liberation. Deconstruction of the texts, whether theological or social scientific, is a part of each author's work. And yet the emphasis in these chapters is much more constructive than deconstructive, and this marks a change from much of traditional feminist and womanist work. The need to justify deconstruction has seemingly lessened, and the need to provide concrete construction that reflects the strengths and strategies of previously marginalized perspectives has taken precedence. Nonetheless, deconstruction is still a necessary and persistent category of interpretation and analysis in any liberation work for ministry.

A third, commonly held interpretive principle is that of transformation. And yet, within that principle is found an example of the importance of debate in building critical norms for interpretation. Although several of the authors emphasize transformation as a key interpretive norm, others challenge the primacy of transformation. Smith characterizes the debate well in her chapter where she writes:

> It is crucial to name this kind of preaching *a ministry of resistance* rather than a ministry of transformation. Though a transformed world is the ultimate hope that undergirds such a ministry, if preachers listen carefully to the oppressed voices surrounding them, they will discern that the language of survival, struggle, and resistance is what permeates these messages of indictment and hope, not the language of transformation. Transformative language assumes a certain measure of privilege and power that neither accurately describes nor reflects the lived realities of oppressed people (see chapter 2).

Townes raises similar points about the need to hold the norms of transformation and resistance together as analysis and interpretation occur. These debates through which agreed upon interpretive principles emerge are central to building shared approaches to theory building without eliminating important voices from the process.

Another interpretive lens that serves to organize the investigations into the literature is that of partnership or collaboration. Both words are used repeatedly throughout this book in a variety of contexts. Collaboration is used as a norm through which biblical and other texts are evaluated as well as a value for research methods themselves. Partnership and collaboration mean that researchers/ministers work mutually and nonhierarchically with those who have not normally been granted equal status or been able to significantly participate in the naming and meaning making of church and world. It also means that diverse perspectives and styles are actively sought so that real collaboration can occur. And it suggests that all of those who seek justice and the transformation of personal and structural realities need to work together toward these common goals, sustaining, confronting, and empowering one another in a shared cause.

Beyond these primary interpretive norms, there are other stated and implied principles for analysis. They include categories such as confession, conspiring, compassion, community, diversity, and reconciliation. These are important interpretive and hermeneutical principles that help the religious leader to approach authoritative texts in theology, psychology, sociology, and the various normative traditions in such a way that they will be able to contribute to building liberating and empowering ministry praxis.

### Theoretical and Theological Resources

Resources are chosen and analyzed by these authors via the categories described above. Resources are claimed as valuable as they are receptive to or speak out of the kinds of experiences that form the ministry and research foci (that is, primarily the experiences of people whose voices have been marginalized and exploited). The resources are explored through the questions raised and norms derived through the careful hearing of and attention to these marginalized perspectives. And these resources, carefully and critically analyzed, provide important insights, transformative strategies, and possibilities of hope for ministry praxis.

There are several issues to be considered when developing theories and practices for ministry done from intentionally liberationist perspectives. First and primary, there are few direct resources about these topics that can be considered and explored for elaboration or contextual shaping. Instead, there frequently are voids in the available literature about pastoral care, preaching, administration, and so on, from feminist and/or womanist perspectives. In terms of the themes of this text, there is minimal literature in any of the topics—especially in feminist administration, mentoring, pastoral care, and pastoral counseling. Both the chapter on administration and the one on mentoring had to rely almost exclusively on empirical research—on the direct experiences of women doing administration and experiencing mentoring—in order to be able to have any source for their theoretical constructions. A lack of specific and focused resources on the particular arena of practical theology being considered, then, is a primary problem for this research.

A second and related problem when discussing resources is the need to draw from associated or cognate literature in order to find relevant categories and trustworthy ideas for theory building. Consequently, many of the authors draw upon feminist and womanist social theory, psychology, and theology as well as the various other forms of liberation theories and theologies. These are important sources as they aid in developing interpretive principles and in gathering more voices of experience across diverse populations. They provide important conversation partners in the methodological dialogue going on in these chapters. However, they are constantly being adapted in order to fit the particular questions raised within these arts of ministry, and there is a risk of overgeneralizing material gathered for one purpose in theory building for a different field.

A third resource problem has to do with the use of sources that were written in contexts unlike the contexts under discussion in these chapters—whether those are differences in time, in assumptive worlds, in focus, or in some other important difference. Obviously, all literature is written in specific time and orientation contexts, but the issue of concern here is that these materials were written in contexts that did not take the perspectives of gender or race or class or sexual orientation into consideration. Rather, they operated from a paradigm with narrow models of "truth" and where particularities were seen as relatively unimportant compared with the universality of "essential" human experiences and their resultant truths. This literature is so fundamentally in conflict with research that understands the centrality of standpoint in theory building and in the practices of ministry, that much of it may be unreclaimable. Nonetheless, sometimes the only literature available in a particular discipline is of this dominant-voiced type, and the question becomes one of starting place. In addition, this literature and its assumptions, truths, and claims are pervasive in what we might call (erroneously) "common knowledge" about the world, about the church, about ministry, about human beings, and so on. Thus they must be considered in any theory building, because nothing is created *ex nihilo*. The process of deconstruction has been and continues to be a crucial tool for revealing the particularities and distortions in theoretical/theological assumptions that have passed for truths. Deconstruction takes place through a variety of means, but one of those means is by placing what has been seen as truth alongside the experiences and voices of those who have not been considered in the creating of those dominant perspectives—especially women, African Americans and other people of color, the poor, gay men and lesbians, the elderly, and those who are not able-bodied. When assumptions and theories are seen as partial instead of as the whole picture, then there is room to begin to rebuild from the ground up or at least to see the radical limitations of these traditional positions.

Another aspect of deconstruction is to use the particular interpretive or hermeneutical principles derived from engaging the experiences of those who have been marginalized as entry and focus points when looking at the traditions. As discussed above, the matrix formed by these interpretive principles becomes the screen through which helpful and relevant insights might be revealed.

Both of these methods of deconstruction are at least implicitly used in the resources chosen by these authors. As they use the Bible, theological studies, and social scientific literature, they take their interpretive principles as primary in choosing particular themes and insights for their theory building. They also use all three of the approaches to theoretical and theological resources described above: building out of an absence of literature (especially in administration and mentoring), using related literature that is in keeping with the key interpretive principles (liberation, transformation, resistance, and so on), and using material that needs appropriate deconstruction (for example, psychological theories, developmental theories, the Bible, and so on).

The resources used by these authors also reflect their particular disciplines and their particular research concerns. Although they use material specific to their particular theological disciplines, they also use materials that help to analyze, both for deconstructive and constructive purposes, class, race, gender, sexual orientation, age, and physical ableness. All of the authors use social scientific resources of various kinds including psychology, developmental theory, psychotherapeutic theory, and sociology. Some of the authors use historical materials (with appropriate deconstruction), especially Townes in her article on womanist ethics where she draws heavily on the history of slavery in the United States. All of the authors use literature written out of liberation perspectives, whether that is material from lesbian theologians, Central American liberation theologians, African-American literary authors, feminist psychologists, or a range of other sources presented explicitly from a liberation standpoint. And all of the authors use, to one degree or another, biblical resources.

It is interesting to look at the primary biblical and theological resources used in these chapters, because they are the result of being chosen through the interpretive principles named above—especially those of liberation and transformation. Several authors use the story of the Exodus—both the whole theme of the Exodus or subplots within that narrative. Many of the writers use the example and witness of Jesus to make a claim upon the readers' understanding of the issues. Some use larger biblical themes or genres such as the prophetic literature, the creation literature, or the parables. Some use stories of healing recorded in the Bible.

The important point is that the Bible is used as primary source in this material, but used in very specific ways. All of the biblical material used is presented as a model or mandate for the elimination of unjust structures and behaviors and for the pursuit of liberation, justice, and reconciliation. Often themes are used that have generally been overlooked in the use of the Bible (Puah and Shiphrah, the juxtaposition of the healing of the woman with the flow of blood and the healing of Jairus' daughter, and other stories of women in the Bible). The Bible is found to be a rich resource when explored through the interpretive principles generated by attention to the marginalized voices.

Theologically, this is true as well. Hess explores Reinhold Niebuhr and others in order to explore and critique notions that are damaging to women. Townes and Holliman look at ecclesiology in ways that create a milieu of liberation, reconciliation, and empowerment. Smith, using a variety of theologians, discusses Christology as it may best reveal the power of God in the lives of all. Scripture and theology become living resources to be engaged in deep dialogue for the sake of feminist and womanist visions and strategies. These are primary resources within each of these chapters, and they serve as vehicles for the constructive efforts of theories in ministry practice.

## Ministry Practice(s)

Ultimately, each of these chapters is written to develop further and implement more liberating and transforming practices of ministry for the betterment of the church and the world. The goal and fulfillment of the work is in how these theoretical constructions about the arts of ministry can be implemented in the congregation and in other ministry settings. Within each constructive proposal for ministry practice there exists a hope that the reflection process used to create these theories of ministry will be part of the ongoing work of ministry. No practice can be sustained as liberating and transforming without a continual process of critical reflection about the practitioner's and the congregation's social locations, about the kinds of interpretive and ethical norms that emerge from those experiences, and about the kinds of resources that continue to generate new insights into theory and practice. Ministry practices must always be tested in their own environments, with diverse populations and perspectives, so that they can be constantly refined and avoid the tendency toward reification and irrelevance. This reflection process, as much as the particular practices themselves, form the core of these proposals. It is easy to become complacent about ministry practices that once were liberating but now serve to maintain a nontransformative status quo.

However, each author in these chapters moves through the descriptive and constructive elements of her work in order to provide the reader with a set of core principles that define the work. It is a core theological assumption and hope reflected throughout this book that it is in the experiencing of these concrete ministry practices that God might be found and God's kin-dom furthered. Those foundational principles are worth summarizing.

For Billman, the essence of liberating and transforming pastoral care, which is always the work of the community, can be captured in two words—collaboration and conspiring. She urges the religious leadership in congregations to take these two images and plumb their depths as they develop theories and strategies of pastoral care together. For her, collaboration is more than a partnership. It is the development of a shared vision of justice and deep care and then the taking on of the hard tasks, co-laboring, to bring those visions to reality. Co-laboring is shared labor and shared rewards. Her sense of conspiring, of breathing together as unjust structures are torn down and relationships of mutuality are built up, brings together the images of partnership, of strategizing, of courage, and of transformation. The work of pastoral care for Billman is ongoing mutual care at the deepest personal and political levels that can be imagined in the life and vision of the church.

Mutuality as a theme is picked up in Hess's work on Christian education. For Hess this profound commitment to partnership and liberation can be found in two images that she uses—hard dialogue and deep connection. These two images, which she holds together in necessary and creative tension, convey the importance of both nurturing environments, which are safe and available for our deepest sharing, and challenging environments, where people can and do say the hard things about their differences and the implications of those differences for their life together. As with most of the other writers, Hess focuses on the marginalized communities and the importance of their being able to say what is important to both the "center" and to one another so that the new constructions that arise will be real and relevant for all. She urges educators to pay attention to the explicit messages they teach, to the messages that they send more indirectly through patterns of power and relationship, and to those things they do not acknowledge or teach but that need to be named for the good of all. Using those images and categories for the sake of an educational process that is empowering and fair is at the heart of Hess's chapter.

For Smith, the themes of weeping, confession, and resistance become the primary vehicles for her understanding of preaching. Smith suggests that resistance, especially, is a key category for this work as preachers attempt to understand the dynamics of evil at work in systems of interlocking oppressions and address those dynamics in their speaking hard truths about them. Although these truths are not easily heard, they must be spoken if the church is to participate in justice making. In order to do this work of radical truth telling, the preacher will create a dynamic dialogue between traditional theological disciplines, including theories of homiletics, and the experiences of those who have been marginalized in the culture. In doing that, the truths that must be spoken will become clear, especially if the preacher will (1) reflect carefully on her or his own theology as it perpetuates the oppression of the marginalized; (2) probe the connections between the various forces of oppression; and (3) listen persistently to the voices of "critique and struggle" outside his or her own social location. For Smith, voice and action belong together.

In the tension between the social and the personal, evident in each of these chapters, Neuger's chapter on pastoral counseling moves back toward the personal. Although she states that "pastoral counseling . . . is about the business of transforming patriarchy," it is clear that the pastoral counselor is asked to empower the people who engage in the counseling to be about the ministry of transformation at the same time that they work to transform their own lives in the direction of wholeness. It is with individuals and relationships that this ministry takes place. Neuger offers four processive images for the work of feminist pastoral counseling. Those four—naming, gaining clarity, making choices, and staying healthy—designate the movement in the counseling partnership where the personal and the political are brought together in each of those phases. The counselee's ongoing health depends, to a great extent, on her or his sense of participation in transforming the harmful dynamics of the culture. The practice of pastoral counseling has to do with helping people to participate in their experiences in the variety of diverse contexts in which they live, and learning to understand those experiences in ways that open up truths rather than suppress them. Using the example of the parables, clarity is in part gained by turning the distortions of patriarchy upside down so that new and more truthful perspectives, with their personal and political implications, emerge. Staying healthy, then, is only possible when one can consistently counter the double-binding messages of an oppressive culture within the self and within the structures in which one lives. This movement between the personal and the social is at the essence of feminist pastoral counseling practice.

Orr's chapter works less at providing a theory of administration and leadership practices and more at hearing how women engage in leadership that may contribute to the theoretical construction in process. Nonetheless, one can catch images of Orr's vision of feminist leadership practice, especially in her theological work. Orr's dominant metaphor for a feminist style of leadership is that of covenant making. For her, this means that leadership means empowering the mutual ministry of all for the sake of liberation and wholeness. Authority, Orr says, is dialogical, shared, cooperative, life-giving, embodied, aiming to uncover the gifts of a diverse community, and working against abuses of power. Authority seeks to restore justice in the world through the sharing of vision and the sharing of story together. Orr suggests that there are four primary tasks for the feminist-oriented leader. First, the leader must be able to address and handle conflict directly, because it is in the conflict over these shifting paradigms that real creativity and justice can be born. Second, the leader will find ways to be both confrontive and appropriately nurturing—"to speak the truth in love." Third, she or he will build and maintain a strong spiritual and theological foundation to the work of leadership that is empowering to all. And fourth, the leader will continue to learn what it means to claim and exercise leadership in liberating and transforming ways. These four tasks, done within the context of covenant making, form the essence of Orr's proposal of leadership practices.

Townes also relies heavily on images of community and covenant in her work on the practice of ethics in the congregation. The emphasis is on the notion of radical truth telling in the community for the sake of justice and for the sake of reconciliation. Townes suggests that this process of truth telling must always exist in the tension between two poles of practice—the pastoral and the prophetic. The pastoral pole reminds the ethicist that all are fragile, even in the midst of good intentions, and that care, nurture, forgiveness, and openness need to be a part of the ethics process. The prophetic pole suggests that the ethicist must seek to discern the will of God, hold the community accountable for justice, analyze the structures of evil and wrongdoing in church and world, create a community that will work together for justice and unity, and work toward "self-critical inclusivity." She concludes with the reminder that it is always important for the ethicist to "wait upon the community" and trust in the ongoing work of the Spirit in the midst of that community of faith.

Finally, in her conversation on mentoring, Holliman works out of two primary images: (1) the intentional sharing of wisdom with another who seeks that experience and knowledge, and (2) the need to offer hospitality to all, especially to those who will be most likely to experience rejection and marginalization rather than welcome. Holliman suggests that mentoring is a necessary activity from those who have found a relatively solid place in nonwelcoming structures for those who are seeking affirmation, reality testing, and welcome. She gives a number of suggestions for how one seeks out mentors and how one participates in a mentoring relationship. However, her recommendations for the ministry practice of mentoring include a conscious attention to hospitality, a belief in the gifts of another and a desire to help those gifts emerge and grow, a willingness to share resources and ideas, and a belief in the power of relationship. For Holliman, mentoring between those who have experienced marginalization in their lives and in their work has fundamentally to do with joining together in a prophetic and liberating solidarity.

These feminist and womanist ministry practices, which bridge the gaps between liberation theories and the traditional and ongoing work of parish-based ministry, contribute to the important dialogue about ministry praxis. They may well serve as important sources of renewal and transformation for a church in the midst of radical transition. If those of us who are engaged in religious leadership in churches are looking for ways to become relevant and vibrant in a world of violence, oppression, and injustice, then we must be willing to move from talk and theoretical/theological abstractions to the concrete and messy work of liberating action. It is time to take the risks of making mistakes in the hope of making justice.

## Implications for Practical Theology

The practices of ministry that emerge in these chapters are not separate from the reflective process discussed in the section on common themes. Each practice is both a consequence of this in-depth set of correlations and a method itself for ongoing critical reflection. No practice described in this book is separate from an ongoing spiral of hearing and testing new experiences within the diverse communities of faith. Practices will have validity only when they can stand the test of both diversity and of transformation in the face of powerful forces of death and destruction.

The approaches undergirding much of the literature within this text seek to articulate a praxis methodology that is committed to privileging marginalized perspectives, to deconstructing texts defined by dominant perspectives to be authoritative for all, and to developing practices that will help resist evil and promote justice and a fullness of life. The method defined in the process of the common themes—the attention to standpoint, the careful naming of experience while walking the tightrope between particularity and claims of solidarity, and of deconstructing, analyzing, and creating resources for the development of these liberating practices—is an important, even central, dimension to practical theology. The spiral that continually moves between and tests assumptions and conclusions within each of these dialogue partners is an ongoing one that keeps the constructive process in practical theology perpetually alive. The development of practices in the midst of this praxis method is both for the wholeness of people and systems and also for the feeding of this reflective and critical process.

The work is new. Many of the arenas of practical theology addressed in this book are initial ventures from feminist or womanist perspectives. These perspectives are offered for the sake of the ongoing conversation through which we are able to be lively participants in God's unending lure toward salvation.

# INDEX OF NAMES AND SUBJECTS